Common Ground
A Course in Communication
Sadler and Tucker

M

First published 1981 by
THE MACMILLAN COMPANY OF AUSTRALIA PTY LTD
107 Moray Street, South Melbourne 3205
6 Clarke Street, Crows Nest 2065
Reprinted 1983 (twice), 1984 (twice), 1985 (twice), 1986,
1987 (twice), 1988, 1989, 1990, 1991

Associated companies and representatives
throughout the world

National Library of Australia
cataloguing in publication data

Sadler, R. K. (Rex Kevin).
    Common ground.

    For tertiary students.
    ISBN 0 333 33814 6.

    1. Interpersonal communication. I. Tucker, Keith.
    II. Title.

302.2

Set in Baskerville and Univers by
ProComp Productions, Adelaide
Printed in Hong Kong

Contents

Preface

Primarily, we are concerned that students develop an ability to use the written and spoken word effectively. Before anyone can make effective use of words, it is essential to have an adequate vocabulary and to know how to use it. To this end we have included chapters on thinking, reasoning, problem solving and on increasing word power.

Because of the vast quantities of information available to us today, it is important that we decide precisely what needs to be communicated, communicate the ideas effectively and then check that our message has had the desired effect.

What we have aimed for is a balance between understanding the communication process and developing confidence in dealing with others by:
- learning and practising interpersonal skills,
- examining various approaches to written tasks,
- knowing how to get the most from reading and listening tasks when on the receiving end of messages.

All too often people assume that because they know how to speak, listen, write and read they can communicate effectively. The numerous exercises contained in this book are designed to sharpen the skills essential to effective communication. Many exercises involve small group participation and role-playing. By encouraging this involvement we hope to provide a meaningful arena in which communication situations can be viewed, analysed, discussed and appraised.

This book will show how to apply sound principles of communication in a variety of situations. The key to mastering the communication skills so necessary in education, in the workplace and in our social lives is practice. Therefore, we provide a full range of examples and exercises to help the student become familiar with the concepts presented in the book.

Common Ground places as much emphasis on oral forms of communication as it does on written forms. Throughout the book, material is presented in small steps to encourage discussion. Each concept is accompanied by exercises so that students can become actively involved in the learning process, mastering the skills as they proceed through the book.

Acknowledgements

The authors and publishers are grateful to the following for permission to reproduce copyright material.

The Herald and Weekly Times Limited for 'Please Don't Die Tonight' by Tess Lawrence; Granada Publishing Limited for the extracts from *Oh, What a Blow That Phantom Gave Me* by Edmund Carpenter; Macmillan London and Basingstoke for the extract from *Smiling* by John Nicholson; John Fairfax and Sons Limited for the article 'Vicious Cycle for Homeless Young People' by Malcolm Brown, and for the article 'Noah'; Penguin Books Australia Limited for the extract from *Confronting the Future* by Charles Birch; A. D. Peters and Company Ltd for the extract from *Reliable Memoirs* by Clive James; Phillip Adams for 'You Too Can Be an Adman' and 'A Simple Guide to Advertising'.

Alan Foley Pty Ltd for cartoons on pp. 3, 4, 10, 13, 16, 25, 35, 44, 51, 60, 61, 73, 74, 79, 90, 92, 102, 130, 215, 217, 220, 221, 229; Mirror Australian Telegraph Publications pp. 172–175; The *Age* pp. 12, 14, 27, 55, 84, 104 (foot), 108, 159, 176, 211, 219, 224, 228; Angus and Robertson Publishers for the photograph from *Tales of Mystery and Romance* by Frank Moorehouse p. 24; Frederick Muller Ltd for the puzzle on p. 111 from *Supermazes* by Bernard Myers; NSW State Cancer Council p. 105; The Herald and Weekly Times Limited p. 104 (top), 161; NSW Department of Employment and Youth Affairs p. 150; NSW Government Division of Inspection Services pp. 184–185; United Press International p. 227.

Cartoon drawing by Rick Amor.
Cover design by Guy Mirabella.

While every care has been taken to trace and acknowledge copyright, the publishers tender their apologies for any accidental infringement where copyright has proved untraceable. They would be pleased to come to a suitable arrangement with the rightful owner in each case.

1 Communication

Definition

'Communicate' and 'communication' are words most of us are familiar with. We find them used in everyday conversations in expressions such as: 'We don't communicate any more, do we?' and 'I just can't communicate with him'. In general terms, we know what people mean when they use the word in these contexts.

Activity 1.A   Communicate!

1. Write down five phrases or words that you consider have the same meaning as the word 'communicate'.
2. Find out what other people in the room have written and compare your answers. Write a number of the responses on the chalkboard and compare differences and similarities in meaning and emphasis. Discuss the meanings that people within the room have assigned to the word.

As this is a book about interpersonal or human communication, not electronics or telecommunication, it would seem appropriate to refine some of these ideas that you have contributed, so that we can clarify what communication is in this context. Unlike some terms and concepts, it is difficult to find an accurate dictionary meaning for the term, as you have possibly discovered above.

Activity 1.B   Defining 'Communication'

1. Write definitions for the following words which represent concepts, ideas and feelings.

tree	work	love
bikini	writing	anger
fish	teaching	drudgery
football boot	sleep	kindness

2. Now that you have tried to define these words, discuss the following questions in class.
   (a) What is the difference between trying to define a word in the first column and a word in the second or third columns?
   (b) In which group would you place the word 'communication'? Explain your placement. Is there possibly more than one reason for this? If so, what are the reasons?

1

3. Here are some definitions of communication. (We have taken fragments of larger definitions so that you can attend to specific phrases.)
   - The transfer of meaning
   - A system of transmitting messages
   - The process by which messages are sent and received
   - The assignation of meaning
   (a) Compare the ideas that you collected on the chalkboard with the above definitions.
   (b) Discuss the following questions in class.
      (i)   How well are the ideas collected in class represented in the definitions?
      (ii) What do the definitions suggest about the act of communicating?
      (iii) Do you consider any of the definitions to be more complete or accurate than any other?
      (iv) Why were four possible definitions supplied, rather than just one?

Interpersonal Communication

The reason for spending so much time defining communication is that it forms the backbone of the ideas contained in this book. If you accept from the definitions that interpersonal communication is the process by which people send and receive messages, then you have the key idea.

But sometimes just sending a message is not good enough. You may be prepared to tune in to a message from another person (that is, to listen with intent to someone speaking or read a memo or letter addressed to you) but in itself this may not mean that the communication has been successful. In interpersonal communication there are three vital elements in achieving success or effectiveness when sending messages: acceptance, understanding and action.

The first point is that there has to be **acceptance** of the message. The receiver of the message has to be able to understand the language that is being used, has to have some knowledge of the other person and be prepared to read, listen or observe the contents of the message. In other words, the receiver has to be in the right frame of mind to tune into the sender and accept the message.

The second feature of successful communication involves **understanding** between sender and receiver. While you may be prepared to accept the message, unless the message is free from ambiguity and unintended meaning there is little point in having communicated.

The third feature is **action**, that is, the result that comes from the communication. As the sender of a message you must be sure that the receiver will behave in the desired way. A short example may help. If you want someone to buy a tomato sandwich for you at lunchtime, you have to guarantee that he will listen to you and thereby accept the message, that he will understand both the language you are using and your motive for asking him to buy you the sandwich, and that the action that comes out of the communication will be that you have a tomato sandwich for lunch.

Communication at an interpersonal level is never an end in itself. Even when we acknowledge someone's presence in the corridor or pass someone on the street and say 'Good day', 'Nice day', or 'How are you?', the communication in itself is of little consequence. What is important in these situations is that you acknowledge the other person's existence, thereby maintaining an open channel with that person, so that when you need to make a purposeful communication in the future you are able to do so. The politeness or acknowledgement of their presence in the simple greeting provides you with this access. Sometimes the exchange in this situation can be less than meaningful.

The one thing that is essential for effective communication is a common ground of experience on which people individually, in groups, and in organizations can focus in order to achieve their aims.

Activity 1.C   What do you Understand?

1. Examine the following statements. In each statement assume that the receiver is prepared to accept the message. Consider the variety of meanings that could accompany any one of these statements. For each statement list the meanings on the chalkboard.

   (a) Would you help this woman, please? (From a manager to a shop assistant)

   (b) I'm hungry. (From a child to his mother)

   (c) Start work at 7.30 a.m. daily. (From a foreman to a new employee)

   (d) Strike! (From a union representative to a group of workers)

   (e) I love you. (From anyone to anyone)

   (f) Jump in the lake. (From the recipient of the above statement)

   (g) You're fired! (From an employer to an employee)

2. Discuss in class how any possible misinterpretations could affect the action for which the communication was designed.

It is within this framework of uncertainty in message transmission that you can begin to understand the complex process that is communication, and from this begin to understand the difficulty of achieving effective or successful communication. When we communicate we need to consider the other person's needs and feelings, and aim for mutual understanding. Communication is not a game where one person wins and someone else loses.

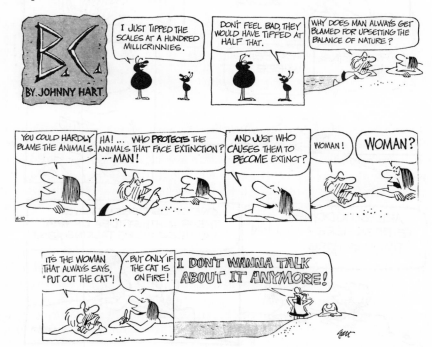

Communication involves more than just sending an information package from one person to another. Communication involves a process of sharing information. In order for this sharing to take place, the communication act must occur under conditions that allow us to make predictions about the impact our message will have on the receiver. Therefore we need not only to consider **what** we will say (message content), but **when** we will say it (communication setting), **how** we will say it (medium) and we need to anticipate the **effect** our message will have on the receiver.

My 'field of experience' must overlap your 'field of experience' if the message or signal is going to have the same meaning for both of us and therefore result in a successful communication. This can be illustrated as follows:

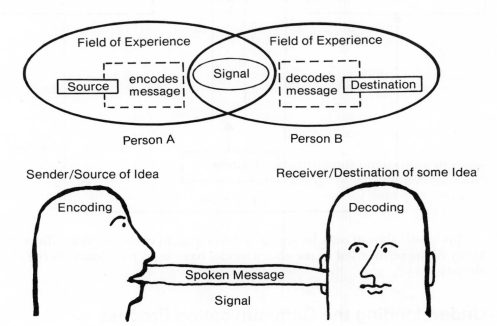

The success or failure of our communication with others is difficult to ascertain. All too often when we write messages, make phone calls, or even pull a face at someone, we assume that the receiver of our message feels as we feel, knows what we know, and will therefore react in the way we desire. When we are involved in the act of communication we make **assumptions** about ourselves, the message and the receiver of the message. We assume that the message will hit the spot with the receiver, leading him in the desired direction or bringing about the desired course of action.

Communication theorists have realised that the above illustrations are inadequate in that they do not provide a complete representation of what happens when we communicate. Many models of communication have been devised to represent the communication process. The one that we have chosen to use is 'the modified information theory model'. Information theory is one branch of communication theory and involves the study of information content in message formation. We will discuss this in Chapter Two.

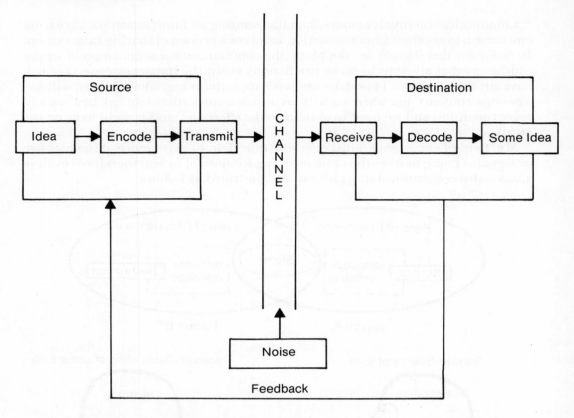

This model should only be seen as a development of the previous illustrations. Many of the terms used in the above model have been mentioned in the chapter already.

Understanding the Communication Process

The **source** or the sender of the message has an idea that he wishes to communicate. He selects both a medium through which the message will be sent and the message content. Selecting the medium and message content is called **encoding** the message. The message may convey instructions, explanations, ideas, attitudes or feelings from the source to the receiver. Once the message is transmitted, it travels quite independently of the source, sometimes becoming distorted simply because the wrong medium was used to send the message. The packaging of the message may have been inappropriate for the type of message being sent. To illustrate this further, if you decide you want to tell someone who is a close friend and who lives nearby that you love him/her, would you:

- write a letter
- send a friend with the message
- call on the phone
- visit
- all of the above?

No matter which medium you select, the message at some point is released by you, and travels through a **channel** to the receiver. The channel may be any of our senses, a page, air waves or might even be seen as an electrical wire when we use the telephone or send a telegram. No matter which channel you use to send a message there will always be distortion, distraction or interference in the channel. This is known as noise. (The concept of 'noise' is developed in Chapter Two.)

Irrespective of how well you have formulated the message and considered the needs of the receiver, there is always the chance that the **receiver** of the message may consider that you have chosen an inappropriate channel through which to communicate, or that you have selected your message content poorly. We have all heard people say 'Why couldn't she *tell* me that?' or 'If he wanted me to remember all those details, why didn't he put the instructions *in writing*?'

Activity 1.D   Sending Messages

1. How would you send each of the following messages? In each situation, consider the channel through which you would send the message and give some thought to the structure of the message content.
    (a) Telling a subordinate that he is not performing his job satisfactorily
    (b) Extending your condolences to a close friend who has just lost a parent
    (c) Instructing a person who has a poor grasp of the English language how to operate a simple hand tool
    (d) Telling a stranger on the street how to get to a railway station that is several blocks away
    (e) Applying for a job
    (f) Telling a boyfriend or girlfriend that you don't want to see him/her again
    (g) Informing an interviewee that he has been successful in getting a job for which he has applied
    (h) Telling an interviewee that he has been unsuccessful
    (i) Informing the council that your household garbage hasn't been collected
    (j) Asking for more money from your boss
2. Why is more than one channel suitable in some of the above situations? What are some of the additional factors that need to be considered when deciding on the medium or channel through which your message is to be sent?

Marshall McLuhan coined the phrase 'the medium is the message'. This is an important concept in interpersonal communication and, hopefully, you have developed some understanding of this through the above activity. What is suggested by McLuhan's statement is that we are influenced as much by the packaging of the message as by the message content. You might like to consider this statement in relation to advertising!

As the examples above show, the receiver of a message can pick up meanings that were sent quite unintentionally by the source. For example, there is the man who sent a case of wine to a business associate to show his appreciation, not realising that the associate was a non-drinker. The intention was there, but the message may have missed its mark. The best way to ensure that the message had the desired effect on the receiver is by either initiating or encouraging **feedback**. As we have shown in the communication model, feedback is the way by which the sender finds out whether the message has reached its destination, how successful his message has been and whether or not the receiver of the message will be prepared to act on the communication. Therefore, feedback can be seen as any response from the receiver indicating understanding and acceptance, or mis-understanding and non-acceptance of the message.

If interpersonal communication is to be successful, one must find out from the receiver *what* has been understood, not *if* it has been understood. By being prepared to get feedback when sending messages our communication with others can be made more meaningful, resulting in a better liaison being established between sender and receiver.

Activity 1.E   I Know What you Said, but What did you Mean?
This will involve everyone in the class and will illustrate:
  • the various levels of feedback that are possible,
  • the difficulty of working without feedback.
One student acts as an instructor. It is his responsibility to give instructions to the class on how to draw a figure on the page. For this exercise everyone will need three pieces of paper and a pen.

Instructions to the Student Instructor
The teacher will give you a drawing consisting of several geometric figures assembled on the page. Your task is to tell the class how to draw the illustration on the page that they have in front of them. You are to give your instructions verbally. Do not use any gestures and do not use the chalkboard. This way you are being unnaturally limited in your selection of channel in the communication. Give your instructions step by step. Do not show the correct illustration until the *end* of the third round.

Instructions to the Teacher and Class
A sample illustration is given below of the type of figure that you might use for this exercise. We suggest that you select a different geometric shape from the one used in the example and use at least six objects in the illustration.

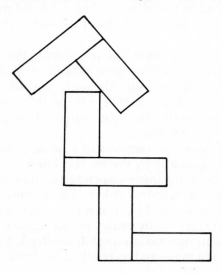

This exercise takes place in three rounds. The same person gives the instructions in each round.

In the first round the class is to ask no questions. Simply listen to the instructions, interpret them as best you can and draw the illustration. The teacher should *record the time* taken for each round, writing this information on the chalkboard along with the accuracy with which students draw the illustration. (This can be judged on whether or not they have drawn the figure correctly.) The teacher should draw the following grid on the board to register the results.

	TIME	ACCURACY	
ROUND 1			No feedback
ROUND 2			Limited feedback
ROUND 3			Complete feedback

In the second round, the instructor gives the instructions again. Students are allowed to ask questions, but only questions that can be answered by the instructor either in the affirmative (yes) or negative (no). Any questions that cannot be answered in this way or any question that cannot be understood should be met with a 'mute' response from the instructor. This, in itself, should give feedback to the class that the instructor has not understood the question. At the end of this round, the teacher should once again check the time taken for the instructions and check the accuracy of the drawings.

In the third round, the instructor and class should enter into open conversation. Dialogue will be established for the first time. By allowing free conversation, many of the misunderstandings of the previous rounds can be clarified and people in the class can check the accuracy or inaccuracy of their illustrations. At the end of this round, when all think they have the illustration drawn correctly, the instructor should draw the figure on the board. The teacher should now complete the grid for the third round.

Questions for Discussion
1. Was an introduction given by the instructor particularly in the first round in order to give the class some idea of the task that lay ahead?
2. What benefit is there in giving people some indication of the goal that is to be reached?
3. Even after allowing for complete feedback in the third round, why might some people still draw the illustration incorrectly? How do 'preconceived ideas' play a role in determining how you alter your illustration from round to round?
4. How did the instructor get feedback in the first round even without questions being asked?
5. How systematically were the instructions given by the instructor?
6. How quickly did the instructor establish a common language with the class, using terms to describe the objects and the placement of them within the diagram?

7. One might expect the time taken to give the instructions to increase as 'feedback' is allowed in each subsequent round. Why might the time decrease?
8. How well did you listen both to the instructor and to the questions being asked by the class members?
9. How much did you take for granted in the second and third rounds?
10. Sometimes when the instructions are given, the instructor calls 'rectangles' 'triangles', or if squares were used, refers to them as 'cubes'. Why is this?

List on the chalkboard the class members' reasons as to why their drawing did not resemble the instructor's at the end of the first round. What does this tell you?

In the above exercise we have the opportunity to note many of the problems that underly all interpersonal communication. We can see that the problems in communication lie not only with the sender in selecting message content and channel but also with the **language** being used, the ability of the receiver to tune in and stay tuned in to the instructions, and therefore decipher or decode the information accurately. In spite of the fact that we may take all of the above things into consideration in communicating, we may still be unable to establish successful or effective communication.

To understand this more fully we must appreciate that much of what goes wrong when communicating is a product of what we bring to the communication situation in the form of our perceptions, attitudes and abilities. These elements will be discussed in the chapters that follow.

THE WIZARD OF ID —   By Parker and Hart

2 Message Sending

The Ingredients in Communication

David Berlo[1], an American communication expert, developed the ingredient model of communication which he called the SMCR model. Berlo took the four major components in any communication: the source (S), the message (M), the channel (C) and the receiver (R) and listed the attributes of each so as to show the complexity of the act of communication.

When making a cake, rebuilding an engine or carrying out an experiment, we must know beforehand what it is that we are working with. The same holds for communication. In the first chapter we examined the **process** of communication; in this chapter we take a close look at the **ingredients** that are present in any communicative act.

BERLO'S SMCR MODEL			
SOURCE	MESSAGE	CHANNEL	RECEIVER
Communication Skills	Elements	Seeing	Communication Skills
Attitudes	Structure	Hearing	Attitudes
Knowledge	Content	Touching	Knowledge
Social System	Treatment	Smelling	Social System
Culture	Code	Tasting	Culture

By itemizing the ingredients or components that are present when we communicate, we can see that even the process models of communication that we presented in the first chapter are far too simplistic in coming to terms with what happens when we communicate. The source may have been influenced in the selection of message content or even the selection of the channel for transmission by something that was **outside the context** of the message. What this means is that one's attitude towards a particular medium such as the telephone may prohibit our use of it when we are communicating. We may not feel confident about our ability to speak in public; therefore we may avoid any situation where the opportunity to do so arises.

---

[1] Berlo, D. *The Process of Communication: An Introduction to Theory & Practice*, San Francisco: Rinehart Press, 1960.

The Source

The source or sender of the message may have poor public speaking **skills** and be unable to address confidently even a small group of people. So when asked to do so, his **attitude** towards himself, the subject matter and even the person who asked him to speak may interfere with the message to be conveyed. Often, we know too little, and sometimes too much about a topic to do justice to it when presenting information. **Knowledge** on a particular topic as well as knowledge of the audience are important determinants of how successful a communication will be, and how readily a message will be accepted. As all communication takes place in some situation, it is important that we consider the **social system** or setting in which the communication takes place. (As an example of this, you do not tell a group of five employees at the local hotel on a Friday afternoon that their services are no longer required.) We are continually reminded in the press just how important **culture** is as a barrier to effective communication. Race, religion, politics and creed in themselves influence our attitude towards others and therefore will influence our communication.

The Message

As much of this book deals with message construction and the successful utilization of language, it will suffice to say at this stage that the ingredients that make up a message comprise:

- **the elements** (letters in words, non-verbal actions or gestures)
- **the structure** (the way the elements are assembled, non-verbal actions linked together)
- the **content** (what the structured message actually conveys in terms of information)
- the **treatment** (through inflection and intonation in our voice we can give a message quite a different meaning)
- the **code** (which indicates that in most messages we are selecting elements from a system from which an infinite number of messages can be made).

Consider the use that Johnny Hart has made of typeface and print size in creating the message in this B.C. cartoon. While there is no meaning in the actual words there is still meaning in the message. How is this achieved?

© FIELD ENTERPRISES, INC., 1977

The Channel

The channels through which we communicate are usually described as the five senses, although some communication theorists like to include the medium of communication (such as the airwaves for oral messages and paper for written messages) when describing the channel.

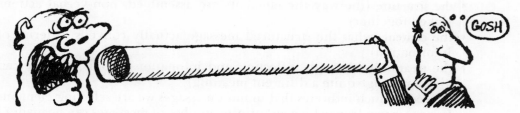

The Receiver

In communication we are both senders and receivers of messages. The attributes of the sender are also the attributes of the receiver, as indicated in the SMCR model.

Activity 2.A   Getting the Message Through

Read the case study 'Alison', and identify the specific ingredients from the communication situation that are contributing or could contribute to a breakdown in communication. Relate your observations and comments back to the SMCR model.

ALISON

Alison had been working in a nursery for nine months. She was interested in plants but not in mixing compost, which was the job she was usually assigned along with the other junior employees. Her boss, an elderly man, always seemed to Alison to derive great pleasure from giving her all the worst jobs. She put this down to the fact that he disliked her because first, she smoked and second, he had said several times, women don't make good nurserymen.

Alison arrived half an hour late one Friday morning. Having clocked on, she resumed a task she had been working on the previous day. Fifteen minutes passed before another junior approached her with a message from the boss.

'Mr Jones told me that if I saw you when you finally got here, I should tell you to pick up your pay from the accountant immediately then go and see him (Mr Jones) in the shade house. Are you in trouble or something, Alison?'

Alison feared the worst! Why?

Communicating Information

Very rarely do we talk simply for the sake of talking, although some people do not necessarily subscribe to this theory. Saying hello to someone on the way to work or exchanging a wave or a smile still has some purposeful end as a communication, in that we use these messages as ways of keeping the communication channels open for the time when we will need to make a purposeful exchange with that person.

When we send messages we are conveying information. We virtually package our information into a speech, letter or report and transmit it to the receiver. At some point in most communications, the sender has to disengage himself from the message and rely on the message package to convey his meaning to the receiver.

Activity 2.B   Messages

1. Read this extract from the gossip column of an overseas newspaper, then answer the questions that follow.

A Composer Whose Affair Hits Sour Note

A composer of international repute has had an off-again, on-again 18 years of marriage with his wife, a Mediterranean beauty. Both have had their lovers but the marriage lasted until recently.

The composer, noted for Broadway hits, movie scores and songs that are now standards, fell in love with a 21-year-old actress who is so beautiful and talented that she is on the verge of major stardom. A top producer just signed her for a five picture deal that could maker her the successor to Barbra Streisand. That gives you a pretty good idea who the producer is.

The young actress had been living with her parents in the San Fernando Valley. Then the composer, madly in love, told his wife that he wanted a divorce and was moving out for good.

After the break, the young actress, also deeply in love with the composer, moved in a Beverly Hills home with him. He wanted to marry her as soon as the divorce went through.

Much hassle with attorneys but that was nothing. The other day the wife discovered the home and barged in an physically beat up the actress, threatening even worse mayhem.

The composer finally pulled his wife off and tossed her out of the house.

More repercussions. All the composer's European friends are siding with the wife. At a tribute to the composer the other night, the so-called friends threatened to boycott the affair if the composer showed up with his girl friend.

The composer buckled and took his wife to the dinner. The girl friend went to a restaurant with one of the town's more famous tycoons who is a very eligible bachelor.

True Hollywood drama. It's a better script than most movies up for the Academy Awards.

(a) What is the writer's intention?
(b) Does he achieve it?
(c) How much 'factual content' could you find in the article?
(d) What information would you need to read the column with understanding?
(e) Why is it more difficult for us to piece together the writer's clues than for someone who reads the column every week?

2. What does the 'B.C.' cartoon suggest about:
   (a) the sending of messages
   (b) the information we place in our messages
   (c) the reception of messages?

Information Content

Possibly the greatest problem we experience in communicating is achieving **conciseness** when encoding messages. We plan talks, write letters, memos and reports, assuming that they contain our message. How often, though, do we get the opportunity to find out if the receiver can decode the message, if the message has been received? How often do we get feedback about the structure of our message indicating that there were either sufficient or insufficient clues to be able to decipher the intended meaning?

Activity 2.C   Decoding

Examine this telegram:

> JACK STOP MEETING SHEBA PARK 1100 FRIDAY TOM.

On a piece of paper, write down *all* the possible meanings. Now collate the information on the chalkboard. How many separate messages do you have?

Tom has had to make assumptions about Jack and the information he has prior to sending the message. What assumptions have you made in your decoding of the message?

The key for decoding the message as Tom desired, is to know that Jack is staying at the Sheba Park Hotel in Tokyo. Jack is awaiting the arrival of Tom, at which time they will have a meeting. The time for the meeting: 11 am Friday. The 'stop' provides punctuation within the telegram as you cannot send 'full stops' and 'commas' via the telegraph.

Because we did not have this common or shared information, our meanings, while possibly close approximations to the intended meaning, were still inaccurate.

Redundancy

In the study of communication, 'redundancy' refers to the parts of messages that do not necessarily add meaning to the message. Redundancy can be useful when we encode and decode messages. The redundant or unnecessary parts of messages do not increase the information content of messages, but they help us break the code. Consider this message:

> th shp tht lft sydny ystrdy hs rrvd n sngpr sfly.

In the above message the vowels have been removed, but because of the *pattern* of the language it is still possible to decode the message accurately. What are some other ways of reducing the length of the message while at the same time ensuring that the message can be decoded?

Because the vowels have been omitted in the example above, it takes more time and effort to decode the message. Redundancy has the effect of reducing uncertainty, and thereby increasing information content. Both verbal and written communication involve a degree of redundancy.

Activity 2.D   Messages Need Pattern

1. By relying on the natural patterning and grammatical rules of our language, decode the following messages.
   (a) _ _ _ engineer had _ _ open valve _ _ release _ _ _ pressure.
   (b) _ _ _ rep_ _ _m_n ann_ _ _d t_ f_ _d t_ _t t_ _ ow_ _r h_ _ b_ _n f_d_l_ _g _ _th _ _ _ pl_ _ _ _ _g.
   (c) the the the a brakes truck it car vehicles cliff on over failed hit rolled both and

2. (a) For each example, which rules did you use to break the code?
   (b) Why were the first two examples easier than the third?

3. Our language patterns itself because it is 'rule governed'. What does this mean?

Repetition

It does not necessarily follow that understanding is increased as conciseness is achieved in messages, although on many occasions this is the case. However, when writing letters, reports or when presenting a formal talk, conciseness *is* necessary.

Because time is so valuable in business it is important that messages convey accurate meanings, that people can read or listen to the message and know exactly how they should act on the information that has been conveyed.

When giving instructions or explanations, sufficient repetition should be included in messages to allow the receiver access to the information. As people tune in and then switch off momentarily to process the information it is important that some repetition be included to allow people to pick up the whole message. If you recall the feedback exercise in the first chapter you should be able to appreciate this point. When the instruction was given in its most succinct form in the first round, how many students drew the figure accurately? What did the repetition provide in the second and third rounds?

Activity 2.E   Check Your Understanding

Answer the following questions, then discuss your answers in class.

1. List three specific situations where redundancy is unnecessary. Why is it unnecessary in these situations?
2. Why is repetition necessary, particularly when giving instructions?
3. Why is it important to be able to differentiate between repetition and redundancy when encoding different types of messages?

Information Overload

Another problem associated with the encoding of messages is information overload, that is, packing so much information into a message that it becomes difficult to know exactly what it is that the sender wants to say. The information may be very well planned, written or spoken, but so unnecessarily detailed that the receiver becomes awe-struck at the complexity or volume of information.

Activity 2.F   Overloading Verbal Messages

Rephrase and restructure the following spoken message to ensure immediate comprehension.

I've asked Jenny and Steve to go on that assignment next Tuesday and to report at 9.30 at our Parramatta office. I told them the office was in Smith Street but they would need to also go to the workshop in Collins Road to check up on the layout. I made it clear to them that they would need to get the plans from Bill Collins before they leave. Jenny and Steve are the new designers we appointed a fortnight ago. What I wanted to ask you is, would you mind going along too and help them if they need assistance?

Activity 2.G   Overloading Visual Messages

1. Examine the following photographs. How is the information content of the two photos different?

2. If we supplement the visual information with the following details, how is the message altered?
    - The man works seven days a week.
    - He has not made a sale all day.
    - It is 4.30 pm.

Sometimes when information is presented, the omission of some detail may bias or change the meaning of the message.

Activity 2.H   Looking Closely

Before the next class, complete the following exercise. Collect some photographs from newspapers of public figures such as politicians and celebrities who appear regularly in the press.

1. Compare several photographs of the one personality obtained from different sources. How does the facial expression change the information being conveyed in the photo? Are there any other features, either of the personality or the photography, that change the meaning in the message?
2. Using the same photographs, examine them in relation to the article or news item that they are designed to support. What additional information is being supplied by the use of the photo? How could a different photograph change the tone of the written article? Would the exclusion of the photograph have any significant effect on the article that you have chosen?
3. Discuss your findings in small groups in class. One person in each group should collate the main ideas and present these ideas to the class at the end of the discussion period.

Noise

Most of us think of 'noise' as any audible disturbance, din or unwanted sound. The concept of 'noise' in the study of human communication has a slightly broader meaning, which is based on the concept of 'noise' used in electronics. If you refer back to the 'modified information theory model' of communication in the first chapter (p. 6) you will notice that under 'the channel' is a noise source. Noise is *any* disturbance or distraction, audible or otherwise that interferes with the fidelity or clarity of the message.

Noise is always present in the channel for the simple reason that when we communicate we do so through a medium: the air waves when we speak, the page when we write, the film when we take photos. When showing a movie, channel noise could be present in many forms. Someone may have left a light on in the room and the image appears faint on the screen. There may be scratches on the face of the film that distract the viewer. There may be a group of people talking in the room, who provide a distraction. These are all forms of **channel noise**.

Some communication theorists go one step further and suggest that another form of noise exists: **code noise**. It is distinct from channel noise in that code noise refers to the inaccuracy with which we use a particular code. If you recall the question at the end of the feedback exercise in the previous chapter that asked: Why might some instructors call rectangles 'triangles', then the answer to this best describes code noise. Quite often there will be little outside interference in the message. The distraction will be in how we **encode** the message or in how we **decode** the message. We may select the wrong word, take a photo of something out of context, or speak to someone using technical jargon when common or lay terms are more appropriate. When we encode messages without giving due consideration to the content of our message we introduce a noise element which makes the decoding more difficult than it should be. The receiver cannot decode the message as the sender wished.

Activity 2.I   The Noise in Messages

1. Where is the noise in each of the following messages? What did the sender mean to say?
   (a) Some old people lose all their facilities.
   (b) Talking about young people like that, you're quite deprived.
   (c) You have to dot and cross every line.
   (d) It's a smart to my face to feel that you have been left out.
2. Noise is present not only in written messages. What do you think the photographer was trying to show in this picture?

Sometimes it is neither the words we use nor the meanings that we attribute to these words that causes a breakdown in our communication with others. The problem quite often is that we want to sound important, or we want to impress our audience. Rather than expressing ideas simply in short sentences, we use 'grotesque syntax', that is, sentence structures that tend to confuse, baffle and bewilder our audience.

Activity 2.J   Say What You Mean!

Read the conversation between a scientist and his child.[1]

'Daddy, I want cornflakes this morning. Must I have porridge?'
    'Yes. It has been suggested by Mummy that, in view of the external coldness, the eating of porridge by you will cause an increase in bodily temperature. Furthermore, in regard to the already-mentioned temperature considerations, your granma-knitted gloves and wool-lining-hooded coat will have to be worn.'
    'May I have some sugar on my porridge?'

---

[1] Quoted in Berlo, *op. cit.*, pp. 73–4.

'The absence of sugar in the relevant bowl has been noted by Daddy at an earlier moment. However, further supplies of this substance are now being brought by Mummy from the appropriate vessel that is present in the kitchen.'

'Daddy, I don't want to go to school today. Why must I?'

'It has been clearly established by several independent investigators that a lack of schooling may lead to a subsequent impairment in an individual's ability to earn money. In addition, other daddies have reported that the particular school for which the present Daddy is paying the fees has been found to be a very good one. Another factor which ought to be taken into consideration here is the comparative freedom enjoyed by Mummy during the period of daytime when, in view of your absence, there is a necessity to consider only Baby and herself.'

'But why must I go to school every day?'

'The previous statement on this matter has been entirely ignored. It seems likely that you were not listening at the appropriate moment. The present speaker's argument is that in the absence of the educational benefits accruing from attendance at a typical school, failure to learn things may occur, and that this deficiency may, on a later occasion, result in unhappiness, secondary to a limited availability of monetary funds.'

'Daddy, Baby's crying. He's always crying.'

'Yes. It has been pointed out that our larval man is particularly vulnerable in this respect. Your observation is in agreement with those reported by both Mummy and Uncle Bill. Several other visitors, however, who have studied the phenomenon in other babies, have contested the apparent uniqueness of this aspect of the behavioural pattern of our particular baby.'

'I like Uncle Bill. When is he coming again?'

'It seems probable, in view of a number of relevant factors, that Daddy will achieve visual contact with Uncle Bill during the coming day. This matter will then be considered.'

'Daddy, how does your car work?'

'This will now be explained to you in simple terms . . .'

Rewrite the father's responses to the child's questions, conveying the same information but stated in simple sentences.

Activity 2.K   Padding in Conversation

1. During the week, listen carefully to people talking and giving instructions and explanations. Listen for the phrases and expressions that are used to 'pad' the speech, such as 'with regard to', 'such that', and 'it can be seen that'.
2. List the expressions that people use.
   (a) How are these phrases used?
   (b) Within the context of the conversation, what value do these phrases have?
   (c) Do they affect the information content in any way?
3. This exercise could be repeated on written material, in the same way as we have suggested above.
4. Discuss your findings, bearing in mind the concepts of noise, information, content, redundancy and repetition.

Activity 2.L   Delusion, or Just Confusion

You might like to use the following statements as the basis for a class discussion. Try to use the concepts already introduced in these two chapters to explain your ideas about these statements. What is meant by each statement?

1. 'He's not articulate, he's verbose.'
2. If you can't convince them, confuse them.'
   or
   'If you can't beat them, baffle them.'
3. 'It doesn't matter how you say it, as long as the other guys know what you're talking about. I've got eight guys working under me and none of them ever complain that they don't understand me!'
4. 'Some people think that if a statement is long, it has to be good. Therefore, long reports and essays *must* be better than shorter ones. I always write more than the required length when writing assignments because I subscribe to the above theory.'
5. 'If you don't use technical expressions and jargon when explaining ideas to customers, they think that you don't know what you're talking about.'

3 Perception

We have probably all heard someone passing comments such as: 'he's one-eyed' or 'she's short-sighted'. When we make these statements we do not necessarily mean that anyone has a vision problem, even though this might be the case. More often than not the comments are made because we have perceived a situation differently from the way someone else has.

One place where many people suffer from these perceptual problems is at football grounds at the weekend. People make inferences about the ability of the referee to see anything clearly, and at one time or another during a game supporters of both teams disagree with a ruling, claiming an 'unfair' advantage to the opposing team. We have all heard someone shout from the crowd: 'Hey ref, you need glasses!'

Football grounds are but one place where perceptual problems occur. When perceptual problems occur it is inevitable that the communication will break down. When a person fails to see another person's viewpoint, quite often an impasse is reached. People blame one another or find scapegoats to accept the blame for the breakdown.

Activity 3.A   What did You See?

Compare these oral reports presented to a football committee after a player had been sent of in a football match.

Player One: It had been a long hard game and I think everyone's temper was frayed. The incident occurred only about five minutes before the end of the match, when I tackled the other player. I suppose I tackled him fairly hard but that's the only way to keep 'em down. I didn't put my knee in, though. The next minute he got up and smashed me in the face, so I just lost my block and flew into him. Then *I* was sent off!

Player Two: He (player one) had it in for me right from the word go. Everytime he came anywhere near me he'd either kick me or try to maim me with his knees or elbows. Even in the last round when we played their team it was 'on'. They haven't got one player who tackles without trying to kill you. It was only a couple of minutes before the end of the match when he tackled me. The referee had acknowledged the tackle and he wouldn't get off me. So I flew into him. Then before I knew where I was, half the other teams were into it.

Now, answer the following questions.
1. The reporting of the incident by the respective players varies. Compare the players' descriptions of the specific events that comprised the total incident. How do the reports differ?
2. What 'generalizations' did both players make? How do these generalizations alter the perception of the incident from both sides?
3. Do you think any details are omitted from either report? If so, what are they? Why have the players chosen to ignore these details?
4. It is obvious that both players while being involved in the one incident, perceived it differently: what are the main reasons for this differing perspective?
5. How do you think the referee 'saw' the incident? What events may have led up to the incident?

6. Both players were involved in the incident. In the heat of the moment, tempers flared, but neither player thinks he is to blame. Because of their involvement, the player's reports are subjective. The man who is supposed to have an unbiased or objective report is the referee. Write his report to the committee. Then have several members of the class read their reports to the class.

Perception is the mental process by which we make sense of the stimuli we receive through our senses. The *Concise Oxford Dictionary* defines 'perception' as 'intuitive recognition' or 'the action by which the mind refers its sensations to external objects as cause'.

In the section that follows we will explore some of the devices we use when we process information mentally, in the act of perceiving. But before we do, try this quick test.

Activity 3.B   Perception Test

1. Arrange the letters O W D E N A R W to spell a new word—but not a proper name, nor anything 'foreign' or unnatural.
2. Allow 30 seconds for this question: If one face of a cube measures 3 cm x 5 cm, what is the area of each of the faces, and what is the total area of all eight faces?
3. Quickly now, how many animals of each species did Adam take aboard the Ark with him? (Note, the answer is not how many pairs but how many *animals*.)
4. Figure out this problem in diplomatic relations: If an international airliner crashed exactly on the French–West German border, where would they be required by international law to *bury* the survivors? (If you cannot work this out in 30 seconds go onto the next question.)
5. If a doctor gave you three pills, and told you to take one every half hour, how long would it require for you to take all of them?
6. Two men played chess. They played five games, and each man won three. How do you explain this?
7. A man living in Wodonga, Victoria, cannot be buried over the border in New South Wales, nor in the Australian Capital Territory, even by the special intervention of the Prime Minister. Why is this?
8. The strange pronunciation of British names: Well you probably wouldn't be caught on C-H-O-L-M-O-N-D-E-L-E-Y or even S-I-D-E-B-O-T-H-A-M, but how about M-A-C-H-I-N-E-R-Y?
9. A farmer had 26 sheep. All but eleven died. How many did he have left?
10. An archaeologist reported finding two gold coins dated 56 BC. Later, at a dinner in his honour, he was thoroughly and openly discredited by a disgruntled fellow archaeologist. Why?
11. If you have only one match, and entered a room to start up a kerosene lamp, an oil heater and a woodburning stove, which would you light first—and why?
12. Quickly now: Divide 60 by ½ and add ten.

Check your answers at the back of the book.

In checking your answers, one of the first things you may have noticed is that not all of the questions have only one answer. Yet when you are answering the questions, we find *an* answer, and then move on to the next question.

Activity 3.C Follow Up
Discuss the following questions that relate to your performance in the test.
1. On completing the test and marking it, how many students counted up their total out of twelve? Why do we find a need to tally our results?
2. Even if you have seen this test before, why might it still be possible to make a number of errors in the test?
3. What has the test revealed about your reading skill?
4. What does the test reveal about our 'rigidity'; 'capacity to generalize'; 'creativity'; and 'awareness'?
5. Why is the test included in this section on perception?
6. Has the test told you anything about yourself?

When we perceive we select, organize and interpret stimuli or information until it has meaning for us. This does not mean that it has the same meaning for other people.

The Perception Process

In Chapter 1 we looked at the **process** by which we interact with others. In the second chapter on information theory we examined the **messages** we construct and send. In this chapter we are examining the third component of the communication network, **perception**. A study of perception enables us to examine the cognitive structures that we use when we are selecting, organizing and interpreting stimuli. Basically, we are examining how people process information and ideas, and how they derive their meanings. This perceptive process forms the basis for our communication and understanding.

Activity 3.D Optical Illusions
On the following pages are a number of illustrations that involve optical illusions. Examine them carefully, then read the text that accompanies each figure.

1. Figure 1 can only be drawn. It is impossible to construct. Examine each corner. Now try to take in the whole object.

Fig. 1

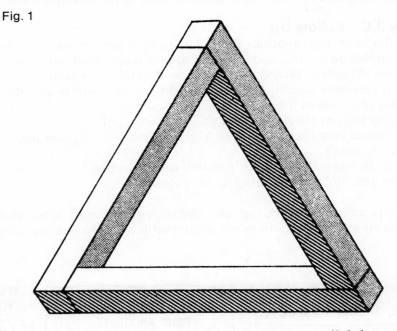

2. In Figure 2, knowledge that the four vertical lines are parallel does not help with the perception of this figure. The lines radiating out from the centre bend the centre lines.

Fig. 2

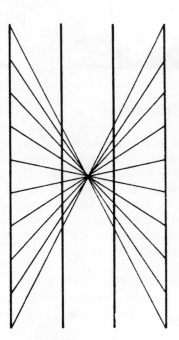

3. Three impossible objects are included in Figure 3 to form an engineer's nightmare.

Fig. 3

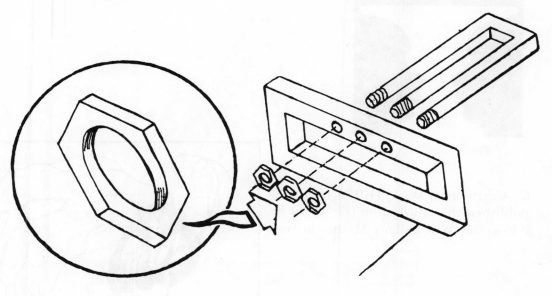

4. Figure 4 is one inkblot . . . but what can you find in it?

Fig. 4

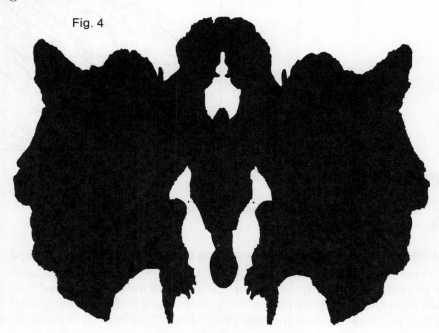

5. In Figure 5, Danish psychologist Edgar Rubin developed this 'reversible pattern' in 1915. Can you see both patterns at once?

Fig. 5

6. A cartoonist, W. E. Hill, originally published this illustration (Figure 6) in 1915 as 'My Wife and my Mother-in-law'.

Fig. 6

Aspects of Perception

The nine sections that follow will help you understand why perception is so important to communication.

1. Our ability to receive stimuli or information through our senses is limited.

Rubin's 'reversible pattern' in Figure 5 and Hill's 'Wife and Mother-in-law' in Figure 6 provide useful illustrations of this point. Rubin maintained that you cannot see both the twin boys (the black pattern on white) and the goblet (the white pattern on black) at the same time. You virtually switch off one image, then switch on the other image. Two distinct fixations or stops are made with the eye. The same holds for Hill's illustration. You have to switch from the young woman to the old woman and back again.

Activity 3.E   How Much Information can you Absorb?

The teacher or a student collects a series of five photographs from newspapers or magazines. They can be photos of people, actions or even scenes. Do not show them to the class.

Five people leave the room. The first person to come in studies each photo carefully. He can take as long as he likes. It is his responsibility to invite the next person in and give that person a description of the five photos orally. Now, the second person gives an oral description to the third person, and so on. It is useful if you tape record the proceedings to see how the information is reduced in subsequent rounds.

When you have finished, play the tape back, show the photos to the participants and discuss these questions.
1. How much information was lost?
2. What type of detail was remembered and passed on?
3. What details survived to the last person? Why do you think they remembered those details?

There is a limit to how much you can see when you go to the movies; there is a limit to how much you can hear when you go to a concert.

> *Concertgoer:* It's a pity the cellist was off-key.
> *Friend:* I didn't know there was a cello in the group!

If we ever have the opportunity to see a movie a second time, there always seems to be things we 'missed' on the initial viewing.

2. Everyone has a different capacity to take in stimuli or information.

Our ability to use our senses effectively and with acuity is determined by the amount of exercise we give each of our senses. Most sighted people do not use their hands and ears as efficiently as they would if they were partially sighted or blind.

Activity 3.F   Making the Most of Our Senses
1. Close your eyes (without falling asleep) and listen for all the different sounds both inside and outside the room. Do this for two minutes. List the sounds. Compare your results with a person near you.
2. Blindfold one person and stand him/her at the front of the room. Five people should now come out and stand in a line across the front of the room. Remove all rings and watches from your hands and wrists. The blindfolded person should move along the line feeling the hands of the five people, trying to identify them. The 'five' should now sit down. Can the blindfolded person find the 'five'? Why? Why not?

Magicians capitalize on speed of movement and distraction to create visual illusions. 'Now you see it, now you don't.'

3. We select or filter stimuli or information from around us.

Most of the time we only see what we want to see and hear what we want to hear.

> *Car driver:* Did you see what that clown in front of us did?
> *Passenger:* No, but I saw the red light you just drove through!

They say that beauty is in the eye of the beholder.

"ANYONE EVER TELL YOU THAT YOU HAVE BEAUTIFUL, BIG BLUE EYES?"

Activity 3.G   Filtering Information

Collect six real-estate advertisements from the press and examine the language that is used. When you have collected and examined the advertisement, answer the following questions.

1. What features of the homes are described?
2. Why do you think this information has been selected for publication?
3. How has the information been filtered? What expressions have been used to describe features of the house?
4. How can this filtering affect your perception of the house?

4. We organize and interpret stimuli and information according to both our past experiences or 'frame or reference' and the situation or environment in which they occur.

> 'I don't eat meat, so therefore the family suffers. When John and I go out he usually orders a pepper steak or a T-bone to compensate. The other night we were visiting friends and we took the kids along with us. We were invited to stay for dinner. When my eldest boy who is six years was asked if he would like a chop to eat, he turned to me and said "Mum, what's a chop?"'

At times it is not only what we say but the way we say it that affects the perception others may have of us. We do not know whether grocery items are expensive or not unless we check the price in another store, in a newspaper or with a friend.

- How wet is a 'wet' season?   To someone living in a hot desert compared to someone living in the tropics.
- How hot is a 'hot' day?   To someone living in London compared to someone living in Sydney.
- How fast is 'fast'?   To a camel driver compared to a race-car driver.

The perceptions that we have are relative to the situations in which they occur. When we find ourselves in foreign countries or unfamiliar surroundings we no longer have the referents on which to base our perception. The judgements we make have little basis for comparison. We may have to establish new behaviours to comply with the behaviours of those around us. Sometimes we may need to have 'behaviours' interpreted for us. The inquisitive tourist when overseas may continually ask questions about what he/she hears and sees. The tourist is creating a 'frame of reference' in order to try to understand what would otherwise be regarded as strange behaviours to that person.

5. We tend to generalize from our previous experiences, no matter how specific or isolated these experiences were.

Sometimes we pinpoint certain features of a person's speech, dress, posture and so on, and only attend to these specific attributes, but in so doing, make sweeping generalizations about that person. Often we view events out of context, and in so doing obtain an unrealistic perspective of what has happened.

When we generalize about the behaviour of certain groups of people we are 'stereotyping' them. In order to see how this occurs, complete the following exercise.

Activity 3.H   Stereotyping

1. Write down your impressions of descriptions of the following people:
    (a) a grandfather
    (b) a customs officer
    (c) a mother-in-law
    (d) a movie star
    (e) a union boss
    (f) a leader of a country
    (g) a public servant
    (h) a mother
    (i) a television news reader
    (j) a greengrocer
    (k) a car salesman
    (l) a policeman
2. Compare your impressions with the impressions of a friend. Then answer the following questions.
    (a) How similar were your impressions or descriptions?
    (b) To what details did each of you attend?
    (c) How did these details form the basis for your overall impression of that person?
    (d) How much access have you had to each of the people listed? How did this access or lack of it affect your perception of each person?

3. Now compare the stereotypes with those of other members of the class.
   (a) Of the people in the above list, which person was most easily stereotyped? Why do you think this occurred?
   (b) How are the generalizations that we make about mothers and grandfathers different from those that we make about movie stars and union bosses?

6. We perceive things as whole units; we pattern information.

This idea has already been developed to some extent in Chapter Two, when we were examining redundancy and repetition. In that section of Chapter Two there are a number of exercises where patterning is needed to be able to complete verbal statements. (See page 17) The way to complete the statements is to identify the pattern. In some sentences vowels were left out; in other sentences whole words were left out; but because of the patterning of our language, you could still read the sentences.

Surrealist painters cause some people to have nightmares. Claims are made that surrealistic paintings are 'not really art' or that they are 'just silly'. One possible reason for these claims is that viewers of the painters cannot find patterns emerging, as is the case with realistic painting. Images appear in random arrays; objects are associated that we do not normally 'see' together.

Musical notes have no form until they are heard as part of a 'piece' or 'score'.

If you turn back to the figures presented earlier in this chapter, particularly Figures 1, 3 and 6, you can best appreciate this point about patterning and viewing whole units of information. With the impossible triangle, try to distance yourself sufficiently to take in the whole shape. What happens when you do this? What happens with Figure 3 under the same conditions? You have to take in the whole of Figure 6 in order to be able to see either the 'wife' or the 'mother-in-law'.

Activity 3.I   Seeing and Perceiving

1. Join the nine dots using four straight lines, without lifting the pen from the page. How does this exercise provide an example of the above point?
2.   C O S   What is the key to the patterning
     X L N   for each of the three lines?
     B D G

There are two further ways in which you can test this 'patterning' concept. When you are listening to the radio, see how long it takes to identify a piece of music (preferably when they do not announce it!). Take a newspaper photo and examine it with a magnifying glass. You will see that it is made up of a series of dots. Now move back from the photo to see the dots merge to form the picture.

7. Our feelings, emotions, attitudes and aspirations flavour our perceptions.

The first exercise in this chapter gives a graphic illustration of this point. Two footballers were both convinced that they were right. Not being at the football ground at the time of the match, we are not in a good position to judge who was right and who was wrong. Even if we had been at the ground I doubt whether or not we could have provided a totally objective view of the situation. Even the referee was in a dubious position. I wonder how many of the altercations between the two players the referee saw leading up to the 'final showdown'?

Quite often in work situations people come into conflict because of their attitude towards work and the conflicting attitudes of the people with whom they have to work.

> Jack Collins had a 'bad' work report filed against him by his foreman. The report was directed to the supervisor of the section. In retaliation Jack submitted a report about the behaviour of the foreman.
>
> Jack was overheard in the corridor last Friday saying to a friend that everything he had said about his boss in the report was true.
>
> The foreman too maintained that everything that he had written about Jack was true.

We seek support from out friends, colleagues and family in reinforcing the perceptions that we have of others. This is the case particularly when we have come into conflict with others, when people do not share our view.

8. We become defensive when other people seem to be unable to acknowledge our point of view or interpretation of a situation.

Jack Collins became defensive because of the implications of what was written in the report. In the foreman's eyes everything that had been written was true. This is where so many problems occur in communication. Not in the sending of a message, or the selection of a medium through which to send the message, but in the heads of the people communicating. Both Jack and the foreman had a right to maintain that there was *truth* in their respective statements.

In Chapter 17 we develop further this theme of self perception and attitude formation.

9. We need to be able to develop an 'empathic relationship' in order to be able to fully understand the other person's point of view.

Some people, like the King from 'The Wizard of Id' fail with their interpersonal communication because they place barriers between themselves and others.

'Empathy' implies more than simply acknowledging someone else's view point. Empathy involves the projection of one's 'self' into the feelings of others in order to comprehend completely how they feel, or to comprehend why they are behaving as they are. Empathy implies a psychological involvement; the relationship must go beyond the superficial. Quite often because of this, people avoid situations that involve emotional contact with others.

The Mind's Eye

The following extracts from Edmund Carpenter's book *Oh, What a Blow That Phantom Gave Me* (Paladin, London, 1976) further illustrate how the perceptive process operates.

> All peoples have the same senses, though not all use them alike. Eskimos have the same eyes as I do, but, though my vision is 20/20, they spotted seals long before I did and continued to watch them long after the seals had disappeared from my sight.
>
> Any sensory experience is partly a skill and any skill can be cultivated.
>
> Charlie, blind since the age of two, spoke with a West Virginia drawl: 'Well, my daddy and me enjoyed deer huntin' every fall. I got to know the sound—twigs breaking—even the weight, just be the way it sounded. My daddy sure was surprised when I got the deer first. He hadn't seen . . .'
>
> Charlie had worked hard to learn to shoot accurately by sound. He used a can with a few pebbles for a target, swinging it just enough to hear.
>
> Wilfred Thesiger, in *Arabian Sands*, tells of a desert Bedouin reading camel tracks: A few days later we passed some tracks. I was not even certain they were made by camels, for they were much blurred by the wind. Sultan turned to a grey-bearded man who was noted as a tracker and asked him whose tracks these were, and the man turned aside and followed them for a short distance. Then he jumped off his camel, looked at the tracks where they crossed some hard ground, broke some camel-droppings between his fingers and rode back to join us. Sultan asked, 'Who were they?' and the man answered, 'They were Awamir. There were six of them. They have raided the Junuba on the southern coast and taken three of their camels. They have come here from Sahma and watered at Maghshin. They passed here ten days ago.'
>
> It's simply a question of training, though that training isn't simple. Reading tracks involves far more than just knowing where to look. Everything smelled, tasted, felt, heard, can be as relevant as anything seen. I recall being out with trackers once and when I stooped to scrutinize the train, they stepped back, taking in the whole. Interpenetration and interplay of the senses are the heart of this problem.
>
> No sense exists in total isolation. Run water into the bath while switching the light on and off—the sound appears louder in darkness and its location is easier to determine. Teach a soldier to strip and reassemble his rifle, then ask him to do it blindfolded and you will find he almost always does it faster without sight. Taste and smell seem stronger in the dark, which may be why

good restaurants are candle-lit. Darkness certainly makes love-making more interesting.

All peoples control their senses, though not always consciously. In our culture, librarians post signs reading SILENCE; concertgoers close their eyes; museum guards warn, 'Don't touch!' Most of us know someone who puts on his glasses before talking on the phone.

How do you think you would react to the following event that Carpenter observed at Mingende Catholic Mission in New Guinea in 1969?

Over a thousand worshippers came to Mass this Sunday, many decked with flowers and feathers, their faces painted, their bodies covered with clay. A few old men were armed, for display, not defence. One woman nursed a baby on one breast, a puppy on the other. Marvellous singing filled the high, old church with its earth floor and log pews. Men with large shells hanging from their noses had to lift these to take Communion. Between services, several clawing, mud-rolling brawls broke out between jealous women, egged on by whooping spectators, but a calm priest slowly drove an ancient truck into each crowd, breaking up the fights, then returned to perform the next Mass. One man wore a photograph of himself on his forehead, in front of his feathers; friends greeted him by examining his photograph.

If we can develop a better understanding of how the perceptual process operates, then hopefully we have a better chance of communicating effectively with others.

4 Non-Verbal Communication

- I knew he was lying, I could see it in his eyes.

- She looked at me, I looked at her, and I knew that she'd accept if I asked her to dance.

- The speech was okay, but he was so unconvincing.

- You can tell by the way he walks.

- You look miserable today.

- You don't think that you'll impress anyone by wearing a dress to an interview for *that* job, do you?

- He stood so close . . . and I felt so uncomfortable.

- When I'm giving a talk to a group I always look for the nodders. Those who nod when they agree with what you are saying . . . and those who nod off!

Some, if not all of the above statements are familiar to us. They are familiar because they are common remarks that people make about one another's behaviour. But each of the statements has something in common, and that is that the behaviour that provoked the responses was **non-verbal**, that is, not spoken or written in what we commonly accept to be our language. This chapter deals with non-verbal communication.

We only seem to think of, and refer to, spoken and written communication as language because we learn how to encode and decode messages using, within our culture, the English language. We know that when we speak, write, listen and read we have a reasonable chance of communicating information, that others will be able to make sense of what we say or write.

- We can attribute **meaning** to words, or examine the **semantics** of the language.

- We can **structure words into sentences** or statements, or examine the **syntax** of the language.

- We know that the language is **rule governed**. I cannot throw words and sentences randomly into any order and hope that they have meaning. I have to consider the **grammar**.

A language therefore is an agreed set of symbols used for communicating. What is suggested in this chapter is that there are elements of language in non-verbal communication. While meanings for non-verbal behaviours cannot be found in dictionaries, cannot be structured into meaningful units such as sentences and are not governed by any rules, we do know (particularly within a culture) what people mean when they communicate non-verbally. Quite often the non-verbal actions do have meanings that are agreed on by people within that culture, sometimes between cultures.

Unfortunately, some people pay little attention to non-verbal behaviours and become blind to the needs, feelings and attitudes of others.

Some of the most important studies in the area of non-verbal communication have been conducted by a British social psychologist, Michael Argyle. One of Argyle's main interests is the way in which we use both verbal and non-verbal signs 'deliberately and unconsciously in the course of social encounters to influence others'.

Deliberate signs are actions such as smiles, purposeful gestures, or indications such as pointing, hugging or touching, whereas the **unconscious** signs are actions such as adopting a particular posture, moving the eye in response to some action, or fidgeting or shuffling when we are anxious or tired.

In examining non-verbal communication we will concentrate on two areas:

- **Kinesics**, or how we speak through our actions, sometimes our inaction, gesture, facial expression, posture and movement.
- **Proxemics**, or how we speak through our proximity to others, whether we touch or allow ourselves to be touched and how we organize the space around us.

Assigning Meaning to Non-Verbal Action

Many of the gestures we use, particularly those gestures made with the hand, carry with them a 'symbolic' meaning. The idea of symbolic meaning when we are talking about non-verbal communication is important. The formation of a sign occurs when we have a **signifier** and something **signified**. The signifier may be a handshake, which in itself signifies 'agreement', 'greeting' or maybe 'comradeship'. Together they form the sign.

Like most signs, though, unless you understand their meaning within a particular context, misunderstandings could occur.

Gestures are movements of any part of the body, but usually hands, arms and feet. They are intended to communicate definite messages. Some of these movements are involuntary, though. The involuntary actions usually reveal an emotional state. Gestures both intentional and involuntary can be used to replace speech, and complete the meaning of verbal utterances.

Activity 4.A   Gestures

1. Make a list of the gestures that people use when they are:
    (a) aggressive
    (b) violent
    (c) anxious
    (d) self-conscious
    (e) tired
    (f) hot
    (g) annoyed
    (h) directing
2. Describe the type and range of gestures used to accompany speech.
3. Many gestures are restricted to certain cultures.
    (a) List any gestures that you feel are universal.
    (b) Are there are gestures that change meaning between cultures?
4. Below are descriptions of some common gestures. What meanings do you associate with them? Compare your answers with the answers of other students in class.

Here is an example: 'laying one's hands on something' according to the *Dictionary of Symbols and Imagery* symbolizes (1) blessing (2) consecration (3) transference of guilt (4) healing (5) on one's own head; mourning.

Try to associate as many meanings as you can with the following gestures.

(a) raising one's hand
(b) placing one's hand on one's breast
(c) two hands joined or clasped
(d) hands put at the side
(e) striking one's hands together
(f) tapping one's foot
(g) shuffling one's feet
(h) crossing one's legs
(i) folding one's arms

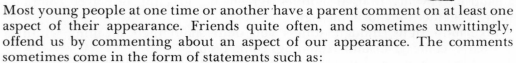

Appearance

Most young people at one time or another have a parent comment on at least one aspect of their appearance. Friends quite often, and sometimes unwittingly, offend us by commenting about an aspect of our appearance. The comments sometimes come in the form of statements such as:

- You're not going out dressed like that!
- What have you done to your hair!
- I *like* your shoes!
- Did you run out of material when you were making that dress?

Sometimes people offend, sometimes people praise, but always people notice our appearance. This is because many aspects of our appearance are under voluntary control. Overall cleanliness, hairstyle and clothing are perhaps the three items that we have most control over, and because we have this control, people notice.

It has been suggested that in our society the majority of young people strive for individuality through their dress and overall appearance. Adolescents want to be seen to be different from children, but not easily identified with their parents and other adults, so they dress to show their individuality. But how do young people dress? How is their dress perceived to be different by children on the one hand, and adults on the other?

If you spend some time observing young people in social gatherings, one of the most striking features is that their dress is individual, but at the same time it is also very conformist. They dress in a similar fashion to their peers. Young people have this ability to be nonconformist conformists. The example of young people is used because dress differences tend to be most significant among this age group. People in all walks of life, by the way they dress, strive to be noticed because of their dress, but at the same time they do not wish to be seen to be significantly different from those with whom they work or socialize.

Activity 4.B The Meaning of Dress

1. Form small groups and complete the exercise. Then, as a group, answer the questions that follow.

    Compile a list of social and work groups and then list the dress that each group adopts. You might also note significant changes in hairstyle and the use of make-up between the groups or occupations. To start you off, here are a few groups that you might like to consider: surfers, office workers, skateboard riders, executives, teachers, nurses, people at a party.
    (a) Is the dress stereotyped for each group? Are there any exceptions?
    (b) What is communicated to the rest of the group if you dress in a similar style to everyone else?
    (c) What could it communicate to the rest of the group if you do not dress in a similar styles?
    (d) Why do you think some people associate the 'wearing of a tie' (for men) as an indication of professionalism?
2. Interview 4 persons who are over 45–50 years of age and ask them how dress conventions have changed, particularly in relation to acceptable work dress conventions! After the interviews, answer these questions.
    (a) How have dress conventions changed?
    (b) What would you consider to be the most significant changes in relation to dress and hairstyle?
    (c) What have been the main trends in dress and hairstyle over the last 20 years?

Because we can manipulate our appearance, we can present ourselves in a particular style and thereby indicate to others how we would like to be treated.

The presentation of self is important. It is through our appearance that others gain their first, and often only, impression of us. While acknowledging that people do judge others on appearance, many people would argue that this is a very artificial way of 'summing up other people' and that dress and appearance can give very misleading clues about people.

How do you feel about this point? It could form the basis for a discussion or debate in class!

Bodily Posture

In some ways we have put the cart before the horse in discussing appearance before posture, but there is no significance in the order. Appearance is, however, quite often determined by the body shape. In the study of human body shape (morphology), three main body types are recognized.

The **endomorph** is characteristically round and fat; the **mesomorph** bony, muscular and athletic and the **ectomorph** tall, thin and fragile. As our overall height and mass are determined for the main part genetically, we cannot change, short of cosmetic surgery, our physical build. But, as we discussed in the previous section, quite often one can minimize differences by adopting a particular style of dress.

Another way in which people communicate feelings about themselves is through their posture. Self-confidence, inferiority, superiority and even internal or emotional states can be communicated through posture. Some young people in adolescence go through a 'growth' spurt where they 'all of a sudden' find themselves much taller, or bustier, than their peers. In order to compensate for this, tall people tend to slump and bustier girls sometimes develop round shoulders. The unfortunate thing that arises from this is that, because the body is growing so quickly in adolescence, it is difficult to overcome the posture in later years. It can therefore affect our posture for the rest of our lives.

So far we have only looked at physiological aspects of posture. Complete the following exercise, then discuss how posture communicates feeling that we may have about ourselves, about situations and about other people.

Activity 4.C   Communicating Through Posture

1. Use stick illustrations similar to those shown to indicate the postures that you feel signal the following feelings and emotional states:
   (a) self-satisfaction
   (b) aggression
   (c) shame
   (d) looking/searching
   (e) superiority
   (f) inferiority
   (g) impatience
   (h) sadness
   (i) disinterest
   (j) anger
   (k) surprise
   (l) relaxation
   (m) tension
2. Compare your illustrations with those of other students.
   (a) What are the main similarities?
   (b) How can the positioning of the hands or head and the stance communicate specific meaning?
   (c) How are dominance and submission communicated through bodily posture?
   (d) How reliably do you think we can communicate feelings about ourselves, about the situation in which we find ourselves, or about others through our posture?

Posture alone sometimes can signal messages, but more often than not with interpersonal behaviour the posture is accompanied by a facial expression, a movement of the eye or a total movement of the head. This is why this whole 'kinesic' area is often referred to as body language.

Facial Expressions

Most writers would agree that the face provides the most accurate messages about one's internal state. The discolouration of the face when you are sick ('You look rather green around the gills today'), blushing when embarrassed or annoyed ('You look rather hot under the collar') and perspiration when under tension all reveal to the people around us 'how we feel'. It is important therefore to watch for these signs when communicating with others. The interviewer who doesn't release some of the tension when he sees the applicant 'perspire' may be placing the applicant or interviewee under unnecessary stress.

Some people can wiggle their ears and tweak their noses, but these actions do not signal meaningful messages. Most of us can only move two parts of our face: our brow, and mouth or jaw. All facial expressions are made by a combined movement of these two parts of our face.

The eyebrows can move from a fully raised position where they may indicate 'disbelief' through a normal position that may indicate 'no comment' through to a fully lowered position that may indicate 'anger'.

The mouth can be upturned indicating 'pleasure' or downturned indicating 'displeasure'.

Activity 4.D   Facial Feelings

1. Collect a series of cartoon frames from magazines. Blot out or omit the spoken dialogue. Next to the frame on your page, indicate:
   (a) the feeling or emotion that the cartoonist was trying to achieve, and
   (b) the parts of the face used, and how they were drawn to achieve this effect.
   Here is a list of terms that may help you formulate your ideas: happiness, surprise, fear, suffering, anger, determination, disgust, contempt, amusement.
2. Test your findings with someone else. Cover up your comments and ask someone to tell you what feeling the character in each of the frames is communicating.

Body Language

A useful experiment to measure just how effective both facial expression and posture can be in communication is to watch a TV drama or movie with the sound turned off. How accurately can you follow the plot?

It is obvious that the head plays a very important part in maintaining a positive stance or posture. But the head can also be used to synchronize speech and indicate reinforcement.

The speaker who fails to accompany speech with either head movement, or intonation, inflection and pitch in his voice is at a loss, mainly because he neither looks nor sounds convincing. Consider some of the key public speakers you see on television or in public. Which speakers have the greatest appeal, the most convincing delivery? Who are they?

Small children become aware of non-verbal cues long before they can speak. The sideways movement of the head, sometimes accompanied by vocalization, gives a child an indication that he should not continue doing whatever it was that he was doing. When verbalization is difficult, perhaps because of noise, the head nod is a most useful way of indicating and giving feedback to others. It can be used to encourage, reward, deny or negate. In combination with speech it can offer a reinforcement to the spoken word.

Eye Movements and Eye Contact

The eye can be used by itself or in combination with a facial expression, to signal someone or indicate a reaction. Speakers who try to look at everyone in their audience (within reason) know whether people are attending to them because their look or fixation is returned. The eye alone has made contact and in this way they receive feedback.

In social gatherings, unless we approach other people from behind, we gain their attention and gather some idea of whether 'it is safe' to enter into conversation with them through eye contact. Some social psychologists suggest that the pupil dilates or enlarges when a positive, elated reaction is received from another person. In fact, they suggest that the eye acts like an exciter bulb.

It has long been accepted that the eyes speak. What is the difference between a stare, a gaze and a glance?

In our culture, we look at things, not people. This could be one reason why people get 'on edge' when someone stares at them. Can you think of any culture where this is not the case?

Bodily Contact

WHERE'D I PUT ME AXE?

Each of us has a 'buffer zone' which extends to a distance of about an arm's length around us. This personal space, our most guarded territory, can cause people great problems, particularly when strangers come into this zone in confined areas. Elevators and crowded public transport provide us with perhaps the best two places to observe people protecting themselves against 'invaders'.

Once we have let someone into this buffer zone, three actions can follow. We can touch one another, smell one another and it is very difficult not to have heightened eye contact. In fact, at such a close range it is difficult not to at least bump into or rub shoulders, with the other person or know whether they have been eating garlic, and it is difficult not to look into their eyes.

Some cultures have strong restraints against bodily contact, particularly in public places. You only need to consider the relaxing of laws in China in the late 1970s which made it possible for young couples to hold hands in public. In many Asian countries it is customary for members of the same sex to walk around arm in arm, an act that within our culture would involve a degree of labelling, particularly for males. An interesting point for discussion is how the taboos against touching are heightened in late childhood and never really relaxed again. Young children are constantly involved in body contact with others, whereas adults are restricted in their contact.

We establish three types of bodily contact: **affective** or intimate contact, **aggressive** contact, and **symbolic** and influencing contact.

Activity 4.E Types of Contact

Rule a page into three columns, one for each type of contact. List under each type the actual contacts that are associated with each type. (Example: kissing for intimate contact, kicking for aggressive contact and shaking hands for symbolic contact.) You may find some actions can be located under more than one heading.

Now, form small groups and discuss the following questions.

1. With whom do you establish each of the forms of contact?
2. Why do some actions fall under more than one heading? What are some of these actions?
3. What are the differences between symbolic contacts such as shaking hands or patting someone on the back, and affective contacts such as hugging or holding?
4. We tend to use methods of influence such as leading by the hand or nudging only with people with whom we have some intimate contact. Do you agree? Explain your reaction to this statement to the rest of your group.
5. How can 'challenging someone's buffer zone' affect your communication with them? Explain your answer in relation to each of the three forms of contact.

Orientation and Territory

In the above section we have tried to emphasize the importance of 'space' to people, and in discussing bodily contact have looked at the space that is most guarded. But we control areas far beyond that buffer zone.

Orientation, or the way we position ourselves in relation to others is a most important consideration for communication in the workplace and in social gatherings. Some people use office space and furniture to strengthen their position within the organization. Some people hide behind furniture. These people may have difficulty earning the respect of their fellow employees. Why do you think this might be?

Inanimate objects such as desks, chairs, cupboards and workbenches and work space can be organized in ways to reinforce an 'inequality of status' between people. The person who does not need to hide behind a desk has a much better chance of communicating with others, rather than communicating his position to others.

Activity 4.F   Using the Space Around Us

Examine the four illustrations which depict a situation where someone has been invited into an office to discuss a matter of equal concern to both parties. Answer the questions that follow.

1. What communication problems could there be in each of the illustrations?
2. What is the best position around the desk for both resident and guest to adopt in order to: co-operate; discuss/converse; negotiate; interview? Do the positions change? Why do they change?
3. Draw the office, re-positioning the desk and indicating the best environment that can be established for inviting the guest in and conversing freely with him.

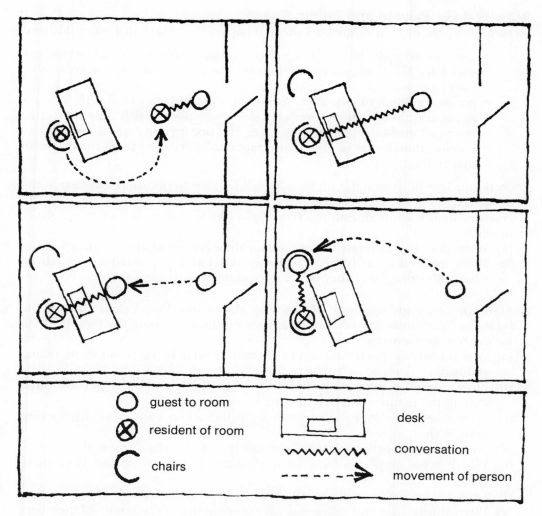

When there are no obstacles such as furniture in the way and when people are not confined by space, they still tend to 'keep their distance' from one another. Closer distances are adopted for more intimate conversations, whereas when we find ourselves in public spaces with strangers, we tend to spread out.

The following activities are designed to get you to make observations of your home and work space, and to make an evaluation of the importance of territory in these places.

Activity 4.G   Private and Public Space

Draw a floorplan of your home on a sheet of paper. Now mark in areas as follows:

- **common ground**: that is, area where everyone (co-dwellers, visitors) can socialize. There are no restrictions on these areas for anyone you invite into your home.
- **personal ground**: that is, areas set aside for each of your co-dwellers. Mark in separately areas that your co-dwellers respect, which they may cross but must acknowledge as your space and occupy only when invited.
- **private ground**: that is, area that is taboo to everyone except the owner of that space.

Even if you live by yourself, you should still be able to divide the area into the three levels.

1. Answer the following questions. You might like to comment on your findings in class.
   (a) What does this exercise tell you about the division of area in your home?
   (b) What importance is placed on furniture (chairs, cupboards, even tables) when 'allocating' territory at the personal and private level?

2. Meet in small groups and discuss the above questions, then discuss the following questions. See how much agreement there is about the way in which we use our 'home space'.
   (a) Are there any particular areas or rooms strictly reserved as personal ground?
   (b) How does the kitchen (particularly the workspace) area get allocated among the people who live in your home?
   (c) How does the allocation of territory differ when you have visitors into your home?
   (d) Are there any seating patterns constantly observed but unstated?
   (e) Which areas or places have been allocated as private space? Why these areas?
   (f) Does anyone in your home lay claim to a specific area?
   (g) What similarities and differences are there between the homes of members of your group in the way in which spaces are divided?
   (h) How important is this allocation of territory to the socialization of people within your home?

3. You may need to amend this activity slightly, depending on your work environment. The purpose of the exercise, once again, is to make observations about the way in which people use the space around them.
   If you work **indoors**, observe the way in which those people occupy the space around them, be it an office, production line, workshop, or retail area. Be sure to take special notice of the way in which *you* use the space around yourself, and the way it helps or hinders your relationships with others. Now answer these questions.
   (a) How does the allocation of space attribute to the overall environment created in the workspace?
   (b) How is furniture used to delineate/define areas?

(c) How is the workspace used by individuals to show their superiority, dominance, or position in the pecking order?

(d) Are there any areas where your movement is restricted because it is 'someone else's territory'? Do you respect their territory? Why?

If you work **out of doors** you might still consider how you function within your workspace. As well as answering questions (c) and (d), you might consider the following questions.

(e) Without the boundaries that can be established through the use of walls, desks, cupboards, windows and doors, are there any ways in which you can maintain personal space or territory?

(f) If you feel you do have a work territory, how do you protect it? From whom do you protect it? Why do you protect it?

If you work **both indoors and out of doors**, you might like to comment on the ways in which the two situations differ in terms of territoriality.

(g) Why do people protect their 'workspace'?

(h) Can you see any danger in people not being able to have a space at work they can call their own?

5 Speechmaking

Kinds of Speech

There are three main kinds of speech. Some are designed to inform, some to persuade and others to entertain. Of course, many speeches do all three of these things in varying degrees.

When you need to explain how something works or to tell how something should be done, or when you present a report or describe a person, place, event, etc., your main purpose is to **inform**.

There are times when you may need to give a speech to **persuade** or convince people to adopt a different viewpoint or attitude or a particular course of action. A persuasive speech involves the use of arguments and logic. However, its success very often depends on the speaker emotionally manipulating the audience.

On very many occasions, such as at weddings, dinners and clubs, speakers set out purely to entertain their audience. They want the audience to relax and enjoy what is being said. While these speeches are not necessarily humorous, many speakers tend to use humorous anecdotes and stories to hold the audience's interest and attention.

Preparing your Speech

The first thing you must do is to work out your **purpose**. It is a very good idea to write down in one sentence exactly what you want to achieve, e.g.:

- believe that smoking is harmful
- understand the working of a petrol engine
- sign a petition for the abolition of the slaughter of whales.

After you have worked out your purpose you should then ask yourself these four questions:

- **Why** are you giving the speech?
- **Who** are the people in your audience? (What are their needs, backgrounds and interests?)
- **What** are you going to say?
- **How** are you going to say it?

Your next task is to **research** your subject thoroughly, and one of the best places to start is the library. You should read any books, periodicals, magazines and newspapers that are related to your subject. Discussions with experts, friends and others can be very valuable as this helps you consolidate the ideas in your own mind.

When you have gathered your material together, you should sort out what is to be retained and what is to be discarded. A good approach is to arrange your information under headings. Select a heading for each main part of your speech and write it on a separate card or sheet of paper, e.g., Why People Smoke. Now list your ideas in a logical order under the appropriate headings. Each main section could then be arranged under subheadings. You may wish to write your speech out in full and read it out aloud to yourself. You will probably need to rewrite and prune sections.

The Structure of your Talk

All speeches should have a beginning, a middle and an end. These divisions are also known as the introduction, the body and the conclusion.

You should use your **introduction** to prepare your audience for what you're going to say. It is important to gain and hold your audience's interest and attention from the outset. A good question to ask yourself: 'What can I say at the beginning to get the audience's attention, and to stimulate their interest?' Some good techniques to use in your introduction are:

- State an interesting fact or make a startling statement.
- Use a thought-provoking quotation.
- Tell a personal interest story.
- Ask a question.
- Use some kind of aid, e.g. slides, chart, overhead projector.
- Tell a joke.

The **body** of your speech should contain all the important information and ideas. This is where you give the facts, evidence, opinions, hypotheses and interpretations concerning your subject. You should be concerned to support your information and ideas with evidence and proof. If you do this, you'll give the impression to your audience that you are an authority on what you're talking about.

In the **conclusion**, your concern will be that your final words will leave an impression on the minds of your audience. A question to ask yourself is: 'What final impression do I want my audience to have?' It is also a good suggestion to summarize your main ideas and reiterate your central idea.

You and your Audience

(1) It is quite natural to experience some degree of nervous tension before giving your speech, so do not be worried by this.

(2) After you have analysed the kind of people in your audience, you should choose an approach that is suited to them. Your approach to an audience of women's libbers would be very different from your approach to a group of burly footballers.

(3) It is very important that you be keen to share your talk with your audience. If you're not interested or involved, how can you expect your listeners to be?

(4) Make your talk stimulating and interesting by inserting human interest details and, when you are relating personal experiences, relive them in your mind.

(5) Speak with conviction, confidence and clarity and use words your listeners can understand.

(6) Be yourself and, if you are using personal experiences, give the actual names and events to breathe life into your talk.

(7) Try to create a lively atmosphere through your words and manner.

You and your Voice

(1) Use your voice to carry meaning and feeling.

(2) Speak clearly so that your voice is audible to all your listeners.

(3) Try to make your ideas flow smoothly across to the audience. Never let your voice become monotonous.

(4) Make sure your voice is pleasant, and vary the speed of your delivery.

(5) Pause occasionally, and stress individual words for emphasis.

You and your Body

You must never overlook the importance of gestures, facial expressions and eye contact. Your body will speak as meaningfully as your voice. It is quite natural for us to use our body when we are talking to one person or to a group of people. Appropriate body movements certainly do help us to direct our listener's attention to the verbal messages being communicated. Head nods can confirm or negate, gestures can indicate direction and reveal mood, and eye contact can make a listener feel that you are attending to him personally.

There are a number of ways of improving your body actions. One good way is to practise in front of a mirror. Another is to study the gestures and body movements of good speakers on television or at public occasions, and yet another is to ask friends or experts to help you identify and overcome any annoying speech mannerisms. Your body and mind should operate as a unified whole.

Activity 5.A   Your Turn: Speech Topics

Some topics lend themselves best to informative speeches, others to persuasive speeches and yet others to entertaining speeches. Select one of the topics and present a three-minute speech to the class. You may decide to concentrate on being informative or persuasive or entertaining or perhaps a combination of all three. In your talk, try to implement some of the speech techniques we have been discussing. One useful approach to develop an understanding of speech technique is to get three people to present a talk on the same topic. Each speaker could adopt a different approach—one to persuade, one to entertain and one to inform.

1. Life is not meant to be easy
2 .The last film I saw
3. The battle of the sexes. Who's winning?
4. Radar traps
5. My kind of music
6. A sportsman I admire
7. Hardened criminals should not be released on parole
8. Planned obsolescence is vital to our economy
9. My chief grievances
10. A television programme I'd like to replace
11. Development of our freeways should be halted
12. Work!

13. My plan to end inflation
14. Leisure time. Do we have too much of it?
15. Trade Unions. Have they outlived their usefulness?
16. Australia, land of . . .
17. There is too much development which is accompanied by the destruction of nature

18. Good grooming is a sign of self respect
19. McDonalds
20. Marriage
21. Most Australians are crude and uncultured
22. Women's liberation. Do they have it already?
23. A book I would take with me to a desert island
24. Politicians
25. Food, glorious food
26. Unusual happenings I have witnessed

27. A place I like to visit very much
28. Things life has taught me
29. Green
30. Keeping fit
31. Prostitution should be legalised
32. Alcohol
33. The motor car does more harm than good
34. Boxing is a blood sport that should be banned
35. Women are inferior to men and always have been
36. The best things in life are free
37. Black
38. The newspaper I like best
39. Socialism. Why fight it?
40. A woman's place is in the home
41. Technical education—the main stay of the space age
42. We should aim to keep Australia white
43. Yellow

44. My solution to unemployment
45. Dole Bludgers
46. Mass media is ass media
47. The smoking of marijuana should be legalised
48. Strikes should be made illegal
49. The generation gap
50. Public transport
51. The youth of today expects too much too soon
52. Five ways of reducing pollution
53. The house I'd like to own
54. My job
55. Public servants
56. The amount of violence in society is on the increase
57. Sex in films should be censored
58. Abortion on demand should not be legal
59. Making money
60. Working women
61. Cancer
62. Talkback radio

"WELL LISTENERS, THAT WAS MRS. SPRONG WHO'S JUST LOST HER JOB, HER HUSBAND'S RUN OFF WITH HER NEIGHBOUR AND HER HOUSE HAS BURNT DOWN.. MAKES YOU THINK EH?"

63. Taxation
64. Compulsory voting
65. Ways of reducing the road toll
66. The army
67. Police
68. Sunday drinking should be illegal
69. Too many of our TV programmes and films have too much violence
70. Education
71. Commercial television leaves much to be desired
72. Improvements I'd make to ABC programmes
73. My favourite charity
74. My favourite comic strip
75. Obedience and respect for authority are the most important values children should learn
76. These days nobody cares about anyone else
77. Road transport
78. Some improvements I would make to some of my courses
79. Jet aircraft are worth all the noise and pollution they create
80. Sex crimes such as rape and attacks on children deserve more than imprisonment; such criminals should be publicly whipped or worse

Activity 5.B   Impromptu Speaking

1. Write topics on cards and have members of the group pick a card face down. Each person then has to speak for two minutes on the chosen topic. A variation of this is to have the names of group members on separate cards and when the topic has been selected from one pile of cards, the name of the speaker is selected from another pile of cards. To give the speaker some choice, two or three topics could appear on one card.

John Smith

Radar Traps
life is not meant
to be easy
Keeping fit

2. Allocate each person in the class a letter of the alphabet and a piece of paper. Next to the letter, each person writes down six to eight of their own speech topics beginning with the letter. The cards are then handed back to the teacher, who reallocates them to members of the class, who then have to select and speak about one of the topics on the card.

B
baked beans
banks
beauty
broken
bosses
books

F
funerals
funny
fat
fashion
furious
fast

T
tennis
toys
tax
toothpaste
terror
test

Evaluating Speakers

In the speech evaluation sheet that follows are a number of questions that will aid you in assessing the content, organization, delivery and language of speeches. Rather than use the whole sheet at once, we suggest that you concentrate on one section. Perhaps ask different people in the room to consider different sections.

Speech Evaluation Sheet

A. Content

1. Was the speaker's purpose clear? ....
....

2. Was the speaker's material interesting and well chosen for *this* audience?
....

3. How well did the speaker know his/her subject? ....
....

4. How suitable and appropriate was the evidence used by the speaker to support his/her viewpoints? (Persuasive speech) ....

Grade 10 9 8 7 6 5 4 3 2 1

B. Organization

5. Did the introduction seize the audience's attention? ....
....

6. Were the speaker's ideas organized in a logical manner? ....
....

7. Was the transition between ideas easily understood? ....
....

8. Was the speaker's conclusion successful? ....
....

Grade 10 9 8 7 6 5 4 3 2 1

C. Delivery

9. Were the speaker's gestures and movements purposeful and effective?
....
....

10. Was the speaker sincere? ....
11. Did the speaker appear to care about communicating with the audience?
....
....

12. Was the speaker's voice pleasing to listen to? ....
13. Did the speaker use sufficient variety of pitch and volume in his/her speech? ....
....

14. How well did the speaker project his/her personality? ....
Grade 10 9 8 7 6 5 4 3 2 1

D. Language

15. Were the speaker's words clear and meaningful? ....
16. Were the speaker's sentences well composed? ....
17. Did the speaker's words suit the audience and the subject? ....
....

Grade 10 9 8 7 6 5 4 3 2 1

6 Listening

Now I hear you, now I don't.
Now I'll tell you, now I won't.

Robert Louis Stevenson once wrote: 'All speech, written or spoken, is a dead language until it finds a willing and prepared hearer'. This chapter discusses the processes of effective listening and then examines a number of situations where listening is the key to effective instructing and speaking.

In One Ear and Out the Other

Some people just don't listen. The adage 'in one ear and out the other' describes fairly accurately what happens in some conversations. One, sometimes both,

parties either don't listen or don't want to listen. This invariably results in a breakdown in communication. People often hear what they want to hear, not what is being said.

Listening, like writing, reading, in fact all our communication skills, must be practised, and can be improved. It involves more than just telling yourself 'I'm really going to listen hard and try to pick up all of this talk'. While this enthusiasm is necessary and should be encouraged, it is simply not enough. You need to know when to tune in and what to listen for, as well as understanding something about your listening capabilities, in order to be an effective listener.

For a start, no one listens intently from one minute to the next. People may look as if they are listening. You may even wonder how they can concentrate for so long on one speaker or idea, particularly when either or both are so incredibly boring. The truth is that while you may be hearing all the time, only for some of that time are you listening, that is, taking in the information, storing, analysing or evaluating the content, and summing up the speaker.

The attentive periods when we are actually listening vary depending on the tiredness, anxiety or boredom of the listener, the stimulation provided by the speaker, and the extraneous noise that makes it difficult to attend to your target. We listen intently for periods ranging from twenty seconds to forty seconds. This is followed by periods when we act on or process the information that we have received. Listening involves this continual process of making sense of what we have heard. If the speaker has our attention and the speech is 'making sense' then we retain more information and recall more details than if the speaker was unconvincing and the content uninformative.

This should not suggest that we do not listen to those who hold opposing views to our own or even that we don't pay them as much attention. We are simply saying that you need to create an amenable frame of mind in order to get the most from your listening.

If we have preconceived ideas about the speaker ('She's a bore', 'He's a ratbag') or about the subject or content of the talk ('I hate political broadcasts'), then we have little chance when we listen of receiving the information content, let alone analysing or evaluating the content objectively. It is only when you have tuned in to the speaker, and thought critically about what has been said, that the listening process becomes effective; it is only at this stage that you develop understanding.

Some Distractions

There are a number of reasons why people fail to listen to what they hear. Distractions can emanate from the immediate environment, from within the listener, and from the speaker.

If the speaker cannot command the attention of the listener, then the listener will attend to stimuli in the immediate environment. The source of this noise or distraction may involve any of the senses. This is why a speaker should not distribute visual material such as notes while he is speaking.

If the listener feels threatened by what he is hearing, his attention may become focused on his feelings rather than on what is being said. If the listener has a different viewpoint or attitude from those being expressed, he may spend his time deciding what can be said in response, and in so doing miss the essence of what is actually being said. The listener can distract himself by being pre-occupied with other commitments and tune out the speaker altogether.

Appearance, mannerisms, accent and even personality can all provide listener distraction. Some of these traits are unavoidable, but nevertheless can distract the listener.

Activity 6.A   Distractions Around You

Watch people in conversation on station platforms, at bus stops, in foyers of cinemas, in wine bars, hotels, corridors, offices, practically everywhere that conversations take place. Attend to the traits that could provide listener distraction. Report back to class with your findings.

If you wish to improve your listening you need to consider the following:

- Concentrate on the speaker and identify the subject of the talk.
- Eliminate any distractions that may introduce a noise source.
- Think about what is being said, and even if you cannot respond to the speaker, listen as if you had to.
- Be empathic. Remember, it could be you giving the talk and there is nothing worse than looking at a sea of vacant gazes.

The Ear Sees

When someone is speaking, we are not only concerned with what the person says, we are also concerned with the way in which he says it. People use hand movements, facial expressions and adopt certain postures to indicate a mood, feeling or attitude. These behaviours either support or detract from what is being said. But people also use vocal expression to enhance the meaning of their message.

The following section on listening is designed to get you to concentrate on what you hear. For the purpose of the exercise you will need to concentrate only on the spoken word in order to see just how valuable the oral-aural mode of communication can be not only in conveying meaning, but in giving us insight into the personality and nature of the other person. The voice can give clues so that you can find out about the person behind the mask.

During the 1930s and again in the 1960s many experiments were conducted to ascertain how well people judge the personality of a person by voice alone. Allport and Cantrill in an article in the *Journal of Social Psychology* in 1934 titled 'Judging personality from voice'[1] wrote:

> Over the radio the rich and informative visual pattern is absent; only the voice and speech remain. The resulting judgement is somewhat fragmentary and uncertain. This situation has already received popular recognition in jokes concerning the disillusionment of those who learn to their sorrow that the radio voice with which they fell in love does not reveal accurately either the appearance or the nature of the possessor.

The radio is only one form of the sound medium where we must make judgements about others through their voice qualities and speech content. In the exercise that follows we would like you to make judgements about people through their voice qualities and speech content.

Voice is 'the vocal expression' which includes factors such as rhythm, intensity, pitch, volume, inflection and vocal mannerisms. **Speech** is the subject matter of the discourse, including dialect, language spoken, vocabulary and sentence structure.

Activity 6.B Making Personality Tapes

This is an exercise to encourage you to listen attentively to the speech and the use of the voice. It is a perception exercise. What do we hear when someone speaks, besides the information or ideas?

Before the next class, arrange for four or five people to make a 3- to 5-minute tape recording of a friend talking on a topic of their choice. The person making the tape should not identify himself by name or in any other specific way. Make suggestions to the person making the tape about a possible subject for discussion.

---

[1] Allport, G. W. and Cantrill, H., *Journal of Social Psychology*, Vol. 5, 1934, pp. 37–55.

Here are some suggestions of possible topics: My Choice of Drinks; Beach Fashion; The Boom in Tennis; My Boss; Bludgers; Bare-Top Barmaids; Male Strippers; My Weekend; Sleep; Unions; Shopping.

Bring the recordings to class for the next lesson and play each of the discourses (talks). Listen to each tape recording carefully. At the end of each recording, answer the following questions and discuss the answers in class. Try to answer all questions.

1. Is the speaker male or female?
2. What age is the speaker? (e.g. 35–40 years, 25–30 years)
3. What sort of complexion does the speaker have? (e.g. dark, fair)
4. Can you think of any other physical features that this person might have?
5. Is the speaker introverted or extroverted?
6. Which political party does the speaker support?
7. What is the job or vocation of the speaker?
8. Would you like to have this person as:
    (a) your boss
    (b) your prime minister
    (c) your employee
    (d) your bank manager
    (e) your teacher?
9. Have you made any assumptions about the speaker? What are they?

It would be useful at this stage if a profile of the speaker, gauged from the student's answers, was written on the chalkboard.

Before finding out the correct details about the speaker from the person who made the tape, discuss the following questions.

10. Which question was answered most consistently by the class members? Least consistently?
11. Was there a consensus of opinion among class members as to the speaker's physical traits (gauged from questions 1–4)?
12. As a class, how reliably did you answer questions 1 to 5?
13. To which specific aspects of the speaker's 'voice' and 'speech' did class members attend in order to answer the questions? Is there any consensus of opinion among class members on these aspects?
14. Which question was the most difficult to answer? Why?
15. Compare your 'picture' of the speaker with the 'correct picture'. How successful do you think voice and speech are as indications of personality?

Listening and Debating

The debate is a useful way of allowing people to discuss the pro's and con's of an issue in an organized way. If you like, a debate is an organized argument.

It does not matter whether you are in a formal debate or debating an issue in a meeting, you must listen carefully to what has already been said by speakers who have supporting and opposing viewpoints. This allows you to build on what has already been stated and find flaws in the arguments presented. There is little point reiterating views that have already been expressed.

Activity 6.C Debate

Conduct a debate in class, either formally as a debate or as an open discussion. Select a topic from the list below or select one that is topical and of interest to the group.

Your debate will be slightly different from a standard debate because each speaker *must* repeat the main ideas of the previous speaker before adding his own ideas. The previous speaker is free to interject if he feels he has been misquoted or misunderstood.

Some ideas for topics:
1. Petrol should be rationed now before it's too late
2. No drinking of alcohol at sporting fixtures
3. The unions will grind Australia to a halt
4. Nudity on beaches should be abolished
5. A four-day working week for all

Listening and Note-Taking

Note-taking is the bane of students' lives. How many times have you given up in disgust when trying to take notes? Why is note-taking so frustrating? Because you don't think you have the salient points! . . . because every time you write something down that you think is important you seem to miss two other points! . . . or because the speaker does not emphasize what he considers to be the key to his talk or lecture!

Different people have different techniques for taking notes. Some people try to take notes verbatim, others sit back and at the end of an interval of time jot down the essence of the talk in their own words. You need to find a method that suits your needs.

Activity 6.D Practising Your Note Taking

In the following exercise, have a student or the teacher read a passage or article from a newspaper or magazine to the class. Make sure it is something of interest to the class. Take notes from the reading. In your note-taking:
1. Try to identify the main points by listening for key words and phrases. Jot these down.
2. Write your notes in point form. Do not try to transcribe long sentences from the talk. Remember, much of what a speaker says is padding designed to keep the talk fluent. You will be helped in this exercise because the material is being read. So . . .
3. Attempt to find a structure in the reading, in the same way that you make sense of a talk. Do you feel that you have grasped the main points being made and written these ideas down in terms you understand? *Think critically* about what is being said. Don't just try to copy it all down.

Activity 6.E Persuasion

As you learned in the chapter on giving a talk, there is more to persuading people and convincing them than opening your mouth. In this listening exercise, arrange to listen to public celebrities such as people in the news and politicians being interviewed either on the radio or on television. Listen for emotional and subjective content, loaded words, appeals to the listener's conscience, and key phrases that the speaker uses.

Bring your information to class. Identify the speaker, discuss the context in which the interview took place, and then comment on the techniques the speaker used to be persuasive.

Was the speaker convincing? persuasive? credible? lucid? erudite?

If more than one person in the class attended to the same speaker, did the listeners attend to the same content and techniques? How did the observations or perceptions differ?

Activity 6.F   Conservation of Conversation

We have already had one exercise where you were to observe the traits of people involved in conversation to identify possible distractions. In this exercise, 'eavesdrop' on conversations for the purpose of identifying how people sustain conversation. How does one person indicate to another that he wants them to continue? Is anything said? Is anything vocalized? How does one person interject or take over the role of speaker when he has been an avid listener in a conversation? How are 'grunts', 'head nods', 'mumbles', 'ums', 'ahhs' and other vocalizations used in conversations?

Telephoning

Some people might as well be talking to themselves when they use the telephone. It is important that you talk *with* the other party rather than talk *at* him. At times this may be difficult, as the other person may not give you the opportunity to get a word in edgeways. The phone is actually quite a useful tool for talking to yourself, having both an earpiece and mouthpiece. The unfortunate thing about this selfindulgent pastime is that *you* may find yourself stuck on the other end of the phone.

However, there are ways of gaining control of the conversation:

- Wait for a pause (no matter how short) and interject with a question to get the person off the topic.
- Continue to ask questions for which you need answers. By doing this you break the flow and remain in control of the dialogue.
- Say that you are busy or in a hurry and that you will ring back in twelve months.

The frustration in using the telephone to conduct your business, make inquiries and seek information comes about because both parties are forced to make assumptions about one another. As you cannot see the other person, you rely heavily on verbal clues and cues to understand the caller and project your own personality.

Hints on Using the Telephone

(1) Identify yourself, and give your number and/or location.
(2) Speak clearly and politely into the mouthpiece.
(3) Attend solely to the caller and concentrate on the inquiry or message.
(4) Be prepared to ask questions in order to clarify information.
(5) Because it is difficult to ask someone to read back your message, repeat relevant information such as order details, names, phone numbers and addresses.
(6) 'Spell out' difficult names and expressions, and product names. Don't just repeat details.
(7) Emphasize key words, phrases and ideas by varying the pitch of your voice.
(8) End the conversation by suggesting follow-up action, or repeat the key point made in the conversation.
(9) Take notes during the call that will be meaningful to you or to the person for whom you are taking the message.

Telepathy and the Telephone

Receptionist: 'Good morning, Boltanut Engineering.'
Caller: 'Hello.'
Receptionist: 'Look, could you just hang on for a tick? I'm tied up at the moment.' [1 minute later.] 'Hello, sorry to have kept you. May I help you?'
Caller: 'Yes, actually I'd like to make an enquiry about . . .'
Receptionist: 'I'm sorry, but you've got the warehouse. The office deals with enquiries.'

Sometimes it's very tempting to slam the phone down in the other party's ear—an effective, but damaging, way of communicating.

You do not know what the other person is doing and he does not know what you are doing, so keep him in the picture. If you are busy, suggest that you will ring back, or ask for a return call at a more convenient time.

Problem Calls

When dealing with problem callers or callers with complaints, keep your cool and gauge the climate of the conversation. There is no hard and fast rule for dealing with people who are upset, impatient or belligerent. Ask questions to get all the facts about the problem. If the customer's complaint is justified, apologize and decide how the problem can be rectified. Decide on the course of action that can be taken. If the customer's complaint is unjustified, be polite but firm and state your reasons for rejecting the complaint.

Explaining over the Phone

Sometimes detailed explanations are necessary in order to create a clear picture of the problem or situation for the person answering the inquiry. Clear pictures are not created by blasting unrelated or poorly thought-out ideas at the other party.

Write down your ideas on a note pad before you call and order them into a logical sequence. Introduce your idea, tell the other party that you would like help with a problem, then begin your explanation. Remember that the other party has specialist information and has probably dealt with many problems similar to your own over the phone. Therefore, it may be better to let him guide you through the problem by allowing him to ask you questions.

Using Jargon

> At regular intervals in its operation the veebleflexer that holds the diagiggle to the opsidynaposcope becomes disconnected from the radiopolydicon. What should I do?

Using technical jargon may be the best way to clarify ideas but may confuse the other party when it is used in a phone conversation. When jargon is used, try to provide an alternative description as well to help clarify the idea in the mind of the non-specialist. In other words, tell the other person what the jargon means.

Phone Messages

There is nothing worse than receiving a phone message that leaves you guessing. Who took the call? When was it taken? Who is Eddy Lyon? Where is he from?

It is a good practice when taking phone messages to indicate:

- time of call
- name of caller (and designation if necessary)
- reference, message
- return phone number, and
- person's name who took the call.

> David,
> Please phone
> Eddy Lyon
> on 6849310.

Answering Services

It can be quite daunting to hear the recorded voice of the person to whom you wished to speak indicating that you can record a message when you hear a beep. Dumbfounded, many would-be callers hang up, never to call again. So much for technological advancements!

If confronted with an answering service, make a brief statement indicating:

- **Name:** who you are,
- **Nature:** what the nature of your business is,
- **Number:** where you can be contacted.

Activity 6.G   I'm phoning about . . .

Here is an exercise in using the telephone. Those students who are not involved in role playing should listen carefully to the dialogue of the people involved in the conversation.

Ask yourself these questions:

- Did both parties sound polite and interested?
- Did the caller indicate what he was after?
- Did the source supply necessary information that expanded the advertisement?
- Did both parties ask relevant questions?
- Did both parties indicate the course of action that was to be taken following the call?

Have students act out the phone conversations that could arise from these advertisements. One student should request the information, the other supply it.

In order to simulate a phone conversation, sit back to back at the front of the class. You might have a number of people make the *one* request for information. Discuss the dialogue in each case.

BRIGHTON
COLLEGE

ACCOMMODATION REQUIRED

Brighton College is situated in Newcastle and provides courses in Physiotherapy, Occupational Therapy, Nursing, Medical Records Administration and Orthoptics.

The Student Union accommodation service requires accommodation in the following categories:

- **FULL BOARD**
- **PART BOARD**
- **HOUSES—FLATS TO LET**
- **SHARE ACCOMMODATION**

If you can assist with any type of accommodation please phone the

Accommodation Officer, 478 1991 at anytime

El Binge Cellars

Applications are invited for the full-time position of

PUBLIC RELATIONS OFFICER

in
El Binge Wine Cellars
to have overall responsibility for promotion, marketing and public relations.
For details
**Phone: I. M. STONE on
682 1798**

MANUFACTURING BUSINESS
FOR SALE

A successful company established 30 years. Proprietors wish to retire. We manufacture sheetmetal products of well known brand, distributed through electrical wholesalers and hardware stores.

The factory is situated approx. 15 km from Adelaide.

Turnover approx. $145,000. For further details

Phone 667 1676

BUSINESS FOR SALE

BRIDAL WEAR MEN'S FORMAL HIRE

This business located in a thriving regional shopping centre is for sale. Don't miss this one. Full price $60,000.

Phone 889 4176 weekdays after 7 p.m., weekends after 1 p.m. for full details.

PLANET

PROMOTIONS

ARE YOU INTERESTED

1. IN SPACE TRAVEL
2. IN INTERGALACTIC SCIENCE
3. IN ISOLATION

IF YOU ARE AND WOULD LIKE MORE INFORMATION, THEN RING 641 7777 FOR AN INVITATION TO ATTEND AN EVENING MEETING ON THURSDAY 6 OCTOBER 1988. WE ARE LOOKING FOR ASTRONAUTS.

7 Complaints and Commands

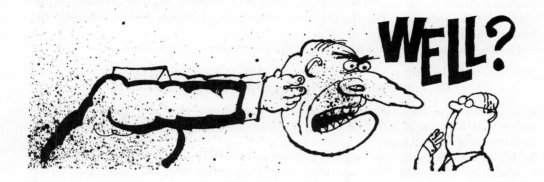

Don't Lose your Head when Handling Complaints

Some organizations employ people to deal specifically with complaints against their organizations. In his book *How to Complain* Christopher Ward writes:

> Complaints departments are by their very existence an admission of a company's incompetence and failure. They say, in effect: We have so many dissatisfied customers that we have to have a whole department to deal with them. Please take your place in the queue.

Be that as it may, the fact is that there will always be dissatisfied customers who have to be dealt with both efficiently and effectively by at least one member of the organization. If the complaint is taken in person or over the phone, the following steps are important:

- Find out exactly what the complaint is and ask questions to get to the bottom of the problem. By doing this you are both showing interest and cutting short unnecessary testimonials and whinging.
- Decide whether or not you can handle the complaint. If it needs to be referred to someone else, now is the time to do it.
- Ascertain whether it is your responsibility, or that of your company to take some course of action. There is little point humouring a customer who purchased goods or services under specified conditions, when those conditions have been breached. Get all the facts.
- Decide what you are going to do and inform the customer of the action that you will take. Negotiate if necessary in order to reach an agreement.

You should not be rude even if the person complaining is abusive. Offer apologies, and give reasons or provide explanations when they are appropriate. Effective listening is the key to dealing with complaints. Nothing will be gained by arguing with the person. Listen, ask questions to clarify the complaint, then decide on some course of action.

Activity 7.A   Complaint Act Outs

Act out some of the following situations in class. For each complaint, have one person complain and have a second person deal with the complaint. An alternative method of conducting the exercise is to have several people act out the same situation.

Having acted out each situation get class members to comment on:

- how the complainer put his case, and
- how the employer dealt with the complaint and the complainer.

If you adopt the alternative method of having a number of students play out the one situation, you might leave the discussion until the end and then compare and contrast the various 'performances'.

1. It's 10 am. You are in a large hardware store where you intend buying a large quantity of goods. You use this store frequently and the service is rarely satisfactory. The customer appears to be a curse.

   There are several employees scurrying to and fro. There are no other customers in the shop. Having stood at the counter for about 8 minutes without being able to attract anyone's attention, you decide to go to the manager's office which is clearly visible at the back of the shop to complain about the service.

2. You purchased a toaster about one month ago but did not use it until this morning. When you plugged in the toaster, it blew up. When you checked the guarantee it read: This toaster is guaranteed for parts and service for a period of 30 days from purchase. Send this card to Brown Toasters Ltd within 7 days for the guarantee to be valid.

   You cannot remember exactly when you purchased the toaster and you forgot to send in the guarantee. Make a complaint either to the service department at Browns, or to the store from which you made your purchase.

3. You live in a home unit. Your upstairs neighbour plays her stereo record-player loudly until quite late most nights.

   It is Saturday night (actually Sunday morning), you have been trying to get to sleep for two hours but the reverberations from the din upstairs continue into the night. It doesn't appear that she is having a party. You've had enough, so you don dressing gown and march up the stairs to her unit to complain.

4. You have hired some scaffolding from Hire It Ltd, the local plant hire firm. As you have finished using it, you stack it in the driveway ready for collection by the firm. The truck arrives to collect the scaffolding and you suggest to the driver to back the truck into the driveway to make it easier to load. As you are running late for work you then leave. On arriving back home from work that night you find one of the two sides gates mangled.

   You find your invoice, and read the small print. There is no indication in the hiring agreement of whether or not the firm is responsible. Complain to the hire firm.

5. You work in a laboratory where glass beakers, pipettes, tumblers and tubes are used continually. You are supplied with the glassware twice weekly. Because of the fragility of the glassware, breakages are inevitable, but rare because of careful packaging and transportation by the firm that supplies you. However,

in the last two deliveries, each consisting of eighty items in four boxes, approximately five items per box have been broken. The firm claims 'all care but no responsibility' in transport.

Phone the supplier and complain.

Giving Orders

An order is a command or directive given to a subordinate indicating that the person should act in a prescribed way. Unlike an instruction, it is not normally accompanied by a detailed description of how the task should be performed. However, a fine line divides the two forms of direction.

Orders can be given verbally, non-verbally or in written form.

Verbal orders may be used where the recipient immediately understands the purpose of the order and is able to carry it out. It is the most direct form of order as it involves person-to-person contact.

Why do 'verbal orders' often cause communication breakdowns at work?

Non-verbal orders may be used where distance, noise or language problems make verbal or written orders impossible. Many non-verbal orders are given using codes and agreed symbol systems. Semaphore and morse code are perhaps the most commonly used codes for this purpose.

Can you think of any other codes that are used to give non-verbal orders?

Written orders may be used where a directive is being given to implement a decision. The written order provides the recipient with a record of the instructions. Written orders are used when the order cannot be acted on immediately or when changes in policy are being made. The most common written form is an order for goods, materials or services.

Activity 7.B   Made to Order

Ask yourself these questions about the following orders.

- How would you give each of the following orders?
- Which medium would you use?

1. Order a subordinate to change company policy on acceptable dress for employees.

2. Order a subordinate (an electrician) to disconnect specific wires from an electrical control board.
3. Order a subordinate to clean a machine.
4. Order a migrant worker who has difficulty with English to change his work location from one suburb to another suburb on the other side of town.
5. Order a roasted chicken from the 'hot window' at the local milk bar.

Verbal Orders

There are three main ways of giving verbal orders: through a command, through a request, and through implication.

In an attempt to change a course of action it may be necessary to use a **command**. However, a command may be inappropriate in certain situations. A command is accepted where danger is present, where there is a strict hierarchy such as in a military establishment, and where you want an order to be succinct.

A **request** order reduces the severity of the directive. Unless you are familiar with the subordinate, the courtesy shown might be interpreted as a weakness in the person giving the order. At the same time, though, the request order is useful in breaking down the resistance of subordinates in having to comply with orders.

Now, look back to the previous exercise and decide which type of order seems appropriate in each case. Then complete the following exercise.

Activity 7.C Changing Commands to Requests

Change the following commands to requests.

- Is there a need to change all of the commands to requests?
- Which commands need not be changed?
- How does the addition of the word 'please' change the tone of the commands?

(a) Get to work by 7.30 a.m. on Monday!
(b) Allan, clean that machine before you go home!
(c) Hold the hammer further down the handle!
(d) Shove off!
(e) You can't come in here!
(f) That work needs to be done again!
(g) There will be a meeting of all staff at 4 p.m.!
(h) Dig a trench from the front gate to the back fence!
(i) Go to the printing office and collect the order!
(j) Wipe your feet before you enter!

If you know the attitudes and habits of the recipient, then **implied orders** are useful ways of giving directives. What is implied in this type of order is not only that the recipient knows his job, but that he will recognize the implication in your statement and act in the desired way.

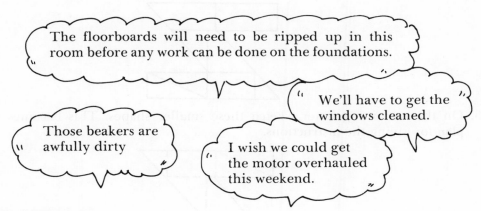

Instructions

All of the tasks and operations we perform in our working lives involve learned behaviours. This implies that at some point, through observation and practice involving trial and error we become familiar with the tasks and operations.

In the workplace, instruction is used to show or teach new operations so that efficiency may be maintained and a satisfactory job completed.

In our day-to-day lives, we give instructions and directions when someone wants to know how to get to a certain location, when a friend borrows a piece or machinery or even when familiarizing a child with the operation of a new toy.

How often have you given instructions and directions only to find out that the receiver has not followed your instructions, or found that what the recipient understood was different from what you meant? If the receiver does not perform the operation as you requested, or does not reach the specified destination, then you, as an instructor, should accept some of the responsibility for the failure. It's no good saying 'Well I told him what to do!' and then expect the person to perform.

Activity 7.D   Test your Ability to Give Instructions

For this exercise you will need to prepare the following material.

1. Take two identical pieces of paper (the same colour on both sides) and draw the same letter of the alphabet, in block form on both pieces of paper. A 15-cm (6-inch) square of paper would be the best size.

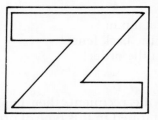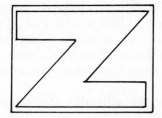

2. Now, cut out the letter shapes. Cut one of the letters into small regular shapes in a way similar to that shown.

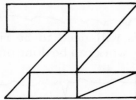

3. On the remaining letter, sketch these smaller shapes. This becomes your **plan** for giving the instructions.

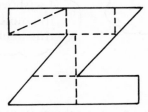

4. Place the pieces that form the letter in one envelope, and the plan of the letter in another.
5. Sit back-to-back with someone else from your class. One person takes the pieces of the puzzle, the other person gives the instructions from the plan.

    This exercise is best played if you use illustrations that have been prepared by someone else, so swap pairs of envelopes and try a classmate's puzzle.

    Try to give the instructions as clearly as possible without looking over your shoulder. Remember this is an exercise in giving *verbal* instructions. Give the instructions without revealing the letter that the pieces form.

A Guide to Giving Clear Verbal Instructions

Preparation: Questions to Ask Yourself
(1) Is the instructee ready to perform this task?
(2) Does he have the necessary materials and is he familiar with them?
(3) Is he familiar with the terms and expressions that I am going to use?
(4) Is there sufficient space to demonstrate and practice the operation?
(5) Do I get on with the instructee so that he will feel free to ask questions and seek help?

Instructing
(1) Create a clear picture of what is to be done. State the overall goal.
(2) Give the instructions in a logical sequence, using terms and expressions that the instructee understands.
(3) Keep the instructions simple. Complex and long-winded instructions could confuse and frustrate the instructee.
(4) Clarify the ideas and encourage feedback. Never ask if he understands. Get him to show you or get him to repeat the instructions to indicate understanding and competence in completing the operation.

8 Meetings

Not Another Damn Meeting

'Not another damn meeting' seems to be a common cry of members of clubs, societies, business organizations and unions who are frequently attending meetings. Why do people hate going to meetings? Why do people become disenchanted with the lack of democracy shown in meetings? Why do people attend meetings through force of habit?

Two of the most frequently occurring reasons for these problems in meetings are that there is a lack of participation by members of the meeting and ineffective chairing of the meeting.

For the purpose of this discussion we will define a meeting as any gathering of more than two persons who have come together for a specific reason, or with a common objective, to discuss matters relating to that cause. This includes all types of meetings from those where a chairperson presides, where motions are proposed, and where minutes are taken; to union and club meetings; to informal gatherings of people who may form a discussion group.

The definition above implies that what each of these groups has in common is that they involve a gathering of people with a common objective. But the majority of meetings have something else in common. Even though the groups may have common interests and objectives, the individuals who comprise these groups have personal needs, interests, aspirations and objectives. Everyone 'knows' how the meeting *should* be run, everyone knows how to deal with difficult and complex issues, but someone else is always to blame. The fault with ineffective meetings always lies with the 'other' person.

In this chapter we will examine the following aspects of meetings: chairing and participating in meetings and running a formal meeting.

Activity 8.A Problems when People 'Meet'

This exercise can either be completed individually at home or in the classroom, or in small groups in the classroom. What we would like you to do is to **list** the specific reasons why people seem to think that meetings are ineffective or unproductive and why many people resent going to meetings and participating in them.

We have already hinted at some reasons why there are sometimes problems in meetings by suggesting that people pursue personal objectives which are not in the best interests of the group.

Examine both the chairperson's and the participant's role within a meeting. When you have compiled your list, either discuss your findings within your group or give your list to another group for comment.

Spend some time now re-examining the points you have made. Could some points that you originally considered negative really be considered to be productive within a meeting? Consider issues such as 'pursuing personal points of view' and 'using formal meeting procedure'. How can these aspects affect how meetings are run?

- What overall conclusions were reached by the class?
- Where do the greatest problems lie in running meetings?

The Role of the Chairperson

It is the responsibility of the chairperson to control the meeting: that is, establish, distribute and then maintain an agenda of proceedings, and control the debate or discussion that flows from the issues tabled on the agenda. In the first exercise it is likely that you attributed many of the failings in meetings to poor control by the chairperson.

The chairperson is the most important person in a meeting, because it is his responsibility to make sure that all matters are dealt with, that appropriate time is allocated to each issue and that everyone present has the opportunity to debate or discuss issues raised.

The chairperson must guide the meeting towards making a decision, direct problem-solving and ensure that everyone is certain of the matters being discussed.

The chairperson should remain impartial to the matters being discussed. If he feels strongly about an issue, he should stand down while the issue is debated. A chairperson should indicate: what the business of the day will be; who will be presenting reports to the meeting; and how much time will be allocated to specific issues. The last point is particularly important where meetings are being held for a limited time, such as during a lunch hour.

All too often the chairperson wears two hats. The chairperson of the meeting may also have a leadership role within the organization. He may be the manager, union boss, or head of department. Problems arise because both the chairperson and members of the meeting have difficulty differentiating between the two roles. On the one hand the chairperson must control the meeting, but on the other hand a manager or supervisor will have *leadership*-type responsibilities. When the chairperson is wearing two hats or performing these two roles at the same time it sometimes becomes difficult to remain impartial in debates, where it is obvious that sides could be taken. At other times because of your position within the organization you may have more information than the other members of the meeting. Imparting the information to keep everyone informed is important, but when the chairperson begins to dominate and not let others speak he is exercising a leading rather than a controlling role.

Participants in a meeting must feel that they both have the opportunity to speak and that they will be encouraged to speak. It is important that the person chairing the meeting be alert to the needs of the members of the meeting. If an issue raised at the meeting directly affects or has resulted from some action by the chairperson because of his/her leadership role, then in many instances the chairperson would be better off standing down while the issue is debated. This allows a 'neutral' person to chair the discussion and both sides of the issue to be presented as a debate. This point is also mentioned under formal meeting procedure.

Activity 8.B   Maintaining Order

How did the chairperson lose control of this meeting of foremen and charge-hands discussing production rates? The organization manufactures sheep-shearing cutters and combs.

Chairperson (Stan):   This meeting will only be brief. I want to let you know about some changes that will need to be made in cutter production in order to accommodate the new order from Laydon in New Zealand. They want twenty thousand B4 cutters and four thousand AX combs by the end of July. What do you think about that, Eric? What production changes will need to be made to fill the order?

Gordon (interjecting):   We haven't produced B4s and AXs for years. The whole . . .

Chairperson: Look! I asked Eric, and besides this order is important. Eric?

Eric: Well, actually, Stan, Gordon has something. We haven't produced B4s and AXs since 1978, when they were superseded by B8s and ATs. Who took the order? Wouldn't the B8s and ATs do the same job?

Chairperson: The order has been taken and a guarantee given that we can supply . . .

Gordon (over the general din):   It can't be done!

Supervisor 1:   We would need to completely re-machine and that would take ages.

Supervisor 2:   To say nothing for the overtime involved.

Gordon: And who's going to retrain the grinders? There's not one man on the comb bench who was here in '78. I'm damn sure I'm not going to!

Chairperson: I realize that a number of things need to be looked into. That's why . . .

Gordon: A number of things! If the front office stopped bloody well thinking how they . . .

Supervisor 3:   We haven't even straightened up the re-work from the last foul-up when we went onto the wider cutters. How much scrap do they expect to cope with in this run?

Chairperson: I agreed with management that the order should be accepted, and I think the problems you envisage will not exist in reality. We *will* go ahead.

It seems obvious that the order should not have been taken. But in spite of this, the chairperson still did not get to the crux of the matter.
1. What did he allow to happen?
2. What was the main issue of the meeting?
3. How should the chairperson have introduced the issue?
4. How would you have approached this situation to ensure some control but still allow each member to have his say?
5. The responsibility for the chaos is not entirely the chairperson's. Why not?

The Role of Participants

'There's no point in going to the roster meetings because we are only *told* of the rostering arrangements. No one gets a say even when we do try to make suggestions about rostering. Jim just tells us when we are expected to come in on weekends.'

This reaction about a meeting 'that wasn't' is quite typical. People go to some meetings knowing full well that they will neither be asked to nor encouraged to speak. Decisions have obviously been made before the meeting and the meeting is held to provide a false form of democracy within the organization. Meetings can be used to inform and instruct. However, every person who attends a meeting should have an opportunity to speak, and discussion (within reason) should be allowed on any issue raised at a meeting. If a two-way face-to-face communication flow is not to be encouraged, then a meeting is not required. Directions, information or instructions can instead by displayed on a notice board.

An active participant in a meeting doesn't necessarily have a say about everything, but rather listens attentively to the proceedings and in this way is alert and ready to supply information, debate, or even interject if the need arises. The active listener is invaluable to the successfully run meeting.

Encouraging People to Participate in Meetings

No matter whether you are a chairperson or participant in a group, or find yourself at a formal or informal meeting, it is important to understand that the interplay of personalities within the meeting will greatly affect proceedings. One unco-operative group member can make decision-making impossible for the entire group.

Here are some stereotypes that you might expect to find in a group.

1 • **The Chatterbox** talks continually, rarely on the topic, and has little of any worth to contribute.

2 • **The Sleeper** is uninterested in proceedings, uses the meeting to catch up sleep. Some have the ability to sleep with eyes open.

3 • **The Destroyer** crushes any and every idea put forward, can always find something wrong with plans, solutions, routines, etc.

4 • **The Rationalist** makes worthwhile contributions, his ideas are well thought out, which makes other group members envious.

5 • **The Trapper** waits for the opportune moment to inform everyone that there has been an error made; tries to trap the chairperson.

6 • **The Know-All** tries to monopolize the conversation, has many good ideas.

7 • **The Thinker** is shy but when he does speak is a great asset to the group.

How would you encourage or discourage each of the above members to make the meeting flow freely, while achieving their utmost co-operation?

Types of Meeting

Meetings are held so that decisions can be made, problems solved and members of staff informed of new procedures and future tasks that will be expected of them. As we have already said, the meeting provides the opportunity for people to become directly involved in the decision-making, problem-solving and on deciding tasks, routines and schedules that will involve the group. These specific functions may require the chairperson to consider not only an agenda for the meeting, but an *internal* agenda, that is, a strategy by which members can deal with the issues at hand. Here are some simple steps to follow:

Decision-Making
1. Establish the specific goal so that the group members know exactly what the overall objective of the meeting is.
2. Discuss any specific barriers that may be faced by group members. Give individual members the opportunity to air their views.
3. List *all* possible objectives before deciding what *must* be accomplished; try to eliminate through discussion personal biases and individual wants.
4. Identify obstacles such as costs, time, manpower, and decide if any of the obstacles could prevent you from reaching your objectives.
5. Compare the alternatives in view of 4 (above).
6. Choose the best alternative and discuss implementation.

Problem-Solving
1. Define the specific problem.
2. Ensure that adequate research has been undertaken to uncover all the relevant facts.
3. Analyse the problem, taking the facts into consideration.
4. If by doing this you arrive at a dead end, then seek opinions about how the problem occurred.
5. Discuss possible solutions.
6. Choose the best solution and discuss implementation.

These brief internal agendas are not intended to be definitive. They are included to show how either a chairperson or members of a meeting might decide how to tackle a problem to allow for discussion, while still arriving at a solution to a problem within reasonable time. The internal agenda simply answers the question: 'How do we go about discussing this problem or making a decision?'

Formal Meeting Procedure

Clubs, societies and unions are bound by their constitutions to conduct the business of that club or society through formal meetings. Many business organizations use formal meeting procedure to keep the meetings efficient and to ensure that the rules of debate are maintained.

If you have ever been to such a meeting you will have no doubt realized that it does not 'flow along' like a friendly chit-chat. 'Motions' and 'amendments to motions' are moved, 'points of order' are called. The meeting is 'called to order', 'addendums' are sought, sometimes someone 'dissents from the chairperson's ruling', and all this happens while you sit in the corner in dumb confusion. It can certainly make you feel helpless because the members of the meeting seem to be using their own language. In a way it is a special language, 'meeting language'.

Motions

All proposals put to the meeting are presented as **motions**. Motions must be clearly worded, as ambiguity could lead to misinterpretation. Motions should be kept in a simple form:

> I move that a marquee be hired for a period of one day for the club picnic on Saturday 11 June.

> Joyce Kipling

The motion having been moved and seconded, it can be debated. The chairperson should call for speakers who oppose the motion. If there are none, the motion can be put to the vote. However, if anyone does oppose the motion, the chairperson should control the debate by selecting alternately speakers for and against the motion. When the debate is finished, someone moves 'that the question be put'. At this time the mover is given 'the right of reply', which allows the mover to answer any questions which have arisen from the debate. Following this, the motion is immediately put to the vote.

Motions cannot be withdrawn without the consent of the mover and seconder. A motion which is tied in voting is lost unless the chairperson exercises a casting vote. There are obvious reasons why it might be ill-advised for the chairperson to exercise this right. What is the main reason?

Motions that are ambiguous, irrelevant to the discussion and inconsistent with previous decisions should be ruled 'out of order'.

Once a motion has been voted on and carried, it becomes a resolution.

Amendments

'Amendments' are proposed alterations to an existing motion. They are moved and seconded like a motion, but the mover does not have the right of reply. Amendments are designed to improve motions. This may be achieved by deleting or inserting words or phrases and/or by substituting other words where an alteration has been made. Amendments cannot introduce a contradiction or direct negative of the motion. Amendments should be clearly worded.

When a motion is being discussed any number of amendments may be suggested. Amendments should be discussed, then put to the vote, one at a time.

An amendment to the motion above might read:

that the words 'six trestle tables and sixty chairs' be added to the motion.

This amendment would be discussed, put to the vote, and carried or lost. If the amendment was carried the motion would now read:

that a marquee, six trestle tables and sixty chairs be hired for a period of one day for the club picnic on Saturday 11 June.

Addendum

'Addenda' are added to the existing motion with the approval of the mover and seconder of the motion. Unlike the amendment, an addendum does not change the intent of the motion. Sometimes the chairperson may suggest an addendum rather than go through the procedure of amending the motion. In the above example, if someone suggested that the number of tables and chairs was insufficient the numbers could be adjusted by way of addendum, provided the mover and seconder agreed with the change. Another addendum might be 'that the marquee only be hired if the weather is inclement'. In the latter example, if the mover and seconder did not agree that this was their intended meaning, then the addendum would be rejected.

Procedural Motions

Procedural motions deal with the conduct of the meeting. If a debate has been in progress for a reasonable period someone may move that 'the question now be put'. A seconder is required, then a vote is conducted to decide if the debate should cease or continue. If this motion is carried, then the motion being debated must be voted on. If the motion is lost, the debate may continue.

Two further procedural motions are 'that the meeting be adjourned' and 'that the debate be adjourned'. If the former motion is carried, the chairperson should seek a motion indicating date, time and venue of the next meeting. The latter motion, if carried, adjourns the matter until another time. This may allow the meeting to continue with more pressing business.

Points of Order

A 'point of order' is called when someone believes that there has been an infringement of the rules of the meeting. The 'point of order' interrupts the speaker and the chairperson must establish immediately if the point of order is valid. He then either upholds the point of order asking the speaker to refrain from making such statements or overrules it, allowing the speaker to continue. Points of order are usually called if the debate becomes unruly, the speaker becomes abusive or the speaker infringes the rules of debate, perhaps by speaking for too long, disgressing or contradicting a statement made earlier. Points of order should not be called when opinions are expressed, as these are acceptable within the rules of debate.

The Role of the Secretary

The secretary has an important role to play in a formal meeting as he records the minutes of the meeting. The minutes should be factual and complete as they constitute the record of a meeting. All names and details should be checked by the secretary as they are recorded. Motions being passed to the chairperson can pass through the secretary so that he can use these to help structure the meeting record. It helps the secretary if the motions are written clearly and with the name of the mover written at the end of the motion. The chairperson may ask the secretary to reiterate details or re-read motions and amendments, so it is important that the secretary's minutes be clear and concise.

The minutes are read at the commencement of the following meeting, at which time the chairperson asks if someone will move that the minutes 'be accepted as a true and accurate record of the previous meeting'. Business arising from the minutes can then be discussed.

9 Interviewing

An interview is a special form of meeting where persons confront one another face to face to share or supply information and ideas. We are all familiar with the job selection interview, but this is only one form of interview even though to most of us it is both the most traumatic and important form of interview. Friends and parents usually ask the question 'how did you go?' or 'do you think you got the job?'

As applicants for positions or interviewees, most of us regard interviews as taxing, if not completely traumatic. We see ourselves in a very one-sided tennis game where the opponent seems to be playing all the winning shots. In this section of the chapter we will look at what makes each type of interview special, and then suggest some ways by which you can improve your interviewing game so that you too can play some winning shots.

The thing that makes the interview special is that it usually involves one party requesting information or ideas (the interviewer) and another party supplying that information or those ideas (the interviewee). This should not imply, however, that one party remains the interviewer and the other remains the interviewee. In fact, in all successful interviewing, there should be a free flow of ideas and a sharing of information. In a job selection interview, the applicant who fails to ask questions severely limits his chance of finding out about the organization for which he might be employed. In an informal interview between persons working in different departments of an organization, both parties should be involved in asking and answering questions, even though the purpose of the interview may be for one party to gather information from the other party. This technique provides both parties with feedback.

Interviews are not always held on a one-to-one basis. The number of interviewers and/or interviewees will depend on the information and ideas being sought and/or the selection of applicant being made. For instance, if some disciplinary action is being taken against an employee, a foreman would best interview the employee on a one-to-one basis. If two employees came into conflict, it might be better for the foreman to take both employees aside together in order to allow each person to air his grievances. Some job selection interviews are held on a one-to-one basis, whereas others involve a panel of interviewers and one applicant. A panel of interviewers might even invite the final applicants into the interview at the same time. An interview of this type would need to be thoroughly prepared and expertly executed.

Interviews range from informal chats in corridors, brief phonecalls where a few select questions are asked, to more formal interviews where special consideration is given to the choice of interviewers, and where there is control over the time and place of the interview.

Most job selection interviews take place in offices, where both interviewer and interviewee may feel ill-at-ease. It should be remembered that there is only so much that you can find out about a person by asking questions. Obviously you cannot test each new applicant for all the necessary skills, as work and educational history and referees need to be consulted to obtain much of this information. However, interviews for skilled tradesmen, technicians and salesmen could be held at the work-site; this would give both the interviewer and applicant the opportunity to ask questions in a less formal setting than an office, where the applicant may feel more 'at home' and where the interviewer can observe the applicant and ask questions that relate specifically to the tasks that may be going on around them.

While offices provide 'a quiet corner' where routine information may be gathered and questions may be asked about the applicant, the office is sometimes not conducive to the performance of these tasks. Consider how the desk might be used, by completing the following exercise.

Activity 9.A   Setting the Scene for an Interview
Examine the following seating positions where A is the applicant and B is the interviewer.

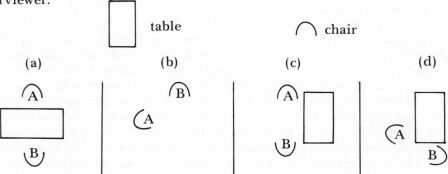

1. How could the seating arrangement affect the interviewing process?
2. Which situation do you think would be most conducive to a successful interview?
3. Does either party have an advantage in any of the arrangements?
4. What is the effect in (b) of removing the desk?
5. If a desk is used, what positive function could it have?

The interviewer in an interview, like the chairperson at a meeting, must have control over the situation. The interviewer must avoid making the interview an interrogation session or inquisition. A congenial atmosphere should be established. The applicant or interviewee who feels uneasy because of the location of the interview, threatened because of the kind of question being asked or isolated because the interviewer seems uninterested, may not be able to create a positive image.

However, some business organizations will deliberately put prospective employees 'through the ropes' just to see how well the applicant copes under pressure. The position for which the applicant is applying may be such that the interviewer needs to know how the applicant can present himself to others, or be forceful and have the ability to argue a case when representing the firm. People involved in public relations, sales, marketing and staff supervision may find themselves in this kind of position. Can you think of any other positions where the interviewer might exert some pressure on the applicant?

An interviewer sums up an interviewee the moment he walks into the room. Gait, standing and sitting posture, gestures, eye movements all give clues to the emotional state of the applicant. If an applicant appears excessively nervous, then the interviewer may need to take steps to relax the applicant. You need to find out what the interviewee knows or how well suited the applicant is for the position, not how nervous he feels about being interviewed. How would you go about relaxing an applicant?

While maintaining a relaxed atmosphere, it is still important that the interviewer needs to be in complete control of the interview, knowing exactly what he requires from the interviewee. Otherwise interviews can be a waste of time.

Types of Interview

The Information-Gathering Interview

The information-gathering interview is concerned only with the collection of information. The information may be fact or opinion. In this type of interview, it is important that the interviewer knows exactly what he wants to know, and organizes a suitable range of questions to ask. He should also consider how much detail or depth of answer is required.

The Problem-Solving Interview

The problem-solving interview, like the problem-solving meeting if used effectively, is one of the best ways of getting to the source of problems in business. As the interview permits an arena for discussion, various attitudes, opinions or complaints about work-related issues can be aired in the problem-solving interview. Under strict control (by the interviewer) the problems can be analysed, solutions sought and possible courses of action discussed. (See Problem-Solving Meetings.)

The Counselling Interview

If an employee is to be disciplined or 'seems headed for trouble', a counselling interview may help sort out the problem. The interviewer must determine the real problem that is to be solved by talking freely with the interviewee, by deciding possible solutions and then establishing a course of action. In situations where an employee has violated customs or rules by which fellow employees work it may be necessary to take disciplinary action. The interviewee should be reminded of the nature of the offence and the custom or rule should be discussed with the interviewee to ensure that the exact meaning has been communicated. The interviewee should be given the opportunity to discuss reasons for his action.

The Appraisal Interview

In many large companies, work or progress reports need to be submitted by supervisors to management. The appraisal interview can be used to discuss progress with subordinates.

The interviewer should be prepared to give his analysis of the interviewee's work performance. The interviewee's performance should be discussed with attention given to the strengths, weaknesses in performance and on deciding how the interviewee can best improve his performance.

The Termination Interview

If a person resigns from an organization it is in the best interest of that organization to find out exactly why the person resigned. On the other hand, if the performance of a staff member is unsatisfactory and he/she is to be dismissed, then it is worthwhile to give the person the reasons for dismissal. This knowledge should prove useful to the person in his future employment.

Before examining the job selection interview in more detail, here are some exercises based on the above types of interviews.

Activity 9.B   Gathering Information Using the Telephone

The most important thing to remember when using the telephone for interviewing is that the other person cannot see the facial expressions and gestures that usually accompany our speech.

Simulate an interviewing situation in class. This can be done by sitting two persons back to back. Select one or more of the following interviews to conduct. The rest of the class should act as observers.

Phone the interviewee to find out the following:
1. How do you get from your home to the interviewee's home by public transport?
2. Which are the best areas for picnicking within two hours drive of your home?
3. How do you change a baby's nappy?
4. How do you start a car?
5. What is the best way to prepare a wall for painting where there is flaky paint?
6. How would you break into your home if you had locked yourself out?
7. How would you find out whether an applicant is suitable for a specific job?
8. How would you conduct an interview effectively over the phone?

Consider the range of questions asked by the interviewer. Did both parties give sufficient feedback? Was there complete understanding by both parties? Were important details repeated?

Concise dialogue is essential for a successful interview. Both parties need to ask and answer questions so that complete understanding will be achieved. Interviewing does not simply involve the interviewer asking questions and the interviewee answering them.

Activity 9.C   Interview Act Outs

Here are some role-playing situations that can be acted out in class.

Counselling Interview

Peter works with a group of four technicians. Together they repair and maintain the electrical system in a large factory. Normally, the four work quite happily together, but over the last two weeks Peter has become quite irritable with his co-workers. Last Friday, while fixing some circuits in the refrigeration plant, he stormed off because you asked him how long he would take to complete the job because the cooling system had to be re-started.

As the supervisor of the technicians, it is your responsibility to make sure that all work groups are functioning harmoniously. Peter's group is not. Interview him to find out what the real problem is.

Appraisal Interview

April has been working for Triumph Industries for nine months, and as is their policy with all trainees, an appraisal must now be made of her progress. The interviewer could be the person who has to submit her report to management.

Create a situation that will be meaningful to the members of your class in which this appraisal interview might take place. You are free to invent details so as to make the situation vivid. Remember what the purpose of an appraisal interview is, and keep this as your main purpose in interviewing April.

The Termination Interview

Judith is the one weak link in your chain. You have an enthusiastic and competent group of salesmen and women, but Judith is not pulling her weight. On four occasions in the last two weeks she has been late for work, with no explanation given. Frequently she has to be reminded to fill shelves, dust stock and serve customers. Considering the patience you have shown her, she has still not impressed you. The rest of your sales team do not need the coaxing you have afforded her.

The purpose of the interview with Judith is to terminate her employment with your company.

The Selection Interview

The main purpose of the selection interview is to select the most suitable applicant for a specific job. The interviewer representing his organization needs to know that he is well equipped to select the most suitable person for the vacant position. The applicant needs to know that he is well prepared for the interview so that he can create a suitable impression. All too often interviewers and applicants alike are ill-prepared for the interview and neither party is sure of where he stands at the end of the interview.

In preparation for the interview, the interviewer needs to consider the following details:

- the **length** of each interview so that all applicants will have a reasonable opportunity to present themselves
- the **questions** that he will ask the applicant
- the **information** and **job details** which he will need to supply to the applicants
- the **profile**, application sheet, or personal résumé supplied by the applicant, with personal details on which the interviewer can base questions
- a suitable **location** for the interview
- the **criteria** that will be used to select the successful applicant. The interviewer will need to ask the question: What qualities will the successful applicant need to have?
- the **composition** of the interview panel. If the interviewer feels that other personnel should be on an interview panel then they should be selected prior to the interview and informed of their role on the panel. This may occur where the position being advertised is one where several qualities are required. The successful applicant may need to possess certain technical skills, leadership qualities and administrative skills so personnel may be required on the panel to check for these qualities.

The interviewee or applicant should prepare for an interview by considering the following details:

- **Answers to likely questions** relating to past employment, education, experience or interest in the position.
- **Job requirements** and **general information** about the company. This not only helps in answering questions but indicates an interest in the position and company.
- **Dress** should be considered, as inappropriate dress could create the wrong impression in the eye of the interviewer.
- **Questions** that the applicant may need to ask the interviewer about any detail of job performance, benefits, salary, promotion or study leave.
- If a **résumé** or **application form** has not been submitted to the employer prior to the interview, it is important to take a résumé with details about yourself outlined on it. (See Letter Writing—Job Application letter for further details of résumé.)

Activity 9.D How do you rate an Interview?

This exercise is designed so that you can either participate in or observe a job selection interview. Use one of the advertisements shown, or write your own relating specifically to your particular interests or vocation. This advertisement should be used as the basis for your selection interview.

<table>
<tr>
<td>

Farrers Nursery
18–40 years

We require a Nursery Assistant in our retail section. A sound knowledge of plant names, growing conditions and required care is highly desirable.

Hours are flexible but weekend work is frequent. Pleasant conditions. Salary negotiable.

Apply in writing stating qualifications and experience to: The Manager, Farrers Nursery, New Growth Road, Doweltown. 2189

</td>
<td>

A.S.I.O.

Our organization is rapidly expanding and we require the services of intelligent young people who are interested in the security of their country.

No experience necessary. We will train you in the skills of this worthwhile profession.

Duties include surveillance, communication checking and other clandestine operations.

Apply in writing to: Roland Sleuth, Personnel Dept., ASIO Capital City, Your State.

</td>
<td>

TV Services
Television Technician

A position is available for a technician in our modern workshop. We service all leading brands of colour television and video cassette recorder.

The successful applicant will have either finished or be in the final stages of the Electronics Technician's Certificate. Pay is according to age and experience.

Phone Andy Stapley on 6419641 for more information.

</td>
</tr>
</table>

You might select three or four persons to be interviewed for the position that you select. Also, select an interviewer, or an interview panel (2–3 interviews, if the position requires a panel).

Interviewers and interviewees should check to see that they have considered each of the details in preparing for an interview.

Set up chairs and desks in the classroom to simulate your interviewing situation. Remember, give consideration to how the positioning of furniture might affect the interview.

When the interviewer(s) have received and read the applicants' résumés, the interviews can commence.

Some points to consider:

- As interviewees and applicants you will need to invent fictitious details about the job, conditions and benefits.
- Tape the interviews and play them back after all applicants have been interviewed. Check to see how confidently the applicants answered questions, how logical and meaningful the questions asked were, and listen to the dialogue between interviewer(s) and applicant to see if the questions were in a meaningful progression and if they were actually answered by the applicants.
- The applicants should remain outside the room and be invited in, as is done in a normal interview. As each interview finishes, the applicant can remain in the room to observe how other applicants cope with the interview situation.
- The students who are not involved in the interview should act as observers. When observing, consider the statements made on the previous pages about the preparation for the interview, and try to answer some of the questions below.

Did the interviewer:
- make the applicant feel at ease?
- ask meaningful questions, requiring both short and longer answers?
- explain the job?
- give the applicant ample opportunity to talk?
- supply necessary information?

Did the applicant:
- present himself positively?
- answer questions thoughtfully?
- ask questions about job, salary and benefits if not supplied?
- display knowledge of job and company?

Because this exercise is fictitious, little can be gained by concluding that person *x* would have got the job. However both interviewers and applicants might comment on what they thought their greatest strengths and weaknesses were. The observers might comment not only on the questioning and answering but on the non-verbal behaviour of interviewers and applicants. Who looked convincing and confident? Why? How?

Conclusion

Interviewing, like all communication skills, is an art. Both parties need to be well prepared for the interviewing session. At the end of a session the interviewer(s) should be in a position to make a selection. It is important that they are confident in their selection, understanding the criteria on which the selection was made.

Occasionally an applicant will come across a difficult employer or even an incompetent interviewer. If caught in this situation the applicant should decide if he thinks he would be happy working for this person. If the answer is 'yes', then he may have to work twice as hard in the interview in order to make sure that he can convince the interviewer that he not only wants the job but that he is the right person for the job.

10 Thinking and Reasoning

Introduction

The use of reasoning to establish the validity of an argument in terms of its bias, its logic and the evidence offered in support of it, is an important part of the communication process. Persuasion is an obvious component of mass communication as in media advertising and propaganda. However, persuading and convincing also plays a part in everyday conversation when opinions are aired and prejudices are paraded. In all such exchanges, whether on the mass or personal level, the use of reasoning is essential in determining just what our own values are and whether a change in them should be resisted or adopted.

Let us examine various areas of argument that are of questionable validity because of faulty reasoning, false claims, techniques of persuasion and other distortions.

Fact and Opinion

> 'The fact is . . .'
> 'I know it for a fact . . .'
> 'The facts speak for themselves . . .'

Conversational openings such as these sound convincing, but we must satisfy ourselves that a fact *is* a fact and not just an opinion. A fact is distinguished from an opinion by **evidence**. In other words:

- A **fact** is a statement that rests on evidence.
- An **opinion** is a statement that relies on belief rather than evidence. 'Oranges have pips' is a fact. The evidence can be seen, felt and even swallowed! 'An apple a day keeps the doctor away' is an opinion. It's based on belief rather than evidence.

Some facts, such as 'oranges have pips', are obvious and can be verified all the time. On the other hand, a statement such as: 'The "dog watch" on ships is from 4 to 6 pm' sounds correct—but that is not enough. Reference to an encyclopaedia or a sailor will verify that the 4 to 6 pm watch is called the 'dog watch'. Such independent verification is often needed in assessing the worth of a claim and, hence, the validity of an argument.

Facts—In Time

There is an area of human experience in which it is difficult to establish facts.

- Elephants are more intelligent than horses.
- Cricket requires more skill than football.

In time, evidence may be gathered that will prove or disprove the factual content of these two statements, but until such time they remain opinions.

Significant opinions

Some statements made about art, culture, the way people live or should live, or about personal taste such as:

- The 'Mona Lisa' is the best known painting in the world.
- Green combines beautifully with gold.
- Delinquents arise from slum environments.
- Snail sauce is a gastronomic delight

are often incapable of proof either now or in the future, but are important expressions of experience and preference and worthy of consideration.

Activity 10.A   Facts and Opinions

Separate fact from opinion.
1. Poverty is confined to Third World countries.
2. Julius Caesar was a Roman dictator.
3. Dogs are quadrupeds.
4. Law of Selective Gravity: an object will fall so as to do the most damage.
5. Boyle's Law: if the pressure on a gas is increased, its volume is decreased.
6. *Jaws* was a best-selling novel.
7. Every individual has in mind a scheme that will not work.
8. Psychiatrists are doctors who do not like the sight of blood.
9. Some of the world's largest birds are flightless.
10. An optimist is a person who hasn't had much experience.
11. Exercise is worth nothing without a calm state of mind to go with it.
12. The USA is a democratic country.
13. Work expands to fill the time available for it.
14. The solid form of water is ice.
15. There are two types of people: those who divide people into two types and those who don't.
16. The moon is a satellite of the earth.
17. Temperature is measured by the thermometer.
18. Murphy's Law: if anything can go wrong it will.
19. A biography is a book about a person's life.
20. A person with one watch knows what time it is, a person with two watches is never sure.

Persuasion in Words and Language

The bias or emotive or persuasive content of some words is a danger to the reasoned, considered appraisal of an argument. For example in:

- She is mean with money

'mean' is a bias word intended to persuade us to agree with the disapproval inherent in the word. However, in

- She is careful with money

'careful' expresses approval of her money management.

   Bias words may distort our reasoned judgement of the worth of an argument. The realisation that words can be deliberately employed to change outlook or attitude shows us that key words in an argument presented to us should be tested or weighed for their bias or emotive or persuasive content. Only when this has been done can an argument be judged factual or objective.

Activity 10.B   Persuasion

1. Supply the missing bias word in each of the following 'I am . . . you are' assertions. (Note: the words you'll need are in the box.)

meticulous	news	doggerel
dictator	slim	quack
old fashioned	foolhardy	vagrant
idealist	extroverted	witty
pessimistic	notorious	exploiter
obstinate	idle	dole-bludger
extravagant	studious	

(a) I am relaxed. You are . . .
(b) I am . . . You are skinny.
(c) I am generous. You are . . .
(d) I am famous. You are . . .
(e) I am daring. You are . . .
(f) I am homeless. You are . . .
(g) I am one of the unemployed. You are a . . .
(h) I listen to . . . You listen to gossip.
(i) I am . . . You are ridiculous.
(j) I am determined. You are . . .
(k) I am aware of possible disasters. You are . . .
(l) I am traditional. You are . . .
(m) I am out-going. You are . . .
(n) I write poetry. You write . . .
(o) I am . . . You are a swot.
(p) I am . . . You are fussy.
(q) I am a . . . You are an exploiter.

(r) I am an . . . You are a dreamer.
(s) I am a doctor. You are a . . .
(t) I am a firm leader. You are a . . .

2. There is another category of words which usually express neither approval nor disapproval but simply state the factual position. These are **neutral** words. In the sequence: mighty, big, monstrous, 'big' is the neutral word.

From the column, select the neutral word that will fit into each of the sequences below:

NEUTRAL COLUMN	APPROVAL	NEUTRAL	DISAPPROVAL
smell	(a) lass		hussy
intelligent	(b) indignant		irascible
speech	(c) childish		youthful
young	(d) gathering		mob
planner	(e) pinch		thieve
girl	(f) zephyr		gust
intensely	(g) chubby		fat
work	(h) address		harangue
annoyed	(i) antique		obsolete
crowd	(j) home		hovel
obese	(k) perfume		stench
house	(l) reformatory		lock-up
steal	(m) brilliant		cunning
wind	(n) strategist		schemer
prison	(o) vocation		chore
old	(p) zealously		fanatically

Activity 10.C Persuasive Advertising

For driving lustre use Car-in-a-can.
Use it on bodywork, windows, chrome, dash—in fact anywhere for soft, deep down richness.
Clean-ride with Car-in-a-can. And if your engine begins to purr you'll know why.

1. **Car-in-a-can**
   (a) Identify the bias words in the ad.
   (b) What is their purpose?
   (c) There are some neutral words used in the ad. Why are they used?
   (d) How is the product linked with an image of smoothness and contentment?

With a LIMBO leather belt, you're halfway
to Heaven.
Styled in elegant cowhide, a LIMBO belt
shows off your taste for fashionwear *and*
your canny sense of the economical.
The LIMBO message—don't waste time,
keep your hips in line. Belt-up and
live it up with your LIMBO.

I'M WAITING...

2. **Limbo belt**
   (a) What needs is this ad designed to appeal to?
   (b) How are bias words used in relation to these needs?
   (c) Write an objective, impartial, purely factual ad for this product.
   (d) Which of the two ads is the more effective? Name the criteria you are using
       to judge effectiveness.

The Analogy

When you say that a person may be likened to a car, you are making an analogy.
Here's how it works:

> Just as a car needs fuel to run, so a person needs food. The engine's pistons
> are the muscles. The fuel pump is the heart. The air filter is the lungs. The
> headlights are the eyes. The tyres are feet (although they don't put on extra
> thicknesses of rubber as the feet put on extra layers of skin to cope with
> friction and movement).

NO DEPOSIT

HERE'S A LITTLE BEAUTY! A GREAT BUY FOR THE FAMILY! WORRY FREE DRIVING!

All these points of similarity go to make up and strengthen the analogy. Of
course, as with most analogies, there are glaring differences that are not mentioned.
What, for example, would you say about the *brain* in the car-person analogy?

This use of analogy highlights quite vividly some of the features of both cars and people.

As a means of highlighting aspects of an idea, the analogy (as long as it's realistic) is above reproach. However, suppose the car-person analogy went on to make this kind of conclusion:

> As we all know, a car's performance is greatly improved if it is run on super-refined fuel. In the same way, a person's performance will show a marked improvement if super-refined foods are the first choice of the person to whom fitness is everything.

A ridiculous conclusion to reach! Yet, the argument from analogy does sound plausible if we accept the similarities and fail to dig out the differences.

Activity 10.D   Fallacy Hunt
For each of the following analogies, give:

  - the two things being compared
  - the main points of similarity

Then point out the fallacies in some of the analogies.
1. Worry resembles an exercise bicycle in that it gives you something to do but takes you nowhere.
2. A young child can be compared to a tree. Both flourish and grow when cared for. And, just as the tree grows naturally beautiful without any restriction so a child may develop naturally and positively without restraints.
3. In factory and shop situations, piped music has been shown to speed up the production of workers. For the same reason, students should be allowed to play and listen to radio while they work in their classrooms.
4. Stand on an ants' nest and you're sure to get bitten. That's why you should always take off when there's a fight—no matter who's getting hurt.
5. A person just cannot change his or her basic nature just as a leopard cannot change its spots.
6. A person's mind is like an umbrella; it works properly only when open.
7. If you wish to be good at guitar playing, you must practise constantly. And, if you wish to be good at relaxing you must practise it constantly too.
8. A human being is mainly motivated by the desire to avoid pain and to seek pleasure. The same applies to animals. The human being is thus mainly an animal at heart.
9. There are certain similarities between an army and a place of learning. In both there are the leaders and the led; in both there is a common goal standing at the end of all the difficulties that must be overcome and the skills that must be acquired. The conclusion: follow and obey your leaders at all times.
10. As night will follow day, so old age will follow youth.
11. One's first date with a girl is rather like a visit to the dentist—a terrible ordeal while it lasts and a happy relief when it's finally over.
12. A little sister is like a bad smell, always around when it's not wanted and always causing embarrassment.

Cause and Effect

Statements about cause and effect attempt to show a definite relationship between two things. However, the true cause is not always apparent to someone who is simply faced with the effect:

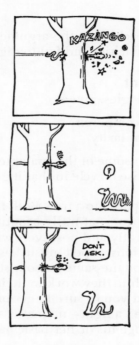

Here, we are in the privileged position of being able to see the single, undeniable cause that leads to the remarkable snake-through-the-tree effect. The ground snake, being puzzled by what it sees, may well have assigned some completely different cause to explain what has happened—for example, that the snake became stuck in some pre-existing hole in the tree.

The rule is: Before assigning a single cause for any given effect, check the evidence carefully.

Another fallacy that can creep into arguments containing statements about cause and effect is the issue of **single** or **multiple causality**. For any given effect there may be not just one but a number of causes.

- hot, windy weather
- drought conditions
- dry undergrowth
- broken glass in abundance

These factors were present on the day a disastrous bushfire began.

The Poker Machine Model

This approach to multiple causality is used particularly in the social sciences. Let's take the probability of a car crash. If only one factor turns up in the 'window', a car crash is probably avoidable. But, if all four turn up, probability tends to certainty.

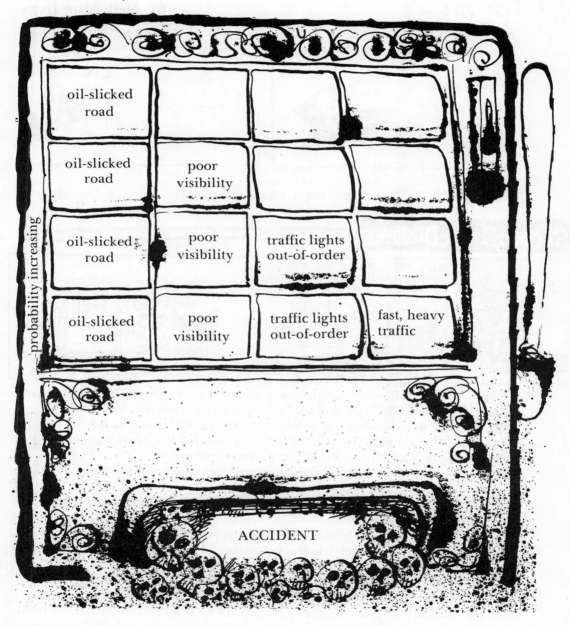

The rule is: Statements giving a single cause to explain complex events (effects) are likely to be simplistic.

Activity 10.E   Single and Multiple Causality

1. Answer these questions on cause-effect situations.

    (a) Is the manager's comment the only evidence we have that the missiles were launched by a group of nurses?

ST PIPS —   **By Neil Matterson**

    (b) Explain the cause and effect relationship that occurs in this Bristow cartoon.

2. Which of the following single-cause statements do you find to be fairly convincing, and which do you find unconvincing? Give reasons.

    (a) Liver ailments are caused by excessive consumption of alcohol.

    (b) The desire to get rich quickly is the reason for the great increase in the number of gambling establishments in recent years.

    (c) The dole system lies behind the great feeling of apathy that has swept through society in recent years.

    (d) The advent of the hand calculator has resulted in a lack of numeracy among school students.

    (e) Swimming produces wonderfully developed shoulder muscles.

    (f) The 'permissive society' is the end product of the widespread affluence that occurred in earlier years.

    (g) Television programmes emphasising violence act as models for violent behaviour in the 'real' world.

    (h) Our education system is failing because of an outdated insistence on rigid authoritarian principles, including strict timetabling and harsh disciplinary measures for minor infringements of rules.

    (i) If your diet is based on carbohydrates you will get fat.

Activity 10.F   Problem-Solving in Groups

For group problem-solving, the class first of all divides into small groups. Each group elects a discussion leader and a secretary. With the discussion leader going to each group member in turn for ideas—and with the secretary recording—the group produces its solution to the problem. Then the secretary presents it to the class.

1. **Think Tank**
    (a) Advise on better ways to present student views to the principal and staff of your school or college.
    (b) Think up a name for a new cat food. Then devise a radio advertisement for it.
    (c) Outline the course you'd most like to see introduced at your school or college.
    (d) The traits of a bad teacher are . . .
    (e) The traits of a good teacher are . . .
    (f) Give a workable and realistic way of reducing the road toll.
    (g) How can the unemployed youth in our society be given a sense of worth and dignity?
    (h) Suggest a plan for better canteen and student facilities.
2. **Posters**
    Here are two posters. The first aims to deter school students from smoking.

DON'T BE A DUMMY

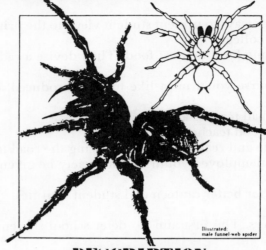

WANTED
FOR MURDER·ALIVE!

Illustrated:
male funnel-web spider

DESCRIPTION

Large, black, shiny spider from 25 to 76mm in body length with long fangs. Normally found on Sydney's north shore in cool, moist habitats. Also known to invade homes. Is aggressive and dangerous.
Do not approach. Keep under surveillance and call 88 9467 for apprehension.

REWARD
Assistance in Macquarie University funnel-web spider research to prevent further tragedies.

The second was designed to get funnelweb spiders for the research programme at Macquarie University. Discuss and plan designs for each of the following.

(a) An anti-smoking poster—unpleasant problems have arisen from students and staff smoking in classrooms, workshops, common rooms, staff rooms and corridors.

(b) A poster promoting assistance to handicapped children—your school or college is organising a fete to raise money to help local handicapped children.

(c) A join-your-student-council poster—talent is lacking in your school council and just at this time a crisis is developing in staff-student relations.

(d) A canteen poster—new lines of foodstuffs have recently been introduced to your canteen and you wish to ensure that students are aware of them.

(e) A poster promoting more and varied student get-togethers—many students are discontented with their present social life.

(f) A free choice poster—your group should suggest a poster to be planned and designed.

3. **Memo**
   Make student recommendations to the harassed principal.

MEMO TO STAFF AND STUDENTS FROM THE PRINCIPAL
SUBJECT: litter and noise
Please read this memo to your classes.

LITTER   On any day of the week, litter can be found everywhere in the grounds of this institution. Lunch bags, drink cans, chip bags, crusts and so on have been thrown about willy nilly by irresponsible people even though waste disposal units have been conveniently located. It shames me, as I'm sure it must shame both staff and students, to bring visitors to the institution under such conditions.

NOISE   Classroom concentration is being badly affected by rising noise levels emanating from the canteen and recreation areas. Sources: loud laughter, raucous conversation, yelling, the clang and clatter of flying drink cans.

Something must be done in both the above areas of rising disturbance. Please discuss with your students.

4. **Rumour Has It . . .**
   In the factory, a couple of machinists have already handed in their notice and departed. You, as the factory manager, are concerned. Their departure seems to be linked to a rumour that is widely believed. The rumour is that the factory is about to be taken over by a multinational concern and many will be sacked.
   Well, you know the rumour is completely untrue.
   (a) Discuss some realistic way of preventing rumours spreading and becoming destructive.
   (b) What is the possibility of some rumours being non-destructive or even beneficial?
   (c) What would be the best policy to adopt towards a known rumour-monger?
   (d) Test the distortion possible in rumours by passing a message (rumour) from mouth to mouth, in a low voice, and checking the original words with the final ones.

5. **Getting Through**
   Your new job is: supermarket personnel manageress. You find you have problems:
   - The General Manager is a much older person, who thinks women should stay at home.
   - He intensely dislikes new ideas.
   - He has no formal qualifications and tends to resent yours.
   - He is seldom seen by his staff.
   - He favours the male members of staff and actually belittles female members of staff.
   - Staff morale is low—there is sickness and a high staff turnover.

- All the staff is ignorant of management's aims and objectives.
- You realise that these problems must be solved if staff morale and efficiency are to be raised.

Discuss the means by which:

1. The manager is to be approached and told of his shortcomings in regard to his relations with female staff and especially in relation to communication problems.
2. How could female staff be brought 'on side' again?
3. How could your personal relationship with the manager be improved?

6. **Threatening Letters**

The usual pattern for debt collection letters is: letter one—'payment is now overdue for . . .' If no payment follows, letter two is sent: 'Since you have not answered our first letter, we are seeking legal advice . . .' and if no payment follows, letter three is sent: 'Payment in full must be made in seven days, or legal action will follow'.

Perhaps a better pattern for debt collection letters might be:

(1) 'We would like to remind you . . .'
(2) 'If you have mislaid our previous letter, we would like to remind you . . .'
(3) 'Has our product reached you in a satisfactory condition and are you completely satisfied with it? If not . . .'
(4) 'If there is some reason why you cannot pay at the moment, please . . .'
(5) 'Are you aware that you are legally required . . .?'
(6) 'We are reluctant to undertake legal action. However you leave us no choice . . .'

(a) Discuss the effectiveness of each letter pattern from the following points of view:
   (i) getting the debt paid,
   (ii) retaining the customer's goodwill.
(b) Discuss other possible patterns of debt collection letters that might be psychologically more rewarding for both creditor and debtor.
(c) Discuss what other options are open to a debt collector besides a series of letters.
(d) Discuss, from the debtor's point of view, the factor (or factors) that weighs most heavily when considering the repayment of a sum of money owed.

Activity 10.G   Brain Teasers

Try to solve the following problems.

1. A detachment of soldiers must cross a river. The bridge is destroyed, the river is deep. Suddenly the officer in charge spots 2 boys playing in a rowing boat by the shore. The boat can hold 2 boys or 1 soldier. Still, all the soldiers succeed in crossing the river in the boat. How?

2. The chef fries bread in a small pan. After frying one side of a slice, he turns it over. Each side takes 30 seconds. The pan can only hold 2 slices. How can he toast both sides of 3 slices in 1½ instead of 2 minutes?

3. There are five houses, each of a different colour and inhabited by men of different nationalities, with different pets, drinks and cigarettes.
   The problem: Who owns the zebra? Who drinks water?
   (a) The Norwegian lives next to the blue house.
   (b) The Japanese smokes Parliaments.
   (c) The Lucky Strike smoker drinks orange juice.
   (d) Kools are smoked in the house next to the house where the horse is kept.
   (e) The man who smokes Chesterfields lives in the house next to the man with the fox.
   (f) The Norwegian lives in the first house on the left.
   (g) Milk is drunk in the middle house.
   (h) Kools are smoked in the yellow house.
   (i) The Winston smoker owns snails.
   (j) The green house is immediately to the right (your right) of the ivory house.
   (k) The Ukrainian drinks tea.
   (l) Coffee is drunk in the green house.
   (m) The Spaniard owns the dog.
   (n) The Englishman lives in the red house.

4. Harry is languishing in jail in Mexico. The jail has multiple locks on the door; the walls are made of concrete extending two storeys into the earth; the floor is made of packed earth. In the middle of the ceiling, about 2½ metres above Harry, is a skylight just wide enough for him to squeeze through. The cell is totally bare.
   One night, in desperation, he has an idea. He starts digging in the floor, knowing he can never tunnel out. What is his plan?

5. How could you put your left hand *completely* in your right-hand front trouser pocket and your right hand *completely* in your left-hand front trouser pocket, both at the same time? (You are wearing the trousers.)

6. Visualize three playing cards adjacent to one another. A four is just to the right of a three, and a four is just to the left of a four. There is a diamond just to the left of a heart, and a diamond just to the right of a diamond. Can you name the three cards?

7. There are 12 one-cent stamps in a dozen, but how many two-cent stamps are there in a dozen?

8. Sam bought a long-playing record that has a total diameter of 30 centimetres. The record has an outer margin of one centimetre; the diameter of the unused centre of the record is eight centimetres. There is an average of 50

grooves to the centimetre. How far does the stylus travel when the record is played?

9. Erica was waiting for her boyfriend to pick her up in his new Jaguar. He was late; the sky clouded over, and it suddenly started to rain. Erica had no umbrella, no raincoat, no hat, and she was far from any awning or canopy. Yet five minutes later, when her boyfriend arrived, she got into the car with her hair and clothes perfectly dry. How was that possible?

10. Jack bought an old horse and a pig for $85. The horse cost $55 more than the pig. How much did Jack pay for the pig?

11. Bet someone that he can't stand with his left foot and left shoulder touching a wall, then raise his right foot.

12. Place eight coins in the shape of the letter 'L', with five coins forming the vertical leg and three the shorter horizontal leg. Bet that by moving only one coin, and using no others, you can put five coins in each leg.

13. Bet that you can drop an egg two metres through the air over a hard surface without breaking the egg.

14. Place a dollar note across the top of two glasses that are at least 10 centimetres apart. Bet that you can put a 50-cent piece on the middle of the note without having it fall.

15. Arrange six matches like this: Bet that you can move three of the matches to make *eight* equilateral triangles.

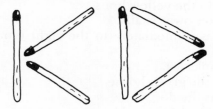

16. Bet your adversary that he can't take off his shoes and socks by himself.

17. Place an empty soft-drink bottle neck-end down on the centre of a dollar note. Bet that you can remove the note without touching the bottle or making it fall over.

18. Bet that you can pick up three matches with a fourth one—all at the same time!

19. Arrange a dozen matches in four squares, as shown. Bet that you can make seven squares by moving just two matches.

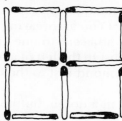

20. Two mothers and two daughters won the daily double at the racecourse. Bet that when they divvied up their winnings—$2100—they each went home with $700.

21. Water flows through these pipes under pressure and can therefore go up as well as down. In the drawing it can flow out of any of the four pipes at the bottom. Can you make it come out of only one of these pipes by opening or shutting not more than two valves?

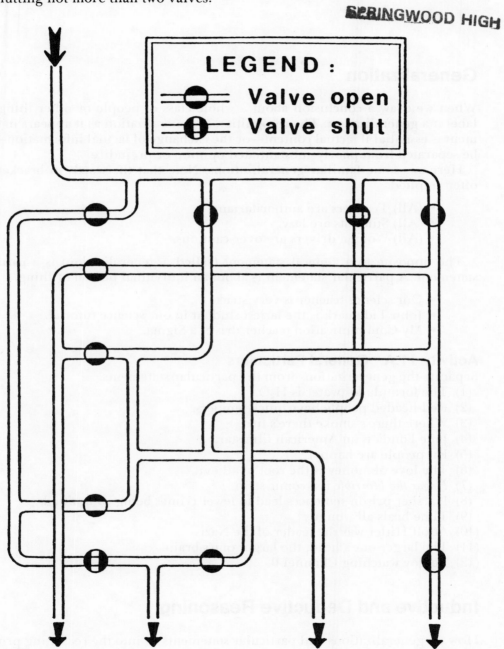

11 Problem-Solving

Generalization

When we draw a conclusion about a whole class of people or other things, we label it a generalization. The recognition of generalization as it appears in argument is essential if factual content — or the exchange of factual information — is to be separated from poorly substantiated opinion or prejudice.

Here are some familiar generalizations. Note that the words in brackets are often implied.

- (All) Teachers are authoritarian.
- (All) Students are lazy.
- (All) Women drivers are over-cautious.

The opposite to a general statement (called a generalization) is a **particular** statement. A particular statement is about an individual person or thing.

- Our science teacher is very strict.
- John Tidemark is the laziest student in our science tutorial.
- My Communication teacher drives a Sigma.

Activity 11.A   General Particulars
Separate the generalizations from the particular statements.
 (1) The formula for water is H_2O.
 (2) Red-headed people have quick tempers.
 (3) Where there's smoke there's fire.
 (4) Jane Fonda is an American film star.
 (5) Fat people are happy.
 (6) The love of money is the root of all evil.
 (7) *Hagar the Horrible* is a comic strip.
 (8) Harsher prison sentences lead to fewer crimes being committed.
 (9) Time heals all wounds.
(10) Adolf Hitler was the leader of the Nazis.
(11) The larger one's head, the larger one's brain.
(12) I enjoy watching Channel 0.

Inductive and Deductive Reasoning

How do generalizations and particular statements fit into the reasoning process? Well, suppose you look around and discover that individuals are smiling:

You take these
special particular
instances

and you make . . .

a generalization:

'Human beings are happy creatures.'

The kind of reasoning involved in moving from particular instances to a generalization is called **inductive** reasoning. The opposite process: moving from a general idea to see whether various particular instances, newly found, conform to it, is called *deductive* reasoning.

In the example of inductive reasoning above, the generalization 'Human beings are happy creatures' is unhappily not true for all human beings. The generalization has been made from too few instances. However, if qualified to: 'Human beings are capable of being happy creatures', the generalization becomes true and acceptable.

Here are three categories of generalization:

(1) Generalizations which are obviously invalid because of insufficient evidence.

   • Black dogs are friendly.

(2) Generalizations which will become valid when adequately qualified.

   • Babies cry often.
   • **Some** babies cry often.

(3) Generalizations which are valid as they stand because they correspond to a wealth of evidence from our own, and others, experience.

   • Emus are flightless birds.

Activity 11.B Validity

Say which of the following generalizations are:
   (a) obviously invalid
   (b) in need of qualification
   (c) obviously valid.
   Give reasons for your choices.
1. Nobody is perfect.
2. Mountaineering is the safest of the outdoor sports.
3. Having high blood pressure increases one's chance of a heart attack.

4. Girls are better at English than boys.
5. Cars are essential to life.
6. People need people.
7. Crime never pays.
8. All soldiers are heroes.
9. The Communist system is a good deal more efficient in its use of material resources than Capitalism.
10. Australia is a land of bronzed giants with healthy thirsts.
11. Christmas only comes onces a year.
12. There is more suffering and disease in India than in any other country in the world.
13. Freedom is the most treasured possession of any human being.
14. Birds are feathered creatures.
15. Animals may be capable of affection but they are incapable of love.
16. Australia is the lucky country.
17. Delinquency originates in slum areas.
18. The policies of the Western world have been responsible for the misery of the Third World.

Reasoning and Statistics

Suppose you are faced with an argument for which the main support is statistical —a graph or figures that prove . . . No doubt you'd be impressed or even over-awed. That is the special aura that statistics carry with them. And yet, any statistical evidence is only as reliable as the **source** and the **sample**, the **presentation** and the **interpretation**. Flaws in these will lead to flaws in the statistical evidence.

The **source** of a set of statistics must be reliable if the statistics themselves are to be acceptable evidence in argument. In the area of breakfast foods consumed by Australian families, the Commonwealth Statistician would probably be a more reliable, and therefore more acceptable source of statistics than, say, Acme Roughage Inc. who might be less than disinterested in slanting results.

The **sample** used in the statistical survey should truly represent the whole group being investigated and should be large enough for generalizations to be made from the sample. If drivers were being interviewed about the condition of state roads, a sample of fifty drivers of pet food vans in the metropolitan area would not be truly representative.

Activity 11.C   Statistical Survey
Read through the following statistical survey and answer the questions that follow.

Social Science teacher Hopegood has been commissioned by the Central Committee of Canteens to prepare a survey on the possible sale of a tee-shirt carrying the imprint, back and front: 'I LOVE STUDY'.

Hopegood prepares his survey with enthusiasm. He prepares a question-naire to be sent out to 4000 students, asking them to tick one of the following:

	tick one
I must have one of your 'I LOVE STUDY' tee-shirts.	( )
I will probably buy one of your 'I LOVE STUDY' tee-shirts.	( )
I am uncommitted.	( )
Tee-shirts usually leave me cold.	( )
I hate tee-shirts.	( )

From the 4000 questionnaires sent out he received 300 replies. They were divided in the order shown above: 80, 52, 47, 45, 76. Delighted, Mr Hopegood sent his results off to the Maths Department. They worked out the following results for Mr Hopegood and the Canteens Committee:

Greatly in favour	26·7%
Interested	17·3%
Uncommitted	15·7%
Not interested	15·0%
Active dislike	25·3%
Total	100·0%

Conclusion: As nearly sixty per cent of students sampled are 'for' the tee-shirt or at least open-minded, my firm recommendation is to proceed with the production and sale of the 'I LOVE STUDY' tee-shirt.

Sincerely,

P. Hopegood.

1. How representative is the Hopegood sample?
2. Why do you think 3700 of those contacted failed to reply to the questionnaire?
3. Is there anything wrong with the product itself that would help to explain the low response to the questionnaire?
4. What kind of person do you think the student is who would bother to answer?
5. Is there any reason to think that some of the 300 replies might not be trustworthy?
6. Can you suggest any way in which the questionnaire could have been altered or followed up to make it acceptable to larger numbers of students?
7. How would this enlargement affect the credibility of the sample?
8. What might be the effect of the decimal places in the results on a reader's mind?
9. Is the effect justified?
10. Comment on Hopegood's conclusion.

Graphs

Graphs are supposed to show us clearly, in picture form, just what a set of figures is all about. However, graphs can be misleading—either unintentionally or intentionally.

(1) The three bananas are designed to show the increase in banana production over two decades. However, this pictogram caused one banana grower to

exclaim: 'That's a lie! Bananas ain't no bigger now than they were in 1960 or 1970!'

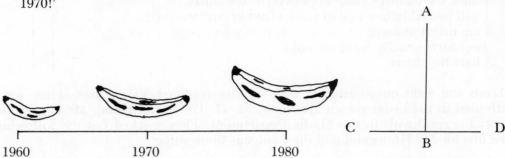

1960   1970   1980

(2) A line on a graph can be misleading in accordance with this familiar illusion. Which is the longer line, A–B or C–D? Actually, both lines are the same in length.

(3) Figures can be played up or played down according to the scale selected. Here's the sort of graph that will show profits shooting up:

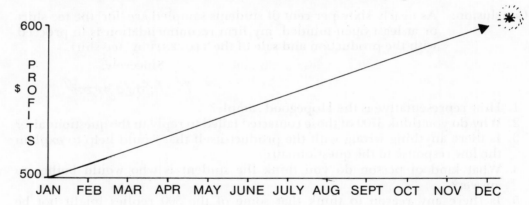

A very persuasive effort! On the other hand, with a wider time scale and a greater dollar range, there appears to be only a miserable advance in profits. A poor effort!

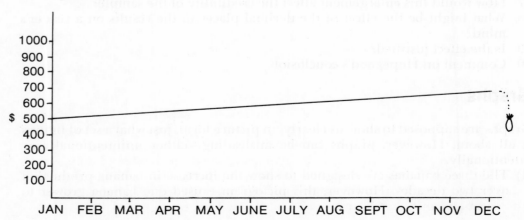

Activity 11.D   The Interpretation

Read through the following and answer the questions.

Vicious cycle for homeless young people

By MALCOLM BROWN

Sydney's homeless young people are locked in a vicious cycle of family and social alienation, unemployment, drugs, alcohol and often vice, two social researchers have found.

And they are only partially helped by welfare organisations.

Gordon Inman and Mark Arnold, researching for Care Force, part of the Anglican Home Mission Society, have found that there is a tendency for homeless young people to gravitate towards the inner City.

But they have found in their report, *Nowhere No-Way*, issued yesterday, that the inner City is not nearly ready or adequately equipped to provide for them.

Leaving home in many cases because of existing impasses in their lives, the young people have faced, on the streets of Sydney, a community whose cold hard face afflicts them with ever-increasing feelings of helplessness and futility.

Mr Inman and Mr Arnold have found that there is an urgent need for government, voluntary agencies and the general community to review their existing ideas about, and policies on, homeless young.

In a series of interviews with 30 of Sydney's young homeless, Mr Inman and Mr Arnold have sought the causes for their condition. In a number of cases, it was the breakdown of family life.

Of the 30, eight had left home because of continual conflict between the parents; nine had left because they could not get on with one or both parents.

Three had left home when they were 10 years old, six when they were 11. Of the 30, 10 had run away from home and 15 had been told to go or left through agreement with the parents. Five had been helped to leave by social agencies.

Comments by the young people suggest a total breakdown, in many cases, in communication.

Dee, 17, said: 'He (father) would come home drunk . . . and hit me around.'

Keith, 15, said: 'The pressure built up and they asked me to leave; but I still keep in touch . . . I still class them as parents.'

Brian, 16, said: 'My father told me to p... off when I bashed him for kicking Ma.'

Deborah, 13, said: 'She was a tart . . . I was in the way.'

Once the break has been made, it tends to be virtually total. Of the 30 youngsters, 25 had no face-to-face contact with their parents whatever and 20 did not even communicate by phone or letter.

Sixteen received unemployment benefits. Eleven received no benefits at all. They lived where they could—seven in a refuge, 10 in a hostel, five in derelict houses. Two on park benches, and six with friends, regardless of how dubious the 'friends' might be.

Inevitably, the young people fall prey to the vultures. Nineteen in the group had taken 'soft' drugs and five hard drugs.

Eighteen had abused alcohol. Four boys and five girls said they had prostituted themselves. Most had been before a court and 24 had been in an institution.

The comments of the young show that, even if they have tried to get work and get out of the depressed rut of poverty, their task has often appeared hopeless.

Art, 17, said: 'I've been after 20 (jobs) in four weeks . . . no _____ luck. They all want bloody experience, but if you can't get a _____ job where's the experience coming from? The world's gone bloody haywire.'

Frank, 16, said: 'What's the use of working for two _____ weeks to lose your dole and then wait two _____ weeks to get back on it again?'

1. What is the source of the statistics given in this survey?
2. As far as reliability is concerned, what strength and weakness can you see in this source?
3. What is the size of the sample used?
4. How representative do you think it is?
5. Say briefly what the survey deals with.
6. The subject of the survey has intrinsic interest. Why?
7. What is the general reason given for the young people leaving home?
8. Explain the 'vicious cycle' mentioned in the title.
9. What need emerges from the findings of the survey?
10. Figures in the survey could be given more impact if presented in picture form. Draw a pie chart to show proportionally where the thirty young people lived. (A pie chart presents data in the form of a circular 'pie'. Slices of the pie show the size relationships of the individual data.)

Activity 11.E   Faulty Generalizations

1. We didn't realise which the most popular soft drinks in our locality were until we watched some children counting the soft drink cans they collected after the football match at the oval last Sunday. They arranged the various brands in their respective piles and the results were as follows:

Zip	60
Sparkle	44
Best-Up	30
Refreshade	15
Swish	5

We now know which companies are selling the most soft drinks in our district.
What comments would you make about the drink can statistics?

2. My girlfriend found a snail in her packet of Greenlife frozen peas. She now tells all her friends and acquaintances not to buy this brand of frozen peas.
Do you think she is right in doing this? Why?

3. A recent survey revealed that four out of five drivers use Pow petrol. It must be the best.

   Do you agree? Why?

4. A testimonial reads: 'Beta powders relieved my headache. You can end you headache troubles too'.

   What comment would you make concerning this testimonial?

The Expert Connection

In any argument, the ultimate appeal to the 'experts' (Professor X states . . . Dr Y has found . . . Research reveals . . .) must be viewed with caution until the so-called expert has had his or her qualifications and credentials checked against the claim made.

Relevancy is a key consideration. Here is one kind of ad we all know well.

Ads or commercials often link one quality with another in the hope that a 'flow' across will occur in the reader's or viewer's mind. In the ad shown, it is from the strength of the superman to the strength of the medication. Notice how an expert in muscular strength has been brought in—but is he also an expert in medication?

In argument, as in advertising, the 'expert connection' must be tested with such questions as:

- Is the expert's knowledge being exercised in the correct field?
- Is the information current?
- Is the expert's objectivity (impartial presentation of facts) beyond reproach?

Activity 11.F   Expert Expertise

In each of the following items there is an expert and a field of expertise. Say whether the expert, in each case, is likely to be qualified or unqualified to pass judgement. Give a reason for each of your answers.

1. General Rommel on desert warfare
2. The manager of the Paradise Tobacco Company on the hazards of cigarette smoking
3. A social worker on vagrancy
4. Lenin on communism
5. A radio announcer on the low quality of TV programmes
6. A well-known atheist on the need for religious commitment
7. The curator of the museum of technology on zoo management
8. Germaine Greer on sexism
9. A dentist on the uselessness of corporal punishment in schools
10. Adolf Hitler on parliamentary democracy
11. The federal treasurer on delinquency
12. A losing punter on a jockey's performance
13. A rugby union hero advertising the finer points of a life jacket
14. A South African police inspector on apartheid
15. Rudolf Valentino on chess

Activity 11.G   Ask the Experts

Choose an expert from the box to go with each of the controversial news head-lines below.

BOX OF EXPERTS

agronomist	almoner	seismologist
penologist	commuter	mycologist
herpetologist	actuary.	speleologist
viticulturist	gynaecologist	ornithologist

Headline	Expert
1. City transport stopped. Public outcry	. . . .
2. Aussies drink more wine	. . . .
3. Prison reform shock	. . . .
4. Poor refused hospital beds	. . . .
5. First test tube birth	. . . .
6. Birds fail to migrate. Experts puzzled	. . . .
7. Earthquake strikes again	. . . .
8. Deepest cave discovered	. . . .
9. Insurance fraud uncovered	. . . .
10. Snake plague in Wimmera	. . . .
11. Drought affects rural economy	. . . .
12. Poisonous fungi mistaken for mushrooms	. . . .

Activity 11.H Assessing an Argument

Many of the elements of reasoning are plainly on view in the following argument humorously slanted by Phillip Adams at some of the extravagances of the advertising world. Read it through, then answer the questions that follow.

YOU TOO CAN BE AN AD MAN

If you'd like a successful career in advertising, you need the Adams Advertising Kit. This exciting set of visual cliches will permit you to write and produce memorable TV commercials.

When I say memorable, the viewer may not remember the specific product, but your general approach will be all too familiar.

Originality is dangerous in advertising. It tends to worry clients and sometimes creates controversy. Better to rely on proven concepts, on ideas with a pedigree. My kit is invaluable as it contains cliches used over and over again by top agencies.

There are nine sets of cards in my kit illustrating cliches of various types. To write a commercial on any subject you simply shuffle them and drop them in random order on your blotter. Then it's an easy matter to add a photograph of your product or service, along with some appropriate phrases.

Before I demonstrate my foolproof system, let us examine the sets of cards.

The slow-motion set: This includes a young child playing with a balloon and a girl running through the mulga in her see-through nightie. As well there's a shot of a young lady tossing her hair about in a dreamy fashion, as though trying to dislodge her dandruff.

The **exciting action** set: This includes race cars circling the track, motor-bikes leaping off a hillock, dune buggies belting through the sand and a young lady in bikini galloping in the surf. There are young men climbing a rock face, shots of yachting on Sydney Harbour and a car crossing the Nullarbor Plain. Last but not least we have the blast off of Apollo-13 at Cape Kennedy.

The **sincere recommendation** set comprises various people saying things like 'I'm never without it', 'It's the best on the market' and 'Take my word for it'. They include Ron Barassi, Captain Bristow, Philip Brady and Mrs Gladys Briggs of Bankstown.

The **appropriate** music set includes an orchestra playing selections from Tchaikovsky, a hairy rock band and hillbilly guitarists.

The **sex and glamour** set is made up of a young man clenching his cheeks and dilating his nostrils, shots of both sexes back-to-camera under the shower, and a collection of radiant young ladies smiling fit to bust.

The **lovable menagerie** set is ideal for pet food commercials or for ads on home heating. It includes an assortment of Siamese kittens, labrador pups, beagles, baa-lambs and a budgie.

The **before** set is invaluable for patent medicine and wig manufacturers. It is made up of people who sadly roll their eyes towards their scalps or who clutch at their backs and foreheads. Some are seriously overweight or are suffering from scurvy or head colds. There is no 'after' set. You contrast your Before people with those from the sex and glamour or sincere recommedation sets.

The **wonderful ingredients** set shows shots of fresh fruit, full cream milk, garden vegetables and thick slices of steak. There are heads of golden corn and a chemist's mortar and pestle. These can be used for food, flour or confectionery commercials or for spots on home medications. I've recently added another card showing grandmother at work in her country kitchen.

The **back to nature** set is proving extremely popular. It comprises shots of sun shining through leaves, babbling brooks, and gum trees in the misty dawn.

Now all you have to do is shuffle your cards and we're ready to go. For example, let's imagine that we want to do a political commercial. With a random selection of cards it would go as follows. First we see a man holding his head ('Is Labor giving you migraine?'). This is followed by a slow motion shot of a girl waving her hair around ('say no to centralised government').

Next you pop in a bit of lettering saying 'vote Democrat for the good life' and you conclude with Barassi saying 'take my word for it'. You might include the Siamese kitten to attract the female vote.

Or you might wish to write a cigarette commercial and the first card to emerge shows a shot of golden corn. 'This is the best Australian tobacco', you'd say, as most viewers wouldn't be any the wiser. Then cut to the girl in her see-through nightie and say 'It's now available in a new, milder smoke'. Girls in nighties go with just about anything.

Next comes the orchestra playing Tschaikovsky, which is a good way to hint at prestige, and you finish with Captain Bristow saying 'it's the best on the market'. All you need to do is add your product's name and price.

You might feel that these examples are over-simple, so let's try a more difficult product, something of a personal nature. Let's assemble a laxative commercial from my all-purpose pack.

These are the cards we deal ourselves. The shot of a baby goat, Mrs Gladys Briggs, a rocket lifting off at Cape Kennedy, the shot of sun shining through leaves, the rock band and a little girl playing with her balloon. We also find a shot of granny in her country kitchen. Now it's a simple matter of assembling them in a logical sequence and adding the appropriate words. Allow me to demonstrate.

First little girl lets go of her balloon ('Feel lighter') then we intercut between the rock band and the sun shining through leaves ('Feel in tune with nature'). We then cut to the rocket and then to the close-up of our product. 'Blast off with Brand X laxative.' Next we cut to the close-up of a mortar and pestle and to grandmother working in her country kitchen. 'Containing the best scientific ingredients, it's like the laxative that grandma used to make.' We conclude with the baby goat ('you'll feel like a kid again') and Mrs Briggs of Bankstown saying 'I'm never without it.'

What could be easier?

1. Is 'cliche' a bias word? Give a reason for your answer.
2. '. . . the viewer may not remember the specific product, but your general approach will be all too familiar.' What kind of reasoning is characterized by the movement from the specific to the general?
3. 'Originality is dangerous in advertising' In reasoning, what kind of statement is this?
4. Why is originality dangerous in advertising?
5. What does Adams mean by 'ideas with a pedigree'?
6. What reason does Adams give for the worth of his kit?
7. What is the method advocated by Adams for producing a commercial on any subject?
8. In the sentence beginning, 'As well there's a shot . . .' indicate an incongruous contrast.
9. In the exciting action set, which outdoor image is laughable? Why?
10. In the sincere recommendation set, a certain insincerity creeps in. How?
11. How is humour introduced to the sex and glamour set by a pun?
12. How much cause-effect relationship is exhibited in the political commercial?
13. Is advertising generally noted for its strong adherence to argument by means of cause and effect? Give a reason for your answer, and find examples from current media advertising.
14. How is 'expert' appeal brought to bear in the political commercial?
15. Why would you be justified in regarding such appeal with suspicion?
16. Comment on the use of analogy in the laxative commercial.

Activity 11.I   Assessing an Argument

Explain why you would reject or accept the following arguments:

1. The government should send all the money at present being wasted on defence to buy food for people starving in underdeveloped countries.
2. Taxes were increased last year. National prosperity increased this year. Therefore the government should increase taxes again if it wishes to increase prosperity still further.
3. The practice of insurance companies charging higher premiums for comprehensive motor vehicle policies for drivers under twenty-five years of age is discrimination against young people. This is unfair. A law should be passed to stop this practice.
4. We as freedom-loving Australians should ban all demonstrations from our streets.
5. It's absurd to pay a tennis player like Borg $1 million a year just for hitting a tennis ball around a court.
6. When a dog is old and in bad health, you kill it to put it out of its misery, and that's just what you should do with hopelessly ill human beings.
7. That man hit my cat. He is an Italian. All Italians are cruel to cats.
8. I have been a teacher for twenty years and I say that students today are not as good as the students I used to teach when I was a young teacher.

Activity 11.J   Problem-Solving the Group Way

For this series of exercises the class divides into small groups. Each group elects a discussion leader and a secretary. With the discussion leader going to each group member in turn for ideas—and with the secretary recording—the group produces its solution to the problem and presents it to the class.

1. **Who Should Survive?**
   There has been a nuclear holocaust. The only survivors left on earth are eleven persons in an anti-nuclear bomb shelter. One month must elapse before the level of radiation in the outside atmosphere falls sufficiently for life to be possible on the earth's surface. However, even with rigid rationing, there is food and water for only *seven* persons for a month. So, only seven out of the eleven can possibly survive. Which ones? Give your reasons. Here are the twelve persons:
   (1) Ian Reed, thirty-seven; white; atheist; manual worker; good health; married; no children; enjoys sport.
   (2) Mrs Barton, thirty-eight; white; M.A. in psychology; counsellor in mental health clinic; good health; married; one child (Andrew) active in community work.
   (3) Andrew Barton, ten; white; in a special school for four years; mentally retarded (I.Q. 60); good health; enjoys his pets.
   (4) Mrs James, thirty-three; Irish extraction; Roman Catholic; Year Ten education; bistro waitress; prostitute; good health; married at sixteen; divorced at eighteen; one child three weeks old (Cheryl).
   (5) Cheryl James, three weeks old; Irish background; good health; still being nursed.
   (6) Denise Warren, eight; black; Protestant; third grade; good health.

(7) Mr Dale, twenty-five; black, agnostic; starting last year of medical school; suspected homosexual activity; good health; seems bitter concerning racial problems; wears trendy clothes.

(8) Mrs Simmons, twenty-eight; Asian; university graduate; civil engineer; married; no children; good health; enjoys sports; grew up in city slum area.

(9) Mr Buckley, fifty-one; white; degree in mechanics; very handy; married; two children; good health; enjoys outdoors and working in his shop.

(10) Father Smith, thirty-seven; white; Roman Catholic; college plus seminary; priest; good health; former athlete.

(11) Dr Green, seventy; Australian; Roman Catholic; doctor in general practice; heart attacks in past five years, but continues to practice.

(12) Nicholas Stephenson, forty-eight; criminal record; heavy drinker and smokes; married; three children.

2. Take it and Leave

After work one day you are dismayed to find that you haven't even got a bus fare in your pocket. You try to get a loan from a fellow employee but he simply says: 'Sorry mate, I'd lend it to you if I could but I'm a bit short myself. Tell you what, slip back into the office—I've just come out and there's no one there—and help yourself to a bus fare from the boss's petty cash. It wouldn't be the first time someone's been into it for their bus fare. The firm owes it to you. Besides that amount from petty cash'll never be missed.'

(a) What are the various forces acting on the fareless employee?

(b) What should he do?

(c) What should he say to the other employee?

3. High-Rise Ideas

As a student or an employee, or even as a member of a club or an association, you would have noticed how difficult it is to move ideas or suggestions upwards through an organizational structure to the administration or management at the policy-making level.

(a) What makes it so hard for the policy makers to listen to, or accept, ideas from below?

(b) What do you believe to be the greatest obstacle to the rise of ideas? Can you speak from experience?

(c) Devise a workable scheme by which ideas or suggestions could find their way through an organizational structure to the top. If possible, use an actual structure you are experiencing or have experienced.

(d) How should a principal or manager be approached with your scheme and persuaded of its value?

(e) How, when and where should your scheme be presented to other students, employees or club members for the first time?

(f) Design a poster advertising the scheme.

(g) What incentives, if any, should be used to encourage the success of the scheme?

(h) What actual mechanical means (e.g. a standardized form) would be used for moving ideas up?

4. **Promotion**

There are many different products coming on the market all the time, and often the success of one rather than another depends on appropriate promotion. Suppose you are able to promote a product or service by means of:

- the mass media—advertising
- quiz shows, cricket or football matches or other sporting events
- sales of samples, badges etc.
- public appearances by well-known personalities

(a) Select appropriate areas of promotion for the arrival on the market of:
  (i)   a new brand of lipstick
  (ii)   a new hamburger
  (iii) a new kind of biro
  (iv)   a new toy
  (v)   a new wig
  (vi)   a new model car
(b) Explain just how the promotion would proceed for each of the new products.

5. **College in Trouble**

The College had a reputation for its well-planned amenities and for its attempts at involving students and staff in the running of the place. Over the entrance way, painted in gold, was:

SELFDISCIPLINE IS THE ONLY TRUE DISCIPLINE

However, no sooner had we entered than we noticed the place was in some sort of trouble. Students were sullen and unhelpful. There was some evidence of damage to facilities. We were at a loss to pin down the *reason* for the bad impression the place was making on us, until we spotted the large, permanent notice laying down the law. It said:

RULE: STUDENTS MUST NOT LITTER RECREATION AREAS

RULE ENFORCEMENT: ANY STUDENT INFRINGING THE RULE IS LIABLE TO BE EXPELLED FORTHWITH.

We had found the trouble!

(a) Explain why the visitors are so sure they have found the problem.

(b) Is the notice reasonable? Should it be rewritten? Should it be scrapped?

(c) Present a report to the college principal outlining the source of the trouble in his organization and making recommendations for its eradication.

(d) Air some of your own experience with hypocrisy in institutions.

6. **Individuality**

You are a teenage girl who has left business college with high qualifications. You have had no trouble in getting a responsible job in a bank. Your difficulties commence when you are assigned counter work which brings you before the general public.

In this new work, your casual teenager gear—not to mention your sandals and beads—are frowned on by your boss. He is the bank manager and is a middle-aged man who has spent all his working life in the bank. He always wears a dark business suit and is conservative in his outlook.

The manager insists on a change in your appearance. You point out that your appearance is an individual thing which hasn't affected your punctuality or your efficiency. None the less he insists that you change your appearance to a more acceptable bank image, and makes an appointment to see you in a week's time so that he can approve the change.

A week has passed and you are due to see the manager. But you have refused to change your appearance.

(a) What options are open to the manager in his approach to his young employee?

(b) Which option is he likely to settle for?

(c) What is the best approach for the girl to take?

12   Word Power

Without words you would find great difficulty in imparting your ideas to others. Your success as communicators vitally depends on your ability to use words. The following exercises have been designed to help you increase your word power.

Activity 12.A   Synonyms

A synonym is a word that is similar in meaning to another word. Write synonyms for the words below. Note that the first letters are given and the number of letters in each word is indicated.

Word	Synonym	Word	Synonym
1. stay	r-----	19. malign	s------
2. unbelievable	i---------	20. clandestine	s-----
3. evil	m--------	21. lengthen	e-----
4. peaceful	t-------	22. adhere	s----
5. abandon	l----	23. round	c--------
6. yearly	a-------	24. empty	v-----
7. cure	r-----	25. smell	o----
8. least	m------	26. plentiful	a-------
9. completely	e-------	27. purpose	i--------
10. abstain	r------	28. understand	c---------
11. adorn	d-------	29. disappear	v-----
12. follow	e----_	30. attempted	t----
13. status	p-------	31. see	p-------
14. tedium	b------	32. hide	c------
15. novice	b-------	33. change	a----
16. fat	o----	34. allow	p-----
17. baffling	p-------	35. strange	p-------
18. intrepid	f-------		

128

Activity 12.B Antonyms

An antonym is a word opposite in meaning to another word. Write antonyms for the words below. Note that the first letters are given and the number of letters in each word is indicated.

WORD	ANTONYM	WORD	ANTONYM
1. beneficial	h------	19. same	d--------
2. poverty	w-----	20. voluntary	c---------
3. temporary	p--------	21. exposed	c------
4. public	p------	22. increase	d--------
5. knowledge	i--------	23. occupy	v-----
6. accept	r-----	24. serious	f--------
7. admit	d---	25. question	a-----
8. include	e------	26. dangerous	s---
9. opaque	t---------	27. ascent	d------
10. superior	i-------	28. apart	t-------
11. legible	i-------	29. innocent	g-----
12. synthetic	n------	30. credit	d----
13. majority	m-------	31. employer	e-------
14. optimist	p--------	32. fertile	b-----
15. expansion	c----------	33. often	s-----
16. synonym	a-------	34. present	a-----
17. energetic	l--------	35. advance	r------
18. initial	f----		

"THIS GOVERNMENT PROMISES THAT TAXATION WILL **NEVER** INCREASE IN THE FORSEEABLE FUTURE!"

Activity 12.C   Key Words

Choose the word or phrase that is closest in meaning to the key word in italics.

1. *Anticipate* trouble
   (a) expect   (b) lose sight of   (c) ponder
   (d) accept

2. Debris *accumulates*
   (a) diminishes   (b) spreads   (c) piles up
   (d) sifts away

3. *Complacency* in suburbia
   (a) self-satisfaction   (b) discontent
   (c) lack of discipline   (d) prosperity

4. Enforced *segregation*
   (a) integration   (b) involvement
   (c) separation from others
   (d) cooperation

5. An *insipid* personality
   (a) spiritless, dull   (b) strong, vigorous
   (c) humorous, fun-loving
   (d) dominant, controlling

6. *Concurrent* publications
   (a) looking the same   (b) running
   together   (c) identical in size
   (d) specialized

7. *Alleviate* poverty
   (a) increase   (b) relieve   (c) alienate
   (d) recognise

8. *Dogmatic* personality
   (a) sensible   (b) logical   (c) unbiased
   (d) tending to force one's own opinions
   on others

9. *Blatant* misuse of power
   (a) hidden and underhand
   (b) conscious   (c) practical
   (d) obvious, shameless

10. High *correlation*
    (a) degree of relationship
    (b) intensification   (c) potential
    for improvement   (d) correction factor

11. *Denigrate* the opposition
    (a) delay   (b) defame   (c) deny
    (d) disturb

12. A *facet* of the problem
    (a) explanation   (b) aspect
    (c) solution   (d) overall view

13. Completely *exonerated*
(a) confirmed in guilt   (b) freed from blame   (c) legalized   (d) involved

14. Sheer *hypocrisy*
(a) sincerity   (b) gratitude   (c) pretended virtue   (d) delight

15. An *expedient* move
(a) advantageous   (b) hasty   (c) unwise   (d) futile

16. *Impervious* to common sense
(a) responsive   (b) not receptive   (c) contributing   (d) impassive

17. A witty *insinuation*
(a) remark   (b) fact   (c) unpleasant hint   (d) phrase

18. A *petulant* child
(a) irritable, touchy   (b) happy   (c) selfconfident   (d) sad, downcast

19. A *vulnerable* area
(a) safe   (b) open to injury or attack   (c) frequently visited   (d) carefully preserved

20. An *audacious* plan
(a) useless   (b) competent   (c) bold   (d) allowable

21. A *prevalent* view
(a) dangerous   (b) proven   (c) widespread   (d) mature

22. *Invariably* sunny
(a) constantly   (b) usually   (c) similarly   (d) universally

23. The *affluent* society
(a) sinful   (b) unemployable   (c) wealthy   (d) disorganized

24. *Simulated* interest
(a) grateful   (b) regretful   (c) alarmed   (d) pretended

25. A *prudent* action
(a) wise   (b) intelligent   (c) courageous   (d) doubtful

26. An *arbitrary* judgement
(a) forcible   (b) demanding   (c) not bound by rules   (d) relying heavily on fact

27. Feeling *enervated*
(a) troubled   (b) ambitious   (c) exhausted   (d) tense

28. Taking an *unequivocal* view
(a) clear and decisive   (b) fully factual   (c) cautious   (d) ridiculous

29. *Vicarious* pleasure
(a) long term and continuous   (b) one
(b) experienced through the medium of other people   (c) religious   (d) completely individual

30. *Coherent* argument
(a) hard to follow   (b) improbable   (c) logically consistent   (d) censorious

31. An *ambiguous* statement
(a) having a double meaning   (b) clear cut   (c) provocative   (d) explanatory

32. An *avaricious* landlord
(a) benevolent   (b) indifferent   (c) greedy for money   (d) emotionally disturbed

33. A short *prelude*
(a) intermission   (b) introduction   (c) addition   (d) conclusion

34. *Lethal* fumes
(a) rendered safe   (b) pure
(c) contaminated   (d) deadly

35. An *innovation* in industry
(a) a rare occurrence   (b) a reaction
(c) a new approach   (d) an amalgamation

36. *Succumb* to exposure
(a) give way   (b) attend   (c) open
(d) immune

37. *Meticulous* attention
(a) superficial   (b) detailed
(c) intelligent   (d) unbiased

38. A stream of *invective*
(a) praise   (b) rational argument
(c) violent abuse   (d) soothing words

39. He claims he was *justified*
(a) shown to be right   (b) proved
incorrect   (c) revenged
(d) deceived

40. *Mutually* advantageous
(a) individually   (b) seemingly
(c) consistently   (d) jointly

41. *Subtle* comment
(a) uncomplicated   (b) elusively clever
(c) unfair   (d) wide-of-the-mark

42. *Erroneous* calculation
(a) unproven   (b) incorrect
(c) complex   (d) errant

43. A *feasibility* study
(a) sensibility   (b) legality
(c) practicability   (d) reality

44. A *gullible* listener
(a) discerning   (b) easily deceived
(c) enthusiastic   (d) critical

45. The social *elite*
(a) working people   (b) technical
experts   (c) best class   (d) unemployed

46. An *interminable* wait
(a) short in duration   (b) comfortable
(c) interesting   (d) seemingly endless

47. The *admonition* was heeded
(a) proclamation   (b) warning
(c) political speech   (d) denial

48. *Comply* with the rules
(a) argue   (b) allow   (c) grant
(d) obey

49. *Contagious* disease
(a) fatal   (b) infectious   (c) individual
(d) lethal

50. *Indifferent* to public opinion
(a) unconcerned with   (b) expert in
(c) outraged by   (d) careful of

51. The *opulent* merchants
(a) unhappy   (b) annoyed
(c) industrious   (d) wealthy

52. The king *waived* his right
(a) retained   (b) relinquished
(c) prolonged   (d) claimed

53. An *odious* crime
(a) forgivable   (b) disgusting
(c) punishable   (d) homicidal

54. A *cursory* examination
(a) hasty   (b) unhurried   (c) thorough
(d) medical

55. The servant was *obsequious*
(a) friendly   (b) deceptive   (c) reliable
(d) fawning

56. The headmaster *placated* the
teacher
(a) abused   (b) pacified   (c) rescued
(d) condemned

57. An object of *derision*   (a) value   (b) contempt   (c) attention
                                      (d) approval
58. An *immutable* rule   (a) unchangeable   (b) harsh
                                      (c) disregarded   (d) just
59. Moving with *alacrity*   (a) hopelessness   (b) tiredness
                                      (c) indecision   (d) briskness
60. *Halcyon* years   (a) changing   (b) ancient   (c) happy
                                      (d) nostalgic
61. A *vacuous* statement   (a) supercilious   (b) stupid
                                      (c) sarcastic   (d) intelligent
62. The caretaker was *amenable*   (a) wise   (b) respected   (c) manageable
                                      (d) stupid
63. He worked in a *desultory* manner (a) energetic   (b) aimless
                                      (c) keen   (d) profitable
64. A *copious* supply   (a) plentiful   (b) scanty   (c) complete
                                      (d) sufficient
65. A *strident* voice   (a) loud   (b) quiet   (c) shrill   (d) sweet
66. A *diffident* recruit   (a) determined   (b) shy   (c) contented
                                      (d) angry
67. An *inveterate* liar   (a) habitual   (b) hateful   (c) imaginative
                                      (d) occasional
68. A *mundane* existence   (a) ordinary   (b) educated
                                      (c) pleasurable   (d) zestful
69. The *zenith* of her career   (a) end   (b) peak   (c) beginning
                                      (d) difficulty
70. *Stingent* laws   (a) just   (b) severe   (c) desirable
                                      (d) chaotic
71. An *obese* child   (a) innocent   (b) active   (c) very fat
                                      (d) diligent
72. A *dearth* of talent in the theatre (a) scarcity   (b) diversity
                                      (c) abundance   (d) superiority
73. A *sardonic* remark   (a) quiet   (b) jovial   (c) sarcastic
                                      (d) confident
74. To take *umbrage*   (a) pleasure   (b) thought
                                      (c) offence   (d) leave
75. His sudden *demise*   (a) happiness   (b) death   (c) arrival
                                      (d) fame
76. An *innocuous* spider   (a) venomous   (b) agile   (c) agitated
                                      (d) harmless
77. The *ignominy* of defeat   (a) disgrace   (b) sadness
                                      (c) senselessness   (d) lesson
78. A *tenuous* connection   (a) strong   (b) metallic   (c) enduring
                                      (d) weak
79. Her speech was *impeccable*   (a) remarkable   (b) coherent
                                      (c) flawless   (d) aggravating
80. A *scurrilous* remark   (a) cunning   (b) abusive
                                      (c) nervous   (d) unusual

Activity 12.D   Column Words

1. From the column, select the antonyms (opposites) for:
   (a) reduce   (e) gradual
   (b) unity   (f) diverge
   (c) join   (g) persuade
   (d) unruly   (h) ungainly
2. From the column, select the synonyms (words with a similar meaning) for:
   (a) significance   (e) detest
   (b) ravage   (f) elucidate
   (c) forbid   (g) contrite
   (d) pretentious   (h) amplification
3. Find the vocations for each of the following:
   (a) one who keeps bees
   (b) one who preaches the Gospel
   (c) one who studies soil and its properties
   (d) one who studies the relationship of life and its surroundings
   (e) one who tests and prescribes for the sight
   (f) one who studies fossils
4. Find the word from the column for each of the following phrases:
   (a) a general pardon
   (b) an exact copy
   (c) one hundredth anniversary
   (d) a conversation between two people
   (e) a jury's decision
   (f) relating to the nose
   (g) a climb
   (h) relating to government
   (i) delay in time
   (j) a note to help the memory
   (k) a light pleasant breeze
   (l) turn to stone

COLUMN WORDS
importance
apiarist
ostentatious
amnesty
sudden
agronomist
penitent
devastate
duplicate
evangelist
political
increase
centenary
palaeontologist
nasal
diversity
postpone
loathe
dialogue
graceful
ecologist
prohibit
verdict
obedient
memo
explain
zephyr
enlargement
separate
ascent
optometrist
petrify
converge
dissuade

Activity 12.E   The Study Of

The suffix '-ology' means 'study of'. Match up each of the following '-ology' words with its correct meaning.

1. biology   (a) study of pregnancy and women's diseases
2. entomology   (b) study of weather and climate
3. astrology   (c) study of water resources
4. anthropology   (d) study of crime and criminals
5. meteorology   (e) study of volcanoes

6.	hydrology	(f)	study of insect life
7.	pathology	(g)	study of the descent of families
8.	sociology	(h)	study of the stars as they influence human affairs
9.	philology	(i)	study of poisons and their effects
10.	criminology	(j)	study of human society
11.	gynaecology	(k)	study of industrial arts and organisation
12.	speleology	(l)	study of human races
13.	vulcanology	(m)	study of life forms
14.	ornithology	(n)	study of disease
15.	genealogy	(e)	study of caves
16.	psychology	(p)	study of human antiquities
17.	technology	(q)	study of religion
18.	toxicology	(r)	study of the mind
19.	archaeology	(s)	study of language
20.	theology	(t)	study of bird life

Activity 12.F   Confusing Pairs

Choose the correct word from the pair in brackets.

1. The (stationary/stationery) car was towed away.
2. The (imminent/eminent) professor was (incredulous/incredible) when told the results of the experiment.
3. Lawyers are able to (cite/sight) previous examples of (liable/libel).
4. The (principal/principle) will now address the assembly.
5. The jet shook the building as it (passed/past) over.
6. What an (ingenuous/ingenious) little device.
7. The yellow of an egg is called the (yoke/yolk).
8. Bathurst is a (populace/populous) town west of the mountain.
9. She spent most of her (vocation/vacation) lying on the beach.
10. There is no doubt that the rain will (effect/affect) the game.
11. The man and women entered into a (marital/martial) relationship.
12. I understand you wish to (wave/waive) your claim to the money?
13. The Prime Minister himself is going out to (canvas/canvass) votes.
14. (Gorilla/Guerilla) forces are being trained in the mountains.
15. He showed great ability to survive in (adversary/adversity).
16. The producer (complimented/complemented) the actress on her success.
17. Raise your hand if you wish to (descent/dissent) from the motion before the council.
18. The groom is asked to (proceed/precede) the bride up the aisle.
19. Unfortunately the problem is (insoluble/insolvent).
20. Shop assistants are expected to be well-dressed and to show (civility/servility) towards customers.

Activity 12.G   Words About People

From the box, choose a word to replace the words in italics.

sagacious	ebullient	irate	ingenuous
garrulous	ludicrous	supercilious	crass
fallible	maudlin	dour	rapacious
implacable	ascetic	brash	raucous
obsequious	parsimonious	arrogant	querulous

1. He was drunk, and *in a silly sentimental state* when I last saw him.
2. She was *shrewd* as well as intelligent.
3. I look back on my *hasty and reckless* youth with shame.
4. What an *innocent and naive* outlook on life!
5. The students found that their teacher was *liable to make mistakes* after all.
6. Today, the college principal made an *angry* speech.
7. Our yoga teacher is *a person who lives a life of austerity in order to gain virtue.*
8. I'm afraid he is rather *gross in taste* when it comes to entertainment.
9. People accuse her of being *overbearing in manner.*
10. I sat behind an *extremely talkative* couple in the bus.
11. The politician was *contemptuously indifferent.*
12. She was *boiling over with enthusiasm* about her new boyfriend.
13. He spends little and, in fact, has been called *very stingy with money.*
14. The public servant was *servile and submissive* towards his departmental head.
15. She was a *sullen, even grim,* old soul.
16. The troops were infamous for their *violent and plundering* behaviour in captured territory.
17. He was *not to be appeased or pacified.*
18. Her behaviour was *silly and laughable* in the extreme.
19. His *fretful and complaining* statements annoyed the rest of the class.
20. Her *harsh, shrill* laughter irritated the rest of the party.

Activity 12.H   -Ic Words

Match each '-ic' word with its meaning.

1. laconic
2. realistic
3. fatalistic
4. sadistic
5. somnambulistic
6. hedonistic
7. agnostic
8. lethargic
9. ecstatic
10. antagonistic
11. nostalgic
12. ethnic
13. mystic
14. militaristic
15. nomadic

(a) one who holds there is no proof of God
(b) one who claims a special, secret link with God
(c) wildly happy
(d) longing for the past
(e) concerning the army or warfare
(f) slow and sluggish
(g) using few words
(h) inexpedient
(i) flattering in a servile way
(j) theatrical action or speech
(k) sleep walking
(l) life-like
(m) practical
(n) obtaining pleasure from cruelty
(o) yielding to the unavoidable

16. impolitic   (p) believing that pleasure is the greatest good
17. sycophantic   (q) disposed to fight
18. frenetic   (r) concerning nations or races
19. pragmatic   (s) wandering
20. histrionic   (t) frantic

Activity 12.1   Word Families

One word of each family is given. Fit the other forms of the word into the sentences.

You are given the first example.

1. **Strong**
   (a) There is a **strong** case for higher unemployment benefits.
   (b) The police wanted to . . . . the law on gambling.
   (c) . . . . of character is needed.
   (d) She objected . . . . to the accusation.
2. **Include**
   (a) There's one other item for . . . . and then the file is complete.
   (b) It is necessary to . . . . emergency rations in the life boat's gear.
   (c) This is an . . . . price.
3. **Evade**
   (a) She was . . . . when asked where she had been.
   (b) Fare . . . . is a serious offence.
   (c) He answered . . . .
4. **Fury**
   (a) The swear word . . . . the teacher.
   (b) There was a . . . . storm last night.
   (c) The policeman's . . . . made him tremble.

5. **Extend**
   (a) .... repairs were needed.
   (b) The flagpole needs an ....
   (c) The factory was .... damaged by fire.
6. **Technical**
   (a) The chief .... made the final decision.
   (b) Industrial .... is well advanced.
   (c) .... change is a daily occurrence.
7. **Prefer**
   (a) Students have a .... for sport.
   (b) Consumers receive .... treatment in that store.
   (c) The college .... chooses teachers with high qualifications.
   (d) They .... the more relaxed atmosphere of the canteen.
8. **Avoid**
   (a) The .... of regulations was a punishable offence.
   (b) The train was un......... delayed.
   (c) There will be an un......... delay.
9. **Employ**
   (a) An .... has responsibilities towards his workers.
   (b) The .... decided on strike action.
   (c) Unfortunately the youth was ....
   (d) Un......... was highest in rural areas.
10. **Decide**
    (a) A .... on the amount will be reached next week.
    (b) It was a .... move to make.
    (c) You must act ....

Activity 12.J   Word Analogies
Give the missing word in each of the analogies. Sometimes the first letters are given to help you.
1. Author is to book as artist is to ....
2. Doctor is to medicine as solicitor is to ....
3. Mechanic is to car as nurse is to ....
4. Teacher is to students as minister is to c.........
5. Plumber is to pipes as glazier is to ....
6. Dentist is to drill as surgeon is to s.........
7. Big is to little as giant is to ....
8. Revolver is to holster as a sword is to ....
9. A general is to war as a judge is to ....
10. Eye is to sight as stomach is to d.........
11. Wool is to bale as strawberries are to p.........
12. Rabbit is to hutch as bird is to a ....
13. Eat is to .... as go is to went
14. Soldier is to barracks as nun is to c.........
15. Sheep is to flock as lion is to p.........
16. Water is to drought as food is to ....
17. Buzz is to saw as .... is to siren
18. Winter is to death as spring is to ....
19. Feline is to cat as e......... is to horse.
20. Fox is to lair as eagle is to e.........

Activity 12.K   Find a Word

instigate	deleterious	unintelligible	raucus
momentous	jargon	renumeration	perpetrated
chaos	charade	supervision	lethargic
symmetry	integral	ingratiate	voracious
fastidious	shrewd	perfunctory	inauguration

1. The shark is known for its . . . . appetite.
2. The earthquake has left . . . . in its wake.
3. She was a . . . . judge of character.
4. The cook was . . . . about having clean utensils.
5. Smoking is considered . . . . to one's health.
6. The client read the contract in a . . . . manner.
7. The hot weather makes students . . . . in class.
8. Naturally you will receive a fair . . . . for your services.
9. The . . . . of the President is a . . . . occasion.
10. She has tried to . . . . herself with her superiors.
11. He claimed that the last election was merely a . . . . and that, in future, elections must be held under proper . . . .
12. Critics stated that the architect's design lacked . . . .
13. The crime was . . . . on innocent victims.
14. Some of the employees were able to . . . . a strike.
15. I'm afraid the legal . . . . in this document is . . . . to me.
16. A battery is an . . . . part of a car's electrical system.
17. A . . . . noise came from the class room.

Activity 12.L   Prefixes

Prefixes are very important in word formation. A prefix is a syllable placed at the beginning of a word to vary the meaning or make a new word. In 'interstate' and 'discomfort', **inter** and **dis** are prefixes.

1. The prefix **tri** means 'three'. Write the missing words, all beginning with 'tri', in the spaces beneath.
   (a) Here is the document in . . . . Please sign each of the three copies.
   (b) A musical . . . . will sing for the audience.

(c) The three-coloured flag is called a ....

(d) The concert is a .... event since it happens every three years.

(e) A .... is a three-legged stand for an instrument.

(f) To .... is to divide into three parts.

2. The prefix **ex** means 'out of' or 'out'. Write the missing words, all beginning with 'ex', in the spaces beneath.

(a) Gas .... when heated. (spreads out)

(b) Living creatures .... carbon dioxide. (breathe out)

(c) The ghost was .... from the building. (driven out by ritual means)

(d) Rebels were sent into .... (out of one's country)

(e) The tunnels were .... (dug out)

(f) We wish to .... all undesirables. (shut out)

(g) The teacher .... in annoyance at the interruption. (cried out)

(h) You have .... the bounds of good taste. (gone out of or beyond)

3. The prefix **bi** means 'two'. Match up the 'bi' words on the left with their meanings on the right.

(a) bisect
(b) bifurcate
(c) binaural
(d) biped
(e) bigamy
(f) bivalve
(g) bilingual
(h) binary
(i) bicycle
(j) bicentennial

(k) having two ears
(l) having two wives or husbands at the same time
(m) having two feet
(n) to cut in two
(o) having two shells
(p) dividing into two branches
(q) composed of two of anything
(r) two hundredth anniversary
(s) commanding two languages
(t) vehicle with two wheels

4. The prefix **inter** means 'between'. Supply 'inter' words for the following.

(a) internal telephone system   inter--m
(b) mutual participation   inter-c---n
(c) between cities   interu---n
(d) interrupt a speech   inter-e-t
(e) clasp together   inter---k
(f) between nations   inter-a-----l
(g) cut or cross mutually   inters--t
(h) come or be between   interv--e
(i) act as a peacemaker between two, pleading for one   inter--d-
(j) stop and seize   interc-p-

5. The prefix **pre** means 'before'. Supply 'pre' words.
   (a) a syllable put before a word   pre-i-
   (b) before birth   pre--t-l
   (c) unduly early   pre--t--e
   (d) foreknowledge   pre---n----n
   (e) go before   pre-e--
   (f) care taken beforehand   pre---t--n
   (g) decide on beforehand   pre-u--e
   (h) see before, in advance   pre-i-w

Activity 12.M   How Well Do You Spell?

Correct spelling is a very important aspect of successful written communication. A piece of correspondence or a report full of spelling errors greatly hinders communication and gives the reader a poor impression of the writer as a potential communicator of information or ideas.

Below are a hundred essential words that *you* should be able to spell. Use the clues to see how well you can spell the words. (N.B. The dots do **not** represent letters.)

1. Food intake is essential and n . . . . y for life.
2. The act of saying or doing something over and over again is r . . . . n.
3. To chase is to p . . . . e.
4. Another word for 'vanish' is d . . . . r.
5. To happen is to o . . . . r.
6. An unmarried man is a b . . . . r.
7. To go faster is to a . . . .
8. A harsher word for to question is to **int** . . . . e.
9. The opposite of comedy is t . . . . y.
10. To fly into pieces is to **dis** . . . .
11. If you are not guilty you are i . . . .
12. Not permanent but t . . . . y.
13. A disagreement can turn into an **a** . . . .

14. The person who lives next door to you is your **n** . . . .
15. To go forward is to **pr** . . . . d.
16. Something that troubles you when you are guilty is your **c** . . . .
17. To **ab** . . . . something is to shorten it.
18. To annoy, attack or trouble is to **h** . . . . s.
19. To **dis** . . . . is to melt in liquid.
20. An ignorant bias against a person of another race is called racial **pr** . . . .
21. To speak in favour of someone or something is to **re** . . . . d.
22. Recreation time is **l** . . . . e time.
23. A paid car driver is a **ch** . . . . r.
24. Something strange and even uncanny is **w** . . . . d.
25. The opposite of deep or profound is **sup** . . . . l.
26. If you find yourself in an awkward position with difficult alternatives you are in a **di** . . . . a.
27. A table of days and months of the year is a **c** . . . . r.
28. Unreadable is **i** . . . . e.
29. One word for 'at once' is **i** . . . . ly.
30. In sport, if you're not a professional, you're likely to be an **am** . . . . r.
31. To go on trying is to **pe** . . . . e.
32. To kill, particularly for political reasons, is to **as** . . . . e.

33. Railway lines run **p**. . . . .**l** or side by side.
34. To **su**. . . . .**d** is to do well and not to fail.
35. A state in which a person lacks awareness of what is going on
    unc. . . . .**ness**.
36. A sudden unexpected happening requiring urgent action is an **em**. . . . .**y**.
37. The Earth's air is called its **at**. . . . .**e**.
38. Another word for a cliff: **pr**. . . . .**e**.
39. A happening, as in: 'On the **oc**. . . . .**n** of my daughter's wedding'.
40. A register of the months and days of the year — **a**. . . . .
41. An advantage enjoyed by only a few is a **pr**. . . . .**l**. . . . .**e**.
42. Another word for a timetable of things to be done is a **s**. . . . .**d**. . . . .**e**.
43. To find guilty or pass judgement on is to **con**. . . . .**n**.
44. Another word for 'helping', as in **aux**. . . . .**l**. . . . .**y** movement.
45. Physical and mental growth and **dev**. . . . .**t**.
46. Sufficient or enough is **ad**. . . . .**qu**. . . . .**e**.
47. Without a name: **an**. . . . .**m**. . . . .**s**.
48. A person noted for good taste and artistic inclination: **con**. . . . .**eur**.
49. To become worse or suffer a reduction in quality is to **det**. . . . .**e**.
50. An advantage or profit is a **be**. . . . .**f**. . . . .**t**.
51. A reproduction of an original but much smaller is a **min**. . . . .**e**.
52. A person who deals with correspondence, etc., in an office: **sec**. . . . .**y**.
53. If something is easy to reach or approach, it is **ac**. . . . .**le**.
54. Introductory, or coming, before, is **pr**. . . . .**l**. . . . .**ry**.
55. Full of care and concern: **symp**. . . . .**ic**.
56. A **u**. . . . .**ous** decision is one approved by all.
57. A wheeled machine such as a car or truck is a **v**. . . . .**le**.
58. Despotic rule is called **t**. . . . .**n**. . . . .**y**.
59. Unusual or out of the ordinary run of things: **ex**. . . . .**y**.
60. A plan can also be called a **s**. . . . .**me**.
61. Fault-finding: **cr**. . . . .**m**.
62. An important chance or favourable time is an **op**. . . . .**t**. . . . .**y**.
63. Retribution or revenge carries the idea of **ve**. . . . .**ce**.
64. Widespread argument is called **contr**. . . . .**y**.
65. Capable of being influenced by something, sensitive to:
    sus. . . . .**p**. . . . .**le**.
66. Another word for inquisitiveness is **cur**. . . . .**ty**.
67. Wasteful, unrestrained — especially in money matters:
    ex. . . . .**v**. . . . .**t**.
68. Not very happy: **dis**. . . . .**f**. . . . .**d**.
69. Something that is obvious and draws attention: **not**. . . . .**le**.
70. Sadness or **mel**. . . . .**y**.
71. Honestly, frankly, genuinely: **sin**. . . . .**ly**.
72. To examine critically: **an**. . . . .**se**.
73. A stress on words is an **em**. . . . .**is**.
74. Another word for oddity: **pec**. . . . .**ty**.
75. A statement that something is good or will last for a certain time:
    g. . . . .**r**. . . . .**e**.
76. Upkeep or support: **ma**. . . . .**ce**.

77. Apart or distinct is a s . . . . p . . . . te.
78. Something that must be done, obligatory: **comp** . . . . y.
79. A group of people elected from a larger group to conduct affairs or business: **com** . . . . t . . . . e.
80. Calamitous: **dis** . . . . ous.
81. To convince is to **per** . . . . e.
82. Put in an awkward position, perplex: **emb** . . . . s.
83. A formal procedure, as in a wedding, is a **cer** . . . . y.
84. A joining together of people or organisations, as with sporting clubs: **as** . . . . t . . . . n.
85. A terrible disaster: **cat** . . . . e.
86. One who puts himself or herself forward freely and without compulsion is a **vol** . . . . r.
87. Health and **h** . . . . e (personal cleanliness)
88. Belonging to the same time or period: **con** . . . . p . . . . ry.
89. Vain or having an inflated opinion of one self: **con** . . . . ted.
90. To take the place of, to supplant: **sup** . . . . e.
91. Reckless from lack of hope: **des** . . . . e.
92. To fail to fulfil a promise or hope: **dis** . . . . t.
93. Board and lodgings: **ac** . . . . t . . . . n.
94. The signing, or taking, over of property as security for money lent: **mor** . . . . e.
95. Too charming or convincing to be avoided: **irr** . . . . ble.
96. Assorted or mixed: **mis** . . . . l . . . . ous.
97. Being **m** . . . . s means 'getting into mischief'.
98. An associate in work is a **col** . . . . e.
99. Disguised by adopting natural patterns: **cam** . . . . ed.
100. The study of the mind: **p** . . . . ogy.

Activity 12.N Tautology

Tautology is the saying of the same thing twice over in different words. For example: 'The twins are exactly identical'. The word 'exactly' is redundant. Sometimes public figures are guilty of tautology. Many of the examples beneath are from the utterances of well established communicators. See whether you can correct the errors.

1. The government has introduced a project that's expected to provide jobs for unemployed people who are out of work. (Radio newsbroadcaster)
2. He was doing his club a bad disservice. (Television commentator)
3. Let's get down to the basic fundamentals. (Sports commentator)
4. 'A free return trip to anywhere and back'. (McDonald's advertisement)
5. We are endeavouring to find the true facts about the petrol strike. (Politician)
6. The soldiers had returned back to their own territory. (Newsreader)
7. The union has no false illusions about support from its own members. (Union leader)
8. There are several past precedents for the government's actions. (Politician)
9. The future prospects of our client are excellent. (Industrial reporter)
10. Free glass of wine on the house. (A sign outside a restaurant)

Activity 12.O   Ambiguity

A sentence that has two or more different meanings is said to be ambiguous. The incautious use of a word with a double meaning or the misplacing of a phrase or clause within a sentence can create doubt as to what meaning you really intend to communicate. Sometimes a degree of unintentional humour is introduced through ambiguity, as many of the following sentences reveal.

1. Sign in butcher's shop: 'All meat in this window is from local farmers killed on the premises'.
2. After the Member for Avalon had seen the seal perform, he was taken to the zoo and given a bucket of raw fish.
3. The lecturers for tomorrow will be found pinned on the notice board.
4. 'Once you've driven a Mercedes Benz car, you're unlikely to drive another'. (*The Bulletin*)
5. When the apartments caught fire, the tenants sought safety in their pyjamas.
6. Women will only be employed after marriage on a temporary basis.
7. At the Rialto theatre a small baby was needed for a scene in a play. A message was sent to Phyllis the theatre nurse: 'Please have a baby by nine o'clock tomorrow morning'.
8. The tenants were forced to leave their houses through unsafe cracks in the walls.
9. Epitaph on a gravestone in Woolwich, London: 'Sacred to the memory of Major James Brush, who was killed by the accidental discharge of a pistol, April, 1831. Well done, good and faithful servant'.
10. 'KEEP AUSTRALIA BEAUTIFUL — use this bag for litter' (Printed on the bottom of a Woolworths bag.)
11. FOR SALE: a house at $20 000. It won't last long so see us now.
12. Health food shop at bargain price, selling owing to illness. (Advertisement)
13. 'Cows Cross Road. Two Fined'. (Headline in *Daily Mail*)
14. We are living in an interesting but quiet district with dogs and children riding tricycles.
15. The man hid the gramophone in the bushes, but watching police arrested him. In court it was discovered that the defendant had a record.
16. Mrs Blank wishes to thank the nurse and doctor for their kind cooperation in the loss of her husband. (North Buck *Times*)

Activity 12.P   Verbosity and Circumlocution

While **verbosity** means the use of a greater number of words than is necessary in communicating an idea; **circumlocution** means 'talking around' or 'not getting to the point' in written or oral communication. Both are characterized by 'wordiness' and both can be a serious hindrance to clarity in communication.

Below are examples of verbosity and circumlocution. Rewrite in simpler terms.

1. The abode was situated in an area of urban deprivation.
2. An abundance of vegetable matter facilitated the discovery of an umbrageous incline upon which to recline.
3. My portmanteau was equipped with an appendage for manual gripping.
4. Incertitude possessed her mind when she considered entering the marital state.
5. The position does possess a fiscal appurtenance which takes the form of a bi-weekly renumeration.
6. Excuse me, but can you acquaint me with the edifice where one may economically partake of a satisfying collation?
7. The guardians of the law were unaware of the fact that the lady was in a state of extreme inebriation.
8. Not an inconsiderable amount of money is being expended on conflagration prevention in naturally vegetated areas.
9. She displayed a lachrymose countenance.
10. His superb physiological competence was unquestionable.
11. The maritime practitioner enumerated digitally the finer points of the vessel.
12. An emolument was allocated to him for his diurnal labours.
13. Comestibles of a delectable nature ingested in overabundance may lead to undesirable obesity.
14. The noxious effluvium gives rise to nasal dilation which can seriously incommode the unwary.

13   Letter Writing

The art of letter writing has been practised for hundreds and thousands of years. In ancient times, scribes were paid to write business letters on clay tablets for merchants who were unable to write. The letters of St Paul in the Bible attest to the importance of letter writing in Roman times.

Today, of course, many of our business transactions are conducted by letter. One of the main reasons for sending letters is to provide the receiver with a written record. Only too true are the words of the Hollywood movie producer, who said that 'a verbal agreement is as good as the paper it's written on'.

Simple Steps to Better Writing

(1) **Decide**
Decide what you want to say.
Decide what you think the reader needs to know.
Decide exactly on the emphasis your letter will need to have.

(2) **Organise**
Jot down all your ideas.
Group similar ideas together so that they may be set out in paragraphs.
Arrange your groups of ideas in a logical and well organised manner.

(3) **Use the Right Tone**
Determine how you want your reader to feel, when he reads the letter. It is certainly better to be pleasant and tactful rather than antagonistic and irate.

(4) **Be Considerate**
Don't answer letters—answer people'. (Jacob Braude)
Tailor your writing to your reader.
Adopt a 'you' attitude rather than an 'I' one.

(5) **Motivate**
Motivate the reader to do what you're asking.
End your letter by pointing the way for the necessary next steps.

(6) **Be Concise**
Use short, simple sentences and simple paragraphs rather than long, confusing ones.
Avoid needless words.

(7) **Be Clear**
Use the simple rather than the complex word.
Use words with which the reader will be familiar.

(8) **Be Accurate**
Make sure your statements and facts are true and accurate.
Use correct spelling, grammar and punctuation.

(9) **Be Vigorous and Direct**
    Use words that are alive.
    Be natural. Don't imitate someone else's style.

(10) **Make Sure the Letter is Complete**
    Check that you have given the reader all the information he/she needs.

BJ/cs   The Macmillan Company of Australia
(1)   (2) 107 Moray Street
                           SOUTH MELBOURNE   VIC   3205

                       (3) 2 September, 1981

The Publishing Manager
Popular Books
1-3 High Street   (4)
MARKETPLACE   9103

Dear Sir,   (5)

re : EVERYDAY ENGLISH - William Nile   (6)

We are at present preparing for publication a textbook
designed to assist the development of language and
communication skills for use at the middle-secondary
level in Australian schools. We anticipate the print run
to be ..... with an approximate recommended retail price of
.....

We are seeking non-exclusive Australasian rights.   (7)

In the book, the author would like to use the black and
white photograph of a bear appearing on page 16 of Popular
Animals by G. D. Green. May we have your permission to
reproduce this material? We will, of course, fully acknowledge
the source of the material as you require.

(8) Yours faithfully,

        Brian Jones

Brian Jones,
Publisher.   (9)

Layout of Letters

Examine the standard layout for a business letter.

(1) **Reference**
Most business firms give a reference to be quoted in the reply. A basic reference consists of the initials of the person sending the letter, combined with those of the typist, e.g. ASH/pb.

(2) **Sender's address**
At the top of the page of all business letters is the sender's address or the firm's letterhead. If there is no letterhead, the address of the sender is placed on the top right-hand corner of the letter. Most typists favour block setting rather than indenting, as this form is easier to type.

(3) **Date**
This is an important part of the letter and is normally written on the line immediately following the sender's address. The three most commonly accepted ways of dating formal letters are:

January 9th, 1984.   9th January, 1984.   9 January, 1984.

(4) **Inside address**
The inside address gives the name, the title and address of the person who is to receive the letter, e.g.:

Mr R. James,
The Public Relations Officer,
W. B. Smith Company,
150 South Street,
Kingswood, S.A. 5062.

(5) **Salutation**
The salutation is the formal way of greeting the reader of the letter. The common kinds of salutations are:

Dear Sir	Dear Madam
Dear Mr . . .	Dear Mrs . . .
Dear Miss . . .	Dear Ms . . .

(6) **Subject**
The subject of the letter is best thought of as a brief title. It enables the reader to know the general topic of the letter. The subject line is usually underlined.

(7) **Body**
The body of the letter is set out in paragraphs. The first paragraph explains the letter's purpose and the last paragraph points the way ahead.

(8) **Complimentary Close**
The complimentary close is placed two lines below the end of the last paragraph. The most used forms are:

Yours faithfully	Yours truly
Yours sincerely	Sincerely yours

(9) **Signature**
Beneath the writer's handwritten signature should appear his typed name and business title.

Writing a Job Application

Your job application is often the first contact you will have with an employer.

An employer will use it to help decide whether you seem suitable for a job and whether or not to give you an interview.

So, it's important to take time and care with your application to make it look good and to provide as much information as possible.

Letter

It is a good idea to write a fairly short letter saying that you would like to apply for a job and attach a resumé to it.

45 Fern Street,
Frimley Green.
5 June, 1980.

The Manager,
Globox Industries,
2 Buckle Road,
WHEATLEY. N.S.W. 2415

Dear Sir/Madam,

I would like to apply for the position of clerk which was advertised in the Sydney Morning Herald on 3 June, 1980.

I have enclosed a resumé giving personal details, qualifications and work experience.

I consider myself to be a most suitable applicant for the job and would be pleased to attend an interview at any time convenient to you.

Yours faithfully,

(Mr) Bryan Chester

Resumé (information about yourself)

A resumé is written on a separate piece of paper. On it, you should put all the information an employer needs to know about you.

Generally, this information can be broken up into four sections:

Personal

Your name, age, address, telephone number.

Educational

Where you went to school, how far you went, details of any other courses you have done or skills you have, e.g. pre-apprenticeship courses, typing ability.

Work experience

Details of any jobs you have done including part-time and holiday; work experience programmes you have been part of.

Other information

Any interests you have, e.g. sports, hobbies, community activities. Names and addresses of people who will give you a reference (referees).

When you have written your resumé, make several copies of it, and you can send one off each time you apply for a job.

and Finally . . .

- Before writing the application get more information about the job. Work out what you need to know and ring the company, factory, etc.
- Make a rough copy of the letter first.
- Watch out for spelling errors. Always check if you are not sure how to spell a word.
- When writing the original letter don't use a scrap piece of paper.
- Write neatly. If possible get the letter typed.
- Don't cross out or write over words.
- If references or birth certificate are required, do not send the original but a photocopy.
- When you give someone's name as a referee, always contact them to let them know.
- Always keep a copy of the letter.

SPRINGWOOD HIGH

Activity 13.A Job Application Letters

1. Go through your daily newspapers and select a job you'd like to apply for. Write a letter applying for the job you have selected. When you have finished, read out both the newspaper clipping and your letter to the class. Get the class to make comments on the effectiveness of your letter.
2. Pretend you have to write a letter applying for one of the positions advertised opposite. Read out your letter to the class.
3. Students, in pairs, exchange their completed letters and their original advertisements. Then acting as personnel officers, they interview the applicants. The class observes each pair in action and then discusses these interviews and suggest improvements.

APPRENTICESHIPS

Fitter and Machinist
Painter and Decorator
Printer
Plumber
Electrical Technician
Carpenter
Cook/Chef

Minimum requirements School Certificate or equivalent.

Selected applicants will be required to undertake specific ability and aptitude assessments.

Handwritten applications giving details of age, school results and interest in the position should be marked "APPRENTICESHIPS" AND ADDRESSED TO:

The Employment Officer

John Brown Company Limited
Box 890, G.P.O.
Sydney, N.S.W. 2001

ANCOR

CLERK/TYPIST
Personnel

We require an intelligent Clerk/Typist to be trained in varied and interesting duties in the Personnel Department of our modern Head Office.

The successful applicant will possess School Certificate or equivalent, be able to type accurately at 45 w.p.m. and will be trained to operate a Word Processor in addition to other duties.

Suitable applicants will be between 16-30 yrs of age.

For further information and appointment, please write to The Personnel Manager, Mr Philip Lynch, Ancor Ltd, P.O. Box 215, Smithfield, N.S.W. 2164

Invicta Australia
TRAINEESHIPS

CHEMISTRY (CERTIFICATE)

PRODUCTION ENGINEERING (CERTIFICATE/DEGREE)

MECHANICAL ENGINEERING (CERTIFICATE)

ELECTRICAL ENGINEERING (DEGREE)

Invicta Australia Pty. Ltd., the largest steel piping manufacturers in Australia, have vacancies for the above positions.
Applicants can be completing their H.S.C. this year or young persons who are studying stage 1 or 2 of a University or Technical College course.
The successful applicants must be prepared to enrol in part time study.
Training will extend to most facets of the course suitable to each applicant. Prospects of advancement are very good and conditions of employment excellent.
For interview appointment write to:

Mr. R. Appleby
Personnel Officer

INVICTA AUSTRALIA PTY. LTD.
1 Mars Road, Chatswood
N.S.W. 2064

S.R.E.

COMPUTER OPPORTUNITY

We have a position available which offers the opportunity for entrance into the computer field. Previous experience is not necessary but you must have both the aptitude and the enthusiasm for a career in computing.
A minimum age of 18 years is envisaged.
Duties will initially involve data control progressing to training in assembler programming.
The computer centre is located on our Melbourne factory site and provides an attractive and comfortable office environment. Parking is available close to centre.
Interested applicants should apply in writing to

Mr. E. Patrick,
P.O. Box 201, G.P.O.
Melbourne, Victoria 3000

Activity 13.B Clear and Correct

When writing a letter, it is not only important that you give the correct information to your reader, but that you use correct English. When you don't use clear, correct English, communication between you and your reader becomes difficult and in some cases breaks down completely. Look at the following examples. They are all genuine extracts from letters sent to various community service departments. They all contain examples of incorrect information or expression. Rewrite each of the examples so that the errors are removed and the correct meaning is made clear to the reader.

1. I am glad to state that my husband died yesterday. I will be glad if you will get me a pension. If you don't hurry up with it, I will have to get public resistance.
2. I cannot get eternity benefit in spite of the fact that I have seen the insistence officer. I have eight children. What can I do about it?
3. I have nothing coming into my house but two sons on the dole. I can do with a pension as I have no clothes on for a year.
4. In accordance with your instructions, I gave birth to twins in the enclosed envelope.
5. I want money badly as quick as you can send it. I have been in bed with the doctor for a week and he doesn't seem to be doing any good. If things don't improve I will have to get another doctor.
6. Re your dental enquiry. The teeth at the top are all right, but the ones in my bottom are hurting terrible.
7. Please send me a form for milk as I am stagnant.
8. My son has been unable to attend school. He has had diarrhoea through a hole in his shoe.
9. Milk is needed for the baby. Father is unable to supply it.
10. Please send me a deserted wife's allowance. I have a baby two months old and did not know anything about it until a neighbour told me.

Activity 13.C   Simplify

1. Here are some extracts from some business letters, which hinder communication because of their failure to be simple and concise. Simplify the language of these letters.

    (a) I hereby acknowledge your order of the fifth instant. I beg to advise you that due to unforeseen circumstances involving the delayed arrival of the toys you ordered, we are unable to supply you forthwith.

    (b) The delay in finalizing your order is sincerely regretted, although I might point out that in sending your original letter you had apparently neglected to include an address.

    (c) I beg to acknowledge receipt of your letter of yesterday's date. I regret to inform you that due to circumstances beyond my control, I am unable to execute your order at the present time. It is anticipated that further supplies will arrive in a fortnight's time.

2. It is important when writing letters that you don't fall into the mistake of using longwinded phrases and hackneyed expressions. Always use simple words rather than complex and involved ones. Look at the following list of clumsy and hackneyed expressions, which have been taken out of business letters. Rewrite each of them in simple natural English.

	EXPRESSION	
(a)	At an early date	
(b)	At the present time	
(c)	Afford an opportunity	
(d)	Be in a position to	
(e)	In the event that	
(f)	We are not in a position to	
(g)	Not withstanding the fact that	
(h)	We acknowledge receipt of your letter	
(i)	At your earliest convenience	
(j)	With regard to	
(k)	I'll give consideration to	
(l)	In the majority of instances	
(m)	During the time that	
(n)	Send it to my attention	
(o)	Three in number	
(p)	We direct your attention to	
(q)	Until such time as we can	
(r)	May result in damage to	
(s)	Due to the fact that	
(t)	Pursuant to our conversation	
(u)	We are in receipt of	
(v)	I beg to inform you	
(w)	For the purpose of	
(x)	I'm writing in reference to	
(y)	I regret to inform you	

Activity 13.D Test your Letter-Writing Ability

A great deal of satisfaction can be had with the following letter writing tasks, particularly if the completed letters are read out to the class.

(1) **Imagine**

    (a) Write a letter to a person who is currently featured prominently in newspapers. Make your letter humorous if you wish.

(b) Get the class to suggest a wide range of comic strip characters, *e.g.* Superman, Wonder Woman, etc. The teacher should jot their names down on the board. Remember there should be a reason for your writing the letter. Make sure you state your purpose clearly in the first paragraph. Now have the class write a letter to one of these characters.

(2) Letters of Sympathy

There will be times in your life when you will need to write a letter of sympathy to a friend or an acquaintance. A letter of sympathy is especially welcome for someone who has suffered a misfortune—a loss of a job, an accident, an illness, a death in the family, the collapse of business, a divorce etc. It shows your concern and caring.

(a) Write a letter of condolence or sympathy to a friend of yours who has endured some kind of hardship or grief.

(b) Explaining the events which led to your letter of sympathy, read your letter to the class. Discuss the effectiveness of your letter.

(3) Letters of Complaint

A carefully written letter of complaint often brings about a righting of an injustice or a change of attitude on the part of the reader. Make sure you adopt a calm approach without the use of threats and antagonism. Be direct and don't apologize for your letter.

Write a letter of complaint on one of the following. (Assume that a letter is the most direct form of communication that you can use.)

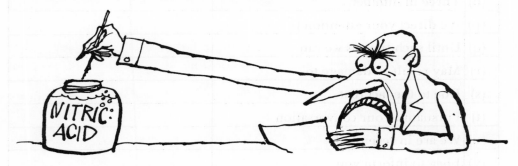

(a) Your new car has just come out of warranty. There are some loud noises coming from the gear box.

Write a letter to the car manufacturer, asking for the fault to be rectified free of charge.

(b) You live in a street which over the years has seen an increased volume of heavy traffic. The local council proposes to improve the surface of the road and at the same time widen it by three metres. This will necessitate the removal of trees on both sides of the street.

Write a letter of protest to your local member.

(c) You are concerned about one of the following:
    (i)   taxation   (iii) road accidents
    (ii) examinations   (iv) strikes

Write a letter to the editor of your local newspaper, expounding your views on the topic.

(4) **Advertising by Letter**

At some stage in your career you may need to write letters which advertise a product you are promoting or service you are providing. In these kinds of letters you should:

- Quickly get the reader's attention and arouse his/her interest.
- Describe and explain your product or service.
- Motivate the reader to action.

(a) Imagine that you have just set yourself up in business as a real estate agent. Write a letter advertising your services, which is to be printed and sent to potential customers in your area.

(b) Imagine that you have just gained the agency to distribute a wonderful new product. Write a letter to potential customers advertising the qualities of your product.

(5) **Letters of Request**

From time to time you'll probably have to write a letter of request. A letter of request is an 'asking' letter. You might ask for a catalogue, a holiday booking, theatre tickets, social service benefits etc. In the first sentence give the reader a clear indication of what you want. Follow this by telling the reader why the information or goods are needed. Then indicate thanks or a possible course of action that the reader may like to adopt. You should also aim to:

- Be specific
- Be simple
- Be brief

(a) You have been failed in a course of study for which you usually gained quite reasonable marks in assignments. The final examination was not difficult. Your attendance has been satisfactory. You suspect that a contributing factor to your failure might be a longstanding personality clash between you and your teacher. For this reason you are reluctant to approach the teacher direct. Write a letter to your principal or head of college asking for a review.

(6) **Letters Saying 'No'**

Even when you have to write a letter saying 'no' to a request, it is of the utmost importance that you convey goodwill. In such letters you should aim to be pleasant and positive. There are a number of stages in saying 'no' in a letter.

- Restate the request and give the other person feedback by stating: 'I know what you're taking about'.
- Give reasons for the refusal.
- Say 'no'. By this stage, the reader should have a good idea that your answer will be 'no' anyway.
- Indicate another course to take emphasis away from your refusal.

(a) Write a letter saying 'no' to a friends request for money.

(b) Write a letter saying 'no' to an invitation to a twenty-first birthday party.

Tone

What is tone? One teacher angrily says to a student: 'Pick up that rubbish', while another calmly asks: 'Would you please pick up that paper?' Both teachers have adopted a completely different tone. The first teacher's tone is angry, aggressive and authoritarian, while the second's is pleasant and cordial. The student's reaction to the first teacher's instruction would probably be one of hostility, while the reaction to the second teacher's question might be one of co-operation.

When we are speaking, our tone is indicated by our voice. It is reasonably easy to recognize whether a speaker is happy, angry, sincere, affectionate, sarcastic, etc., just by the very sound. However, when we are writing letters we have to rely on our choice of words to indicate our tone. There are as many tones as there are attitudes. Here are a few basic tones to give you some idea of the range available.

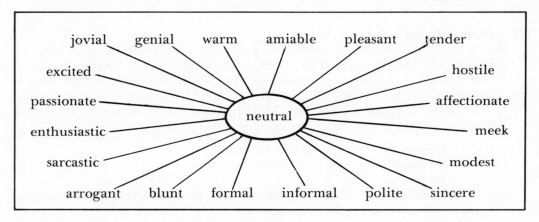

Activity 13.E   Identify the Tone

See whether you can identify the tone in each of these examples.

1. We sincerely appreciate the loyalty you have shown our firm over the last three months. (Business letter)
2. Keep Off The Grass. (Sign)
3. Of course our politicians need an increase in salary. Look at their hovels and rags. (Newspaper editorial)
4. Investigate the problem immediately and submit a report as soon as possible. (Manager's letter)
5. Palatial unit fastidiously decorated by discerning owner. Grande entrance foyer adjoins flowing lounge. Impressive dining room opens to sunny tiled patio. (Advertisement for unit)
6. You failed to state your size: therefore we cannot send you your boots. (Business letter)
7. Homes in our district are being demolished for the new freeway. This is intolerable. Homes are more important than motor cars. Why should people's homes be sacrificed on the altar of the great god motor car. (Letter to the editor)
8. I advised you in my last letter that the stock will arrive on time and it shall. (Business letter)

Activity 13.F

The following letter of complaint was written by a young business executive. (The names have been changed.) He received immediate action from the car company involved. Read the letter through and answer the questions.
1. What is the tone of this letter? Do you think it is the right one? Why?
2. Why did the young business executive write this letter?
3. Why do you think the car company reacted immediately to this letter?
4. Do you think the young executive was justified in writing this letter? Why?
5. Do you think the writer has organized his ideas coherently? Why?
6. What criticisms can you make of this letter?
7. Do you think this letter is clear and concise? Why?
8. In what ways do you think this letter is (a) vigorous and (b) natural?

The Managing Director,
The A.B.C. Car Company of Australia Limited,
Sydney Road,
Sydney N.S.W. 2000

Dear Sir,

I must congratulate the A.B.C. Car Company on the production of what must surely be the most hopeless car on Australian roads today. If not the 'most hopeless' then certainly the most fault-ridden vehicle in years and, I trust, for many more years to come. The model, yes of course, the now famous '. . . . .'!

Our company maintains a number of vehicles for its executive staff, and I was recently unfortunate enough to have my company purchase a new '. . . . .' on my behalf, a decision which I will obviously regret for some time to come.

With only 4000 kilos on the clock, the car has been plagued with mechanical trouble commencing from the moment of delivery, when it was discovered that the doors would not lock and the passenger's window could not be wound down. Despite the fact that my position imposes heavy responsibilities and demands on my time, thus necessitating extremely tight time schedules, I have, during the short time I have had the car in my possession, experienced the following problems with the machine.

- The clip on the motor-end of the accelerator cable fell off, stranding me miles from anywhere and finally costing me some five (5) hours time delay.
- The heater controls were extremely difficult to use and finally became useless. A delay of some fifteen (15) days elapsed before a new cable could be brought from Melbourne. It is expected that this will be fitted shortly, and I will once again have a heater which is functional.
- I was stranded again, once more on an extremely busy day, with a pierced radiator hose resulting in a boiling and overheated motor. This time some four (4) hours was lost.
- The motor is still 'missing' under pressure. Despite the matter having been mentioned on two occasions, the vehicle has been in for repairs and service.
- The driver's door closes slightly off centre, perforating the rubber seal around the inside door surrounds. The rubber has now been replaced but wind howls through a gap between the rubber and mental frame whilst the car is in motion, and water absolutely pours in while the car is being washed at an automatic carwash centre. I understand the door is to be completely refitted in the near future.
- The thermostat was faulty, necessitating the installation of a new one.
- The steering-lock device is broken and as such is completely useless.
- The passenger-side front parking light globe has blown and necessitated replacement—perhaps this could be considered 'normal'.
- The heater/fresh air controls would not and still will not close off completely.
- The driver and passenger door windows are in my opinion scratched, and have been in this condition since delivery.
- The motor does not cut out 'cleanly' when the ignition is switched off, but rather continues to 'shudder' for some seconds on many occasions.
- The internal rear vision mirror was regularly moving out of position, although I think I have now rectified this problem myself.
- No tool kit was ever received with the new vehicle. Admittedly, through an oversight, I have failed to bring this to the attention of the suppliers.

In forwarding this correspondence to you, I do not expect the A.B.C. Car Company to come rushing out to discuss my problems with me. I do respectfully request, however, that very serious attempts are made to reduce such mechanical faults in a machine costing in the vicinity of $10 000. Numerous complaints of a similar nature regarding the '. . . . .' have been received by me from friends and acquaintances since my troubles began, and I must regretfully advise that any comments I personally have to make with people with whom I come into contact with regarding the '. . . . .' will do little for sales of vehicles produced by the A.B.C. Car Company of Australia.

Yours faithfully,

R. Jones

General Manager

14 Report Writing

What is a Report?

A report is a document which contains facts and information on a specific subject. Sometimes it makes recommendations for the reader to act on. A good report helps to clarify the reader's thinking on the subject.

Reports play an important role in most large organizations where managers and overseers are unable to make particular decisions until they have the necessary data or information from their subordinates. It is through the reading of reports that people within organizations are able to run their companies more efficiently. A report provides a permanent written record.

ST PIPS — By Neil Matterson

Types of Report

The Memo(randum) Report

Most companies use memo reports within their organization and many companies have their own standardized memo forms. The memo report is the least formal but most used report in business writing. It is designed for easy reading. Most longer memo reports use subject headings to help guide the reader through the ideas being presented. The memo report will tend to have fewer parts than other types of reports. It begins by explaining the circumstances which led to the need for it to be written. It then presents information and data to the reader, draws conclusions and makes recommendations where necessary. As well as writing a subject heading which gives a clear indication of the contents of the memo, the writer should also indicate not only his own name and the name of the person to whom it is being sent, but also their designations. The writer should not forget to sign the memo.

```
┌─────────────────────────────────────────────────────────────┐
│  ┌──────────────┐                                            │
│  │ M MACMILLAN  │                INTER-OFFICE MEMO           │
│  │   AUSTRALIA  │                                            │
│  └──────────────┘                                            │
│   TO: ..................          FROM: ..................    │
│   SUBJECT: .............          DATE: ..................    │
│ ═══════════════════════════════════════════════════════════ │
│                                                              │
│                                                              │
│                                                              │
│                                                              │
│                                                              │
│                                                              │
└─────────────────────────────────────────────────────────────┘
```

Activity 14.A   Writing Your Own Memo Report

Try your hand at writing your own memo report.

You work in a laboratory where dangerous flammable liquids and chemicals are used. To comply with safety regulations, you are required to supply a brief report on the safety provisions of your laboratory. The report should be submitted to your manager, Mr White, who will forward the information to the fire department.

Organize the information beneath and use headings to structure it. (Note that the items are not in a logical and coherent sequence.)

1. Fire extinguishers are located in prominent positions every five metres around the laboratory walls. They are serviced regularly by the fire brigade.
2. A ducted exhaust system operates above each of the four work areas in the laboratory. The exhaust system is not linked to any other existing ventilation system.

3. Two fire blankets are located at each of the two entrances to the laboratory.
4. The laboratory has a fume cupboard for odorous substances.
5. A first aid kit is located on the front laboratory wall.
6. A respirator is contained in the first aid cupboard.
7. A stretcher is attached to the wall outside the laboratory.
8. Fire drill is conducted once a month.
9. One member of your staff, Don Sutherland, has been trained in first aid and Red Cross procedures.
10. All new personnel are given a six-hour induction course in safety procedures.
11. Each laboratory attendant is provided with a dust coat and protective eye, hand and footwear for use within the laboratory.

The Letter Report
This is a short report sent to someone outside your organization. It takes the form of a letter, with addresses, date, salutation, etc., but many also use subject headings to separate each section.

The Long Report
A long report tends to be more formal in language and structure than a short report. A formal report is usually directed at a larger audience and may deal with complex and detailed technical matters. Most long, formal reports (except those compiled jointly by a group) are written in the third person. The reason for this is that many report writers feel that if pronouns such as 'you' and 'I' were used the long formal report could have the appearance of not being objective. On the other hand, in a memo or letter report, the use of the pronoun 'I' often gives the report a sense of directness.

Planning and Preparing Your Long Report

What Is Your Purpose In Writing Your Report?
In a clear, concise sentence write down the purpose or objective of your report. Your purpose or objective will generally encompass some or all of the following:

- to provide information
- to analyse facts
- to put forward ideas
- to recommend a course of action

Who Will Read Your Report?
Knowing your reader's attitude will help you, the report writer, to determine your approach to your subject. You should consider the following questions:

- Who has requested the report?
- Who is likely to read the report?
- What does the reader want to know?
- What does the reader already know about the subject?
- What is the reader's point of view and background?
- How is the reader likely to use the report?

What Is a Good Report?
If your reader is able to readily obtain the ideas and information he needs from your report, then the report is successful. If you follow these rules you will be well on the way to writing a good report.

- **Correctness** — Make sure that your facts and figures are accurate, correct and verifiable.
- **Clarity** — Select words that make your meaning clear.
- **Coherence** — Arrange your thoughts in a logical sequence.
- **Conciseness** — Aim to make all your information relevant.
- **Completeness** — Make sure that all the necessary information has been included.
- **Consideration** — Try to have consideration for your reader's point of view.

How do you Collect Material?

You need to collect all the facts and ideas you can that are related to the subject of your report. If you are a thorough report writer, you will gather your information from many sources. You will probably make use of techniques such as observations, interviews, discussions, surveys, questionnaires, bibliographical research and investigations.

Taking Notes

It is a good idea to jot down all your facts in note form. Be sure that you take careful and complete notes so that when you come to read them later all the important facts will be at your disposal. It is also wise to include the source of your material.

Interviewing

If you are obtaining information by interviewing people, take notes of the interview so that you will be able to refresh your memory when you are writing up your report. Prepare a list of questions to take with you to the interview. It is generally a good idea to explain fully to the person you are interviewing your reason for asking questions. As you are taking your notes of the interview, try to be as inconspicuous as you can and keep your eyes on the person's face as much as possible.

Questionnaire

A questionnaire is a good way of collecting reliable data when you cannot interview people personally. When making up a questionnaire it is crucial that you state your questions clearly so they will not be misunderstood. Be sure that you don't make sweeping generalizations from the data gathered in your questionnaire.

Literature Searches

A bibliographic research involves the reading of all kinds of publications on the subject of your report—books, journals, laboratory reports, bulletins, articles, etc. Many report writers make up a separate bibliography card for each publication they consult. The card usually would contain (i) the library card catalogue number of the book, (ii) the author's name (iii) the title of the book (iv) the facts of publication (name of publisher, city of publication, year of publication and the edition) (v) and sometimes specific page number references.

Graphics

A report should make appropriate use of visual aids. However you should only include graphics, diagrams and photographs which will help clarify the written content within the body of the report. This practice will help to prevent the report from becoming too bulky or disjointed. It is better to include non-essential graphics in the appendices of your report.

Number Systems

Once the topics have been arranged in sequence, each topic will then be further divided into smaller sections and finally into paragraphs. The subdivisions and paragraphs will need to be numbered so that the reader will readily be able to refer to any points that he may wish to discuss with you after he has read your report. Of course, if the report is very short, notation may be unnecessary.

There are two widely used number systems used in report writing, the **letter-number** system and the **decimal numbering** system. Whichever form you adopt you must make sure that you are consistent throughout your report.

LETTER-NUMBER	DECIMAL NUMBERING
I.	1.0
A.	1.1
1.	1.1.1
a.	1.1.1.1
(i)	1.1.1.2
(ii)	1.1.1.3
b.	1.1.2
(i)	1.1.2.1
(ii)	1.1.2.2
(iii)	1.2
2.	1.2.1
a.	1.2.1.1
(i)	1.2.1.2
(ii)	1.2.2
b.	1.2.2.1
(i)	1.2.2.2
(ii)	2.0
B. 1.	2.1
a.	2.1.1
(i)	2.1.1.1
(ii)	2.1.1.2
b.	2.1.2
c.	2.1.2.1
2.	2.1.2.2
a.	2.2
b.	2.2.1
c.	2.2.1.1
II.	2.2.1.2
A.	2.2.2
1.	2.2.2.1
a.	2.2.2.2
(i)	
(ii)	

The Principal Parts of your Report

Long reports have most of the following features:

- Title page
- Letter of transmittal
- Table of contents
- Summary (or synopsis)
- Introduction

- Body of the report
- Conclusions
- Recommendations (or discussion)
- Close
- Appendix
- Bibliography

Title Page

The title page identifies the report. It should include the title, the author, the reader for whom the report is intended and the date of completion. The title itself should be accurate, complete, concise and informative.

Letter of Transmittal

The letter of transmittal, which is sometimes referred to as a 'cover letter', is often considered an introduction to the report. The letter of transmittal explains on whose authority the report was written and gives a brief summary of the report. In some cases, the letter of transmittal would be attached to the title page.

Table of Contents

Any report longer than a few pages needs a table of contents. The table of contents reveals the major and minor divisions of the report and provides the reader with the skeletal structure. By doing this it also introduces the number system employed in the report. The table of contents provides a list of diagrams, tables and appendices.

Summary (or Synopsis)

It is particularly desirable to summarize your report. The busy, overworked reader needs a brief statement of what the report is all about.

Introduction

The introduction clearly states the problem which led to the writing of the report and explains the purpose or the objective of the report in relation to the problem. The introduction serves mainly to give the reader enough background information to understand the body, the conclusions and the recommendations.

If the introduction is well written, forceful and convincing, the reader is more likely to read the whole report carefully, and thoroughly examine the report's findings and recommendations.

The introduction also indicates the problems encountered, the writer's method of research and his resources of information. It gives a concise picture of the methods used.

Body of the Report

The body usually makes up the bulk of the report. In the body you present all the pertinent facts that you have gathered and you explain exactly how you arrived at your findings. In the body you should use meaningful headings to guide the reader through the information.

Conclusions

Your conclusions are most important to your report. After the reader reads your data and the results of your investigations, he will want to know their significance. The reader will tend to ask: 'What does all this mean?' It is important therefore that you give your reader a clear statement of the conclusions you have reached from the facts. In doing this you are relating the conclusion to your original objective in uniting the report.

Recommendations (or Discussion)

The reader of your report now will want to know what course of action is to be taken. The writer should put forward a solution based on his conclusions. If there is more than one possible solution, the writer should indicate the one he thinks is to be preferred and explain his choice.

Close

The close consists of the report writer's signature, the title of the report and the date.

Appendix

The appendix contains important supplementary material, which, if inserted in the main body of the report, would impede the flow of the report. The appendix is usually made up of materials such as photographs, tables, charts, maps, diagrams, statistics, experimental results, graphs, etc.

Bibliography

The term 'bibliography' means a list of books. If you wish to quote from books, journals, articles and other references used in compiling your report, you will need to have a bibliography at the end of your report. The entries in the bibliography are linked in alphabetical order.

Books:
Author(s): surname, then initials or given names
Title (underlined)
Edition (if not the first)
Publisher
Place of publication
Year of publication

Example of correct punctuation: Cooper, B. M. *Writing Technical Reports*. 3rd edn. Penguin Books, Middlesex, Eng., 1967.

Journal Articles:
Author(s): surname, then initial(s) or given names
Title
Title of the journal (underlined)
Volume, then number or part (if any)
Year of publication
Page numbers

Example of correct punctuation: Evans, G. W. The Biological Functions of Copper, *Chemistry*, 4 June 1972, pp. 9–21.

Style

Your Words

Clarity is most important when you are writing your report. For this reason use common, everyday words as often as you can. Being precise is another essential step towards writing a good report. Always use the precise word that fits your need rather than a vague or inappropriate word. Your words should be alive, but you must not make the mistake of using emotionally loaded words. When you have finished your draft report, it is a good idea to go through it, eliminating words that are unnecessary.

Your Sentences

Of course you should aim to be concise and to the point. For this reason the majority of your sentences should be short and simple. However, if you use several short simple sentences one after the other, then your writing will tend to appear rather childish. This is why you must try to vary your choice of words and the length of your sentences and paragraphs. If you do this, your writing will not become monotonous for your reader.

Hints for a Good Report-Writing Style

- Be sure that your report is easy to read and understand.
- Treat your subject in a rational and objective manner.
- Make sure that the conclusions that you reach are valid.
- Be accurate with your spelling, punctuation and sentence and paragraph construction.
- Present your information concisely and with a lively style.
- Follow a writing style which is suited to your reader.
- Make sure your ideas are in proper sequence.
- Make your report communicate.

Revising Your Draft

Now that you have completed the first draft of your report you will need to check it through thoroughly and make alterations and corrections. You will probably find the following check sheet very helpful. As you read through your draft report, ask yourself these questions.

Check Sheet

1. Have all the facts been supplied?
2. Have all the facts and references been checked for accuracy?
3. Is the information complete?
4. Is all the material relevant?
5. Does the report accomplish what was intended?
6. Has the problem been accurately defined for the reader?
7. Has the necessary background material been provided for the reader to understand the situation?

8. Does the report meet the needs of your readers?
9. Is the organization of the report logical?
10. Has the material been properly subdivided?
11. Does the subject of the report advance in clearcut stages?
12. Does the report flow smoothly and easily from one idea to another?
13. Is the emphasis of the report in the right places?
14. Does the conclusion of the report leave the reader with the desired point of view?
15. Do the conclusions and recommendations emerge logically from the findings?
16. Will the reader reach the same conclusions as those in the report?
17. Do the conclusions form a firm basis for the recommendations?
18. Has use been made of illustrations to give the report greater clarity?
19. Have headings and the numbering system been used to good effect?
20. Are more organizational devices, such as headings, needed?

Language
1. Is the style appropriate for the content of the report?
2. Is the tone positive?
3. Are the words exact and living—concrete rather than abstract?
4. Are most of the sentences short and simple?
5. Is there any wordiness to be removed?
6. Does the writing have variety?
7. Are the grammar, spelling and punctuation accurate?
8. Are the paragraphs clear and coherent?
9. Do the ideas of the report flow smoothly?
10. Have you kept closely to your subject?

Activity 14.B   Writing a Report
Try your hand at writing a report on one of the following.
1. Write a report on the sporting facilities in your suburb. The mayor has asked you to prepare this report.
2. Investigate student parking facilities near your college. Write a report on your findings and make recommendations for possible improvements. Submit these to the principal of your college or the police department.
3. Your college principal has become alarmed about the amount of graffiti appearing on the toilet walls of your college. Write a report on this problem with recommendations for its solution.

4. Write a report to the lecturer-in-charge of one of your college courses and present your own ideas and recommendations for improving the course.
5. Imagine you have been given the task of purchasing for your employer a new automobile. The following facts should be kept in mind.
   (a) The car must not cost more than $15 000.
   (b) The car is mainly to be used for driving around the city.
   (c) The car will be driven by both male and female drivers.
   Write a report in which you recommend the model your firm should purchase.
6. Write a report examining public transport facilities for disabled people travelling to and from the city. Submit your report to the Council For The Disabled.
7. Write a report to your manager or employer presenting your own ideas for improving efficiency and saving costs in the firm/institution which is presently employing you. Make sure you give convincing details of time, materials, manpower, etc., being used to better advantage.
8. A business firm is interested in purchasing a piece of machinery or equipment, which you are using in your college workshop. Your lecturer has requested that you write a report for the business firm explaining the advantages and disadvantages of this piece of machinery.
9. You have recently been involved in an accident. A bus ran into the back of your vehicle while you were stationary at a set of red lights. Your insurance company is in doubt about who is to blame. It has requested that you write a report giving full details of the accident.
10. Write a report for your boss on the effectiveness of communication within your organization.
11. Write a report on things that annoy you in your college. You may be annoyed by such things as (a) the food in the cafeteria (b) lack of heating (c) litter (d) poor library facilities. Submit your report to the registrar of your college.
12. You are incensed by the spate of nude bathing on a beach you frequent. Write a report to your local council, explaining the problem and making recommendations for changes to the present situation.

Activity 14.C   Super Sleuths

A good deal of fun can be had while you practise some of the report writing skills that you have just learned. First of all, form yourselves into groups of three or four. Each group is to have a leader, a super detective who is to organize and lead his/her team of investigators to a solution of one of the following cases:
1. The Case of the Socket Wrench
2. The Case of the Crash on Control Curve
3. The Case of the Big A

Each member of the super sleuth's team has a specific role to play. One member will need to be the secretary, whose task it is to collect and assemble in a logical order all the information and findings established by his/her group. Other members will become investigators, bringing back the vital information which is to be integrated in the total report. The finished report with the case solved will be orally presented to the news media (your class) by one of the sleuths from your group. Classes get a lot of enjoyment from listening to the reports of other groups and listening for inconsistencies in the information presented.

Once each group has undertaken to solve a case, the members will need to work closely together as they invent fictitious details, plot the story through, reach conclusions and perhaps make recommendations.

As you go about solving your case, keep in mind some of the report writing skills you should be concerned to implement. Know exactly what your purpose is. Then make sure you uncover all the relevant evidence and evaluate it. The conclusions that you eventually reach about your case should emerge logically.

Now it is the task of each group to select one of the following cases to investigate. Happy detecting!

1. **The Case of the Socket Wrench**

   Malcolm Mugger (pictured) has been convicted of the murder of Brenda Body (pictured) a model, who had taken her car to Mugger's garage for repairs. She was found, shot dead, in the boot of her car, two blocks from the garage. Mugger's socket wrench was lying beside her. What really happened?

2. **The Case of the Crash on Control Curve**
   Barnaby Grudge, the worldfamous racing driver was killed in this crash at
   Brando Hatch racing circuit in England. The official race inquiry stated that
   the accident occurred through driver error. Barnaby's team mate and close
   friend Carl Ferrari (pictured) suspects that there was foul play. The police are
   now investigating. What really happened?

3. **The Case of the Big A**
   Agnes Appian was last seen at Essen Railway Station in South Germany on
   her way to Castle Neuschwanstein, where she was to stay with her uncle,
   Count Ludwig von Grappler. Her father has asked the police to find out what
   has happened to Agnes.

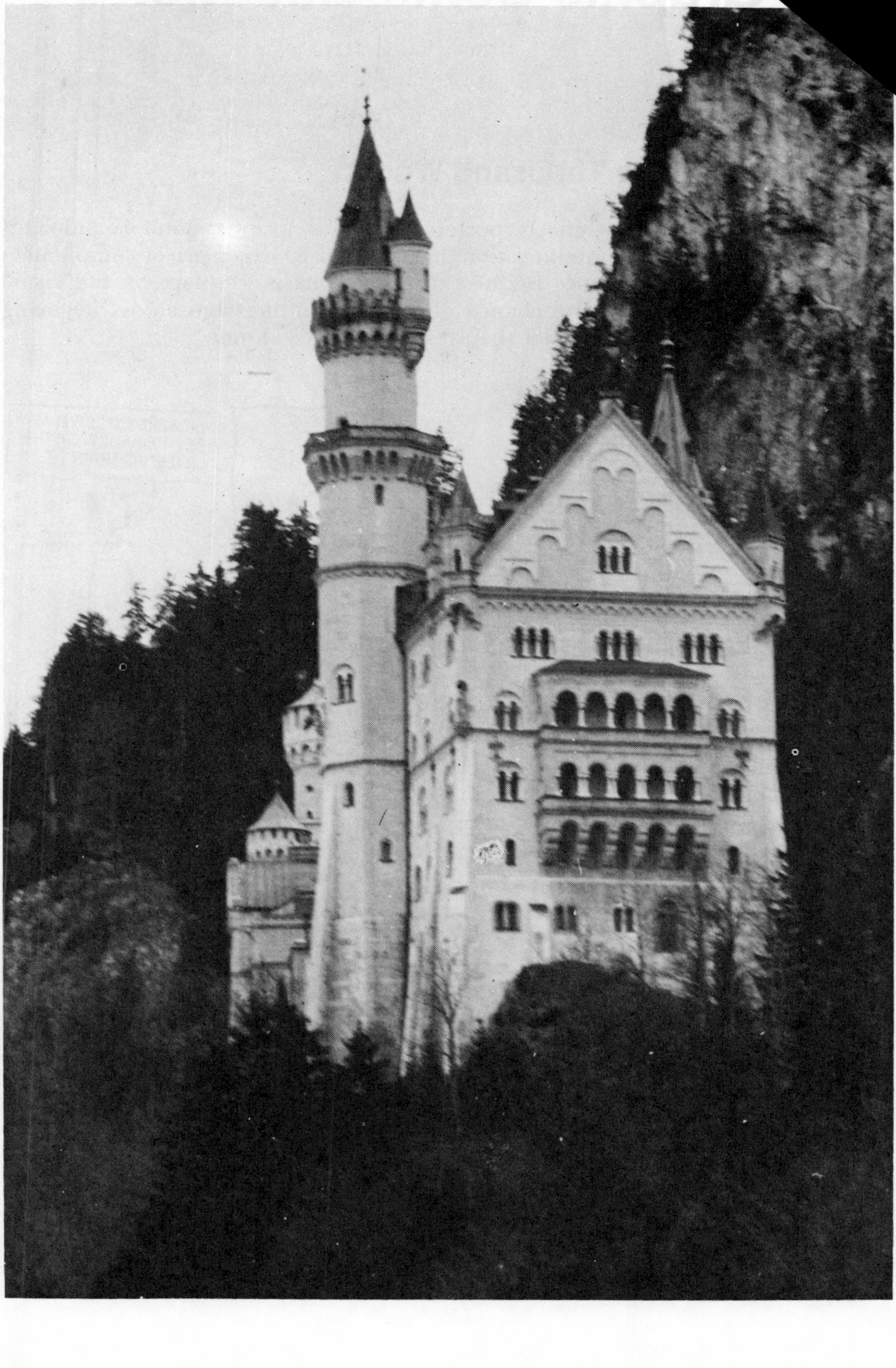

phic Communication

nts a Thousand Words

strations, charts, posters, diagrams, graphs, symbols and signs
rms of communication that can be used to replace or complement
written and spoken messages. Because of the emphasis we place on the visual
mode of communication, the chance of getting our message across by using
visual stimuli is probably greater than if we use words alone.

Activity 15.A   Communicating with Signs

1. What do the following signs and symbols represent?
   (a) A symbol of a closed fist
   (b) A hammer and sickle; a bear; an eagle
   (c) A skull and crossbones
   (d) A snake or serpent
   (e) A heart
   (f) A cross or crucifix
   (g) A fish
   (h) A trident
2. How many of the following signs can you visualize and describe, or draw?
   (a) Red Cross
   (b) United Nations symbol
   (c) International Youth Hostel Accommodation
   (d) 'Nuclear-free' zone
   (e) Plimsoll line
   (f) Surrender (indication of)
   (g) This Way Up
   (h) Use No Hooks
   (i) Fragile
   (j) Christianity

Signs which utilize pictorial images overcome the problem of communicating to people who speak diverse languages. Signs become self-explanatory because the number of possible meanings is restricted. Airports, major transport systems, and international sporting venues are just some situations where pictorial images are used in signs.

Activity 15.B   International Images

Design a set of signs employing pictorial images suitable for an international audience. You might like to consider the signs that have been used at the Olympic Games in recent years. Your signs should indicate and include:
1. Male and female toilet facilities
2. Smoking and non-smoking areas
3. Car park areas/non-parking areas
4. Directions to bus and train facilities
5. Banks, post offices, and an information service
6. Accommodation and eating facilities

Typeface and Mastheads

Hundreds of newspapers and magazines appear on newsstands every week. There are also thousands of newsletters, journals and magazines distributed through organizations. One feature on the front page of all of these publications does not change, or at least does not change frequently, and that is the **masthead**. The term is probably derived from 'head of the mast', or top of the ship's mast, hence the analogy of the top of cover, or banner on a magazine or journal.

Magazines propped up on gondolas in newsstands quite often can be differentiated only by their distinctive typeface and masthead. Each magazine may be easily identified because of this block of type. The masthead is extremely important when you consider that most magazines with similar subject content employ similar layout and design for their cover and that the magazines are usually the same size.

There are many distinct type families and each family has its own particular appeal and style. Some type families are interpreted as being

modern, delicate, fine   Futura Book

complex, fancy   Candice Inline

fine angular   MICROGRAMMA

antique   Fraktur Bold

This variety in type makes it possible to select a typeface that is in keeping with the message.

Activity 15.C

1. Bring a magazine to class or organize it so that everyone brings in a different magazine. Discuss the following questions.
   (a) How would you describe the typeface used in the specific masthead?
   (b) Is the typeface in keeping with the image that the magazine is trying to create?
   (c) How many different typefaces are used in the magazine?
   (d) How does the use of different typefaces affect the presentation of the magazine?
   (e) Is the masthead used anywhere else in the magazine to reinforce the image on the reader? Where this occurs, is the typeface similar to that used on the masthead?
   (f) Are any symbols included as part of the masthead? What is their function as part of the masthead?
2. Examine the typeface and print used for movie advertisements in newspapers, on theatre billboards, and placards.
   (a) Have the typeface and print added anything to the advertisement? How?
   (b) Has the movie title become a symbol? Why do advertising companies employ this technique?
3. Go to a public library and examine the use of mastheads over, say, the lifetime of a newspaper.
   (a) How has the masthead changed?
   (b) Why do you think it changed when it did?
   (c) Did the change in masthead reflect a change in the layout of the newspaper? How?
   (d) Compare the size, typeface used. What do these changes suggest to you?

Graphs

When we compile research data, and records involving the tabulation of figures, and we want to summarize or illustrate our findings, we run into the problem of finding a suitable medium. To discuss the findings using words would involve verbosity and repetition. Graphs are a convenient way of presenting such data.

You need to know that you have selected an appropriate graph or chart. You need to know that you are not misrepresenting your data.

LIFE-OF-THE-PARTY NOVELTY COMPANY

What is wrong with each of the following presentations? The presentations may be persuasive but in each case there is misrepresentation or distortion of the data.

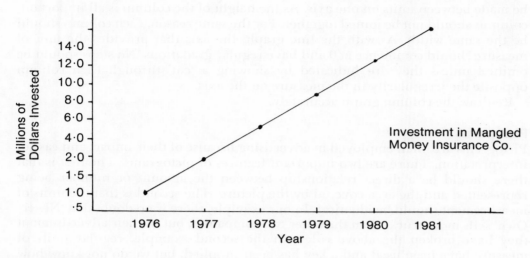

Line Graphs

Line graphs show a trend. You should be able to plot any point on the line and, within reason, it should give a reading on both the horizontal and vertical axis. For this reason, on a line graph both axes have to be continuous. One of the most frequent faults in graphing information is using a line graph when a column graph or bar chart should have been used. If you examine the column graph you will see that the information could only be presented in a column graph because the horizontal axis is not continuous. Each unit of this axis is separate. There is no relationship between the colleges, and in fact the colleges could occupy any position on the horizontal axis. The line graph should have regular gradations on the vertical axis, and should commence at 0.

Re-draw the line graph accurately.

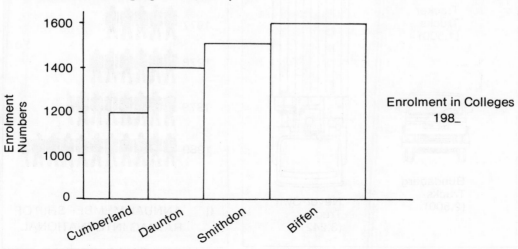

Column Graphs and Bar Charts

The only distinguishing feature is that columns originate on the horizontal axis and bars originate on the vertical axis. They are used when comparisons need to be made between units on one axis. As the height of the column is all important, columns should not be joined together. For the same reason, each column should be the same width. As with the line graph, the axis that provides the unit of measure should commence at 0 and have regular gradations. No steps should be omitted unless they are indicated by showing a 'cut' through each column opposite the irregularity in the measure on the axis.

Re-draw the column graph accurately.

Pictograms

Pictograms are often employed in advertising because of their impact and ease of interpretation. There are two important features of pictograms. The first is that there should be a direct relationship between the amount or number being represented and the area covered by the picture. The second is that the units of measurement should be identical. In our example, there is no doubt that 'Never-Own' sells more trucks than the other two companies, but in their advertisement they have broken the above rules. In the second example, regular units of measure have been used and a key has been supplied, but we do not know how many persons are represented by a partial figure, an arm or a leg.

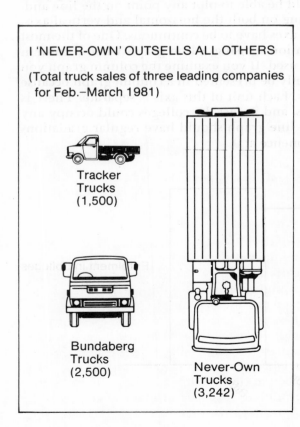

I 'NEVER-OWN' OUTSELLS ALL OTHERS

(Total truck sales of three leading companies for Feb.–March 1981)

Tracker Trucks (1,500)

Bundaberg Trucks (2,500)

Never-Own Trucks (3,242)

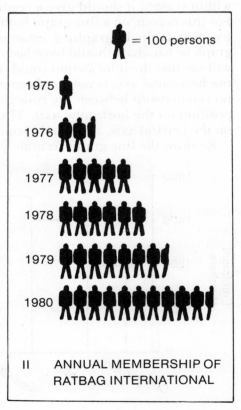

= 100 persons

1975
1976
1977
1978
1979
1980

II   ANNUAL MEMBERSHIP OF RATBAG INTERNATIONAL

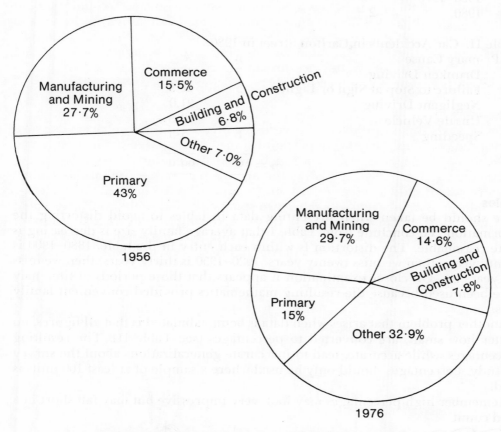

Comparison of Sector Contributions to Gross National Product

Circle or Pie Charts

The circle or pie chart is a useful way of dividing up a whole unit. If you wanted to illustrate how you spend your wages, how the monies of a club are spent, how the human resources of a country are divided between different industries, then the 'pie' can be easily cut up into meaningful pieces. It is important to label each unit carefully, indicating the percentage represented by a segment.

Parallel pie charts are convenient ways of showing comparisons. However, because the comparison is being made 'between the units that make up the whole', both pies or circles should remain the same size. When comparing the contribution made by primary industry in 1956 and 1976, note that the 43% (1956) in real terms might represent only fifteen million dollars, whereas the 15% (1976) might represent twenty-seven million dollars. As it is difficult to compare the area of circles accurately, it is difficult to judge the quantities represented.

Table I. Average Family Size in

1880–1900	5
1920–1950	4
1960–1970	3
1980	2

Table II. Car Accidents in Carlton Street in 1980.

Primary Cause	n	%
Drunken Driving	7	36·8
Failure to Stop at Sign or Light	5	26.3
Negligent Driving	4	21.0
Unsafe Vehicle	2	10·5
Speeding	1	5·3
n =	19	99·9

Tables

Care should be taken when presenting data in tables to avoid distorting the information. To conclude from Table I that average family size is decreasing is quite reasonable. The distortion is within each entry in the table. 1880–1900 is twenty years, then we miss twenty years: 1920–1950 is thirty years, then we miss ten years . . . On closer examination it appears that those periods of time may have been used because the resulting mathematics provided convenient family sizes.

Another problem that arises when data is being tabulated is that all figures, no matter how small, are converted to percentages (see Table II). The resulting percentages, while accurate, lead to inaccurate generalizations about the survey or study. Percentages should only be used where a sample of at least 100 units is used.

Remember high percentages may look very impressive but may fall short in a head count.

Enrolments are up 50% Jim

Oh! You have 2 students in your course this year

Activity 15.D   Presenting Numbers Visually

You have been asked by the course co-ordinator to prepare a graph to indicate both the growth in the number of subjects available as electives for your course and the growth in student numbers. The graph or chart that you prepare is to be included in a report that will be sent to the government. The theme of the overall report is 'The Growth of Cranium College 1970–1980'.

Here is the data from which you have to work.

SUBJECT	YEAR		
	1970	1975	1980
1. Brain Surgery	23	29	35
2. Mud Brick Building	14	23	107
3. Grape Peeling	16	24	39
4. TV and Radio Repairs	10	15	16
5. Carpet Weaving	18	24	36
6. Mountain Climbing	16	28	14
7. Contemp. Literature of Mongolia	9	9	9
8. Gambling	—	—	10
9. Preparation for Unemployment	—	5	25
Total	106	157	291

Figures indicate actual enrolment figures in each subject.

Posters

We are probably most familiar with attention-grabbing graphic design through our contact with commercial advertising. However, there are other places where design can be used to gain your attention and convey a message effectively. There has been a trend in recent years to replace written signs with signs that employ symbols and graphics. As well as being attention-grabbing, graphics tend to be more universally accepted and have the ability to overcome language barriers. This is often important in the workplace where people from various ethnic backgrounds work together, where signs are ignored because of over-familiarity, or where safety needs to be maintained.

Posters can be used to inform, instruct, give directions and warn people of danger.

Activity 15.E   Posters

1. Here are some industrial safety posters distributed by the New South Wales Department of Labour and Industry. Examine each poster carefully. Now answer these questions.
   (a) How does each poster gain its impact?
   (b) What use has been made of visual rather than verbal language?
   (c) How do the two forms of language support one another?
   (d) Where could each poster be used in a workplace?
   (e) How often do you think you would have to change or replace the posters to avoid over-familiarity?

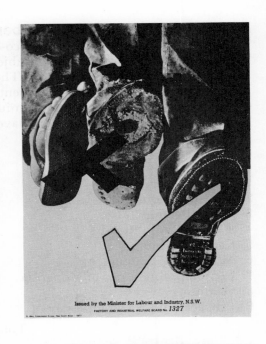

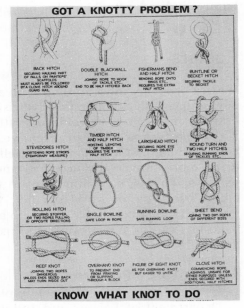

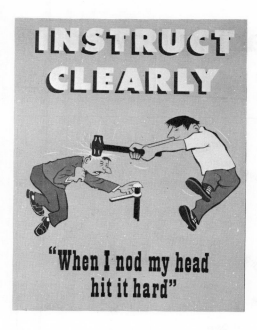

2. Design your own poster. Highlight the need for safety, outline a process involving several steps, or *illustrate* a technique. Use a piece of cardboard or a large sheet of paper. Here are some ideas.
   (a) The safe use of tools, or building plant such as power tools, ladders or scaffolding
   (b) Protecting the bystander on industrial sites
   (c) Safe use of chemicals or insecticides
   (d) Handling explosives
   (e) Working with electricity
   (f) Industrial noise
   (g) Working near or with moving machinery such as conveyor belts or lathes
   (h) Protective clothing
   (i) Thinking and planning before acting
   (j) Using fire extinguishers
   (k) Packaging fragile goods
   (l) Lifting heavy loads
   (m) Road safety
   (n) Instructions for using a tool
   (o) Working regulations

Bring your poster to the next class. On the back of your poster indicate where you would envisage the poster being used. Give specific details (e.g. the poster would be attached to the door of the laboratory, or the poster would be pinned to a noticeboard in the tea room). Do not indicate your intended message as this should be self-evident.

Pin up your posters around the room. You might like to use this exercise as the basis for a discussion. Comment on the merits of the various posters. Ask yourself the same questions about the class-produced posters as you did about the sample posters.

16
Increase Your Reading Power

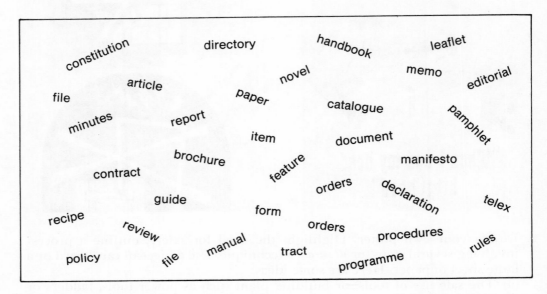

How do you survive the avalanche of printed communication that continually bombards you as you study or work or simply go about your business of living as a citizen in this highly complex, information-centred world?

Good Reading Habits

These may be summed up as follows:

- Try to read at an above-average to fast reading rate. Here is a range of reading speeds for straightforward prose, e.g. newspaper articles:

SPEED (words per minute)	READING RATE
150–240	slow
240–250	average
250–300	above average
300–450	fast
450–550+	very fast

Each improvement in your reading rate must not be at the expense of your comprehension or understanding of the ideas and facts you are reading. So, always link your reading rate to a high score on your retention and recall of the information.

- The nature of the piece of writing will determine your rate of reading. The easier the material, the faster your reading rate. Always have an aim in mind as you read. To extract the main idea from a paragraph, read the topic sentence (the sentence containing the main thought) and rapidly read the other sentences containing supporting evidence, other examples etc.
- Read silently and without lip movements. Meaning is more important than sound.
- Try to read with total concentration—with the aim of retaining and recalling what you've read. The better your concentration, the fewer regressions (back tracking movements of the eyes) you are likely to feel in need of.
- Generally, read for the idea behind the words rather than for the words themselves.

Eyes Across The Printed Page

As the eyes move along a line of print, reading takes place. However, the act of reading is not something smooth. The eyes move across the print in a series of jumps and pauses called 'fixations'. It is during the pauses or fixations that the eyes see a span of worlds which is translated into meaning by the brain. Both jumps and fixations are performed unconsciously.

The mossies are big in the Territory . DDT has no effect on them.

An average reader takes about five or six fixations to cover a line of print. As reading ability improves fewer fixations are needed to read a line of print. Also, with improved reading ability, a shorter time—a fraction of a second—is spent on each fixation.

A difference between an average or good reader and a poor reader is that the poor reader continually regresses, i.e. skips back to make certain that a word has not been missed or misunderstood.

- **A poor reader's eye movements**: Fixations followed by regressions.
  Note: Many poor readers move their heads instead of eyes from one fixation to another. This means that the person does not exercise his eye muscles and therefore will get very tired when reading.

One time a big mosquito landed on the tarmac at Darwin airport

Another bad habit is subvocalising. When a reader is subvocalising he is actually mouthing the words he is reading. This should not take place in silent reading unless a new word is being learned.

- **An average reader's eye movements:**

They pumped fifty gallons of petrol into it thinking it was an aeroplane

- **A good reader's eye movements:** Fewer fixations, more words included/ recognized in each span of fixation.

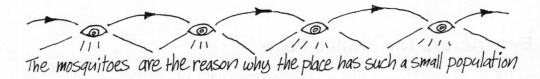

The mosquitoes are the reason why the place has such a small population

Keep these aspects of reading theory in mind as you look at various techniques for more rapid and more effective reading. In the reading exercises in this chapter, you will be given the opportunity to get some idea of your normal reading rate. This is only intended as a guide. In order to improve your reading speed, as in any skill, you need to practise every day.

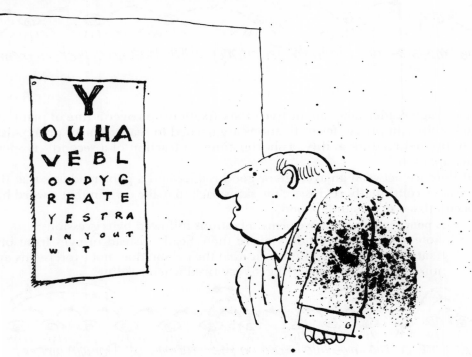

Pre-Reading

Pre-reading will provide you with a framework of the main ideas in a piece of writing. Use pre-reading when your aim is to see whether a piece of writing is going to be of value to you and whether you need to go into it in more detail.

Here is how it works. From any piece of written or printed material you feel has potential for your needs, read only the title, author, introduction, and the topic sentences of each paragraph (a topic sentence is the sentence in a paragraph—usually the first sentence—that gives the main idea or topic that the rest of the paragraph will deal with). Finally, read the concluding paragraph for a summary of the piece of writing you are considering.

Diagrammatically:

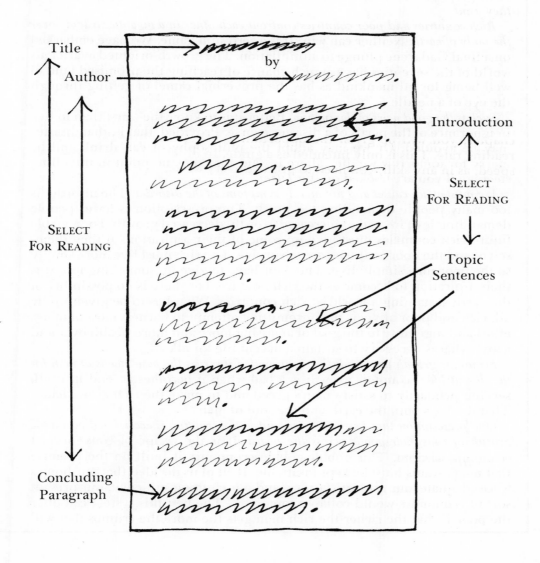

Activity 16.A   Pre-Reading

Pre-read the following passage with the aim of extracting the main idea. To help you, the important sections of the passage have been printed in italics. When you have finished, you will be asked to choose what you consider to be the main idea from a number of alternatives.

CONFRONTING THE FUTURE
Charles Birch

A way of life which has brought affluence to a third of mankind in this century now threatens the demise of all mankind. The skies are darkening, the heavens are heating up, the seas are being poisoned, lakes and rivers dry up, forests and fields disappear as we draw the last drops of life blood from the veins of the earth. Too many people, demanding too much, destroy their source of life in trying to get what they want.

Rich countries and poor countries confront each other in a gigantic struggle over the body of earth. Neither can win. It is a zero sum game. We have embarked on a final Gadarene plunge to annihilation. The growth-oriented avaricious world of the seventies has as much chance of reaching the promised land of well-being for all mankind as has the proverbial camel of getting through the eye of a needle.

Such is the good news of damnation. Better it is to know the worst than to live in ignorance of the perils of a disaster course. Provided, that is, that disaster may be avoided. Or we may adopt the philosophy of eat, drink and be merry for tomorrow we die. There is, said someone, no point in travelling steerage if you are booked on the *Titanic.*

We must attack causes and not merely symptoms of the disorder. The disorder is too many people demanding too much. The prescription is fewer people demanding less; instead of increased growth, decreased growth. For a viable future rich countries must give up some of their aspirations if they themselves and the poor countries are to survive. The rich must live more simply so the poor may simply live. The poor have to give up something too. It is their aspiration to become as the rich now are. For there is no possibility of the earth sustaining a world of rich countries. What has to be given up by all, rich and poor alike, is the unremitting attempt to harness most of man's effort and ingenuity to the goal of amassing more and more wealth over and above what is necessary to sustain a decent life for all.

Economic growth is a good; that is, provided it serves the basic needs of man for the decent life. Economic growth is a bad when it becomes an end in itself, serving primarily to satisfy man's greed and to make the rich grow richer. That destroys both the earth and the soul of man.

One prescription that has been tried and found wanting is accelerated economic growth of consumer goods across the board. It is the recipe of conventional economic wisdom. This gobble-gobble economics is built on the premise that man's wants must be kept insatiable. If all of us decided that our homes were adequate, our cars satisfactory, and our clothing sufficient, our present sort of economics would collapse tomorrow. The best this system can offer the poor is that the richer the rich man gets the more the crumbs that will fall from his table for the poor to pick up. The rich get richer while poverty is left untouched.

There can be no development of the undeveloped nations without redistribution of the world's wealth. The needs of the needy must be filled before the greeds of the greedy. Existing marketing systems between the nations fail to achieve this. Goods go not to those who need them most but to those who can afford to pay—the rich. Redistribution of the world's wealth involves reduced economic growth in rich countries and increased economic growth in poor countries. One must go down for the other to come up, contrary to conventional economic wisdom that sharing is a myth. Redistribution also demands of the rich countries that they cease to strengthen powerful vested interests that delay or stop social and political reforms in poor countries. Sacrifices required of the rich countries are willingness to put up with temporary dislocation of industry and temporary unemployment that may follow reduction of tariffs on goods from poor countries. Payment must also be made in the coin of one's own person; accepting limits to incomes, reduced choice in consumer goods and reduced purchase of luxuries.

The prescription is not one of zero economic growth but reduced growth in consumer goods by rich countries and increased growth in services of health, education and welfare in both rich and poor countries alike.

[700 words]

Use your pre-reading to choose the main idea of the passage from among these four alternatives:
(a) The goal of life on this planet is a level of existence which will enable the world's nations to sustain life although this inevitably involves a reduction in the provision of services.
(b) The rich and the poor countries of the world are locked in a struggle for possession of the world's resources. But whichever wins, the results will be the same—untold misery and suffering for the human race.
(c) The uncontrolled consumption of world resources is threatening the existence of the human race. The answer is a decrease in demand and a redistribution of the world's wealth to enable the world's people to live an adequate life.
(d) There is fundamental disagreement among the nations of this earth on how scarce resources should be used. The poor countries want economic control; the rich countries demand endless economic growth.
Check your answer on page 234.

Rapid Reading

Now, having grasped the main idea from pre-reading, turn back to the passage and read it completely. Time yourself from the first to the last word. The passage contains 700 words. To find your rate of reading, divide 700 by your reading time. Check with the scale on page 186 to find where you stand.

If you read the passage in 2·5 minutes, your reading rate is 280 wpm. (words per minute) Checked with the scale on page 186 you will find you have an *above average* reading rate.

Record your result like this:

READING TIME ____ minutes

READING RATE 700 ÷ ____ minutes

= ____ wpm

Tick your finding: slow/average/above average/fast/very fast

Activity 16.B Comprehension

Test yourself for comprehension or understanding of the passage by saying whether each of the following is TRUE or FALSE.

(a) A third of mankind is threatened by demise.	T	F
(b) In the confrontation over the body of earth the rich countries will win.	T	F
(c) It is useless to remedy merely the symptoms of the disorder.	T	F
(d) Too few people are demanding too much.	T	F
(e) Growth must be limited.	T	F
(f) Both poor and rich countries must give up some of their aspirations.	T	F
(g) Mankind must use effort and ingenuity to amass more and more wealth.	T	F
(h) A decent life for everyone should be the aim of economic growth.	T	F
(i) When economic growth becomes an end in itself it is good.	T	F
(j) The accelerated growth of consumer goods is called 'gobble gobble' economics.	T	F
(k) Redistribution of the world's wealth can lead to the development of the poorer countries.	T	F
(l) Redistribution involves increased economic growth in rich countries and reduced economic growth in poor countries.	T	F
(m) Reduction of tariffs on goods from poor countries may involve some industrial upsets and some permanent unemployment in the rich countries.	T	F
(n) Essential services would be increased in both rich and poor countries.	T	F

Check your answers on page 234, and record your Comprehension Score.

Skimming

This is the technique of speed reading with the sole aim of locating a certain point or fact in a piece of writing. When you skim, look for the word shape. The word shape for 'communication' is different from the word shape for 'propagation'. When the point or fact is located, cease skimming and read for detail to 'fix' the context.

Activity 16.C   Skimming

Locate the 5 facts listed below by skim reading the passage. Stop when you reach a fact to read more slowly and pick up details which describe and explain it. Test yourself on your grasp of the fact by answering the questions that follow the passage.

1. Laughter lines
2. Body language
3. The movement of muscles
4. The professional smile
5. Types of smile

Smiling

If you doubt that smiling is an important habit, try a couple of simple experiments. First, take a close look at your own face in a mirror, and then compare what you see with a photograph of yourself as an adolescent. Some of the changes will be idiosyncratic: you may have grown a moustache or acquired lasting scars from a car crash. But if you want a more accurate idea of what your face has been doing in the years since the picture was taken, concentrate on the new lines which have appeared, because these have been formed by use. You will find that the deepest are the laughter lines which curl away from the bottom of your nose and end somewhere beneath the lips. If this surprises you (you may think that you don't often smile) it is because smiling is rarely a deliberate, consciously directed action—which is in fact its greatest strength. Smiling is perhaps the most powerful single technique for non-verbal communication (NVC) we possess, precisely because the effectiveness of NVC, or 'body-language', lies in the fact that its signals are outside the full conscious awareness of the person who is sending them. The ambiguity and subtlety of NVC signals increases their impact, and may on occasions make them more useful than spoken language in telling other people what we feel about them.

If this seems implausible, try another experiment. Talk to someone without allowing yourself to smile; you will find this difficult, but possible. What will be less easy is getting the same person to talk to you again, because there is something decidedly unnerving about a conversation with someone who never smiles.

The great advantage of the ambiguity of NVC is that if the message it conveys doesn't please the person at whom you are directing it, you can always claim that they have misunderstood you. Suppose you laugh when someone is telling you about a misfortune he has suffered, and he reacts coldly, saying that it is no laughing matter. You can then protest that you weren't laughing *at* him (ridicule), but *with* him (sympathy). Unlike smiling, laughter is in fact rarely used to express sympathy, but you still have a much better chance of retrieving the situation than if you had committed to words your true sentiment: that you find it extremely funny that he has broken his leg ski-ing. Both smiling and laughter have this ambiguity, and it is no accident that smiling involves the laughter lines. So far as the movement of muscles is concerned the two activities are very similar, laughing being a more intense form of smiling. But when we study the circumstances in which people smile or laugh, it becomes clear that the two are not completely interchangeable.

What is the meaning of a smile? When a human adult smiles, he may be indicating any one or more of at least six different things. The following description of an imaginary social worker's morning illustrates some of them. Before seeing his first client, we find him sitting in his office, looking at the pleasant view from his window, and smiling. He saw a good film last night, slept well, and is thinking how much happier he is in his job than his brother-in-law. His smile is a simple expression of *happiness*. But when the first client of the morning arrives, his expression becomes noticeably exaggerated as he assumes the professional smile which is designed to convey both *sympathy* with the client's problem and *reassurance* that he is in good hands. Details of the saga which is then related are clearly meant to be funny, so the social worker smiles to show mild *amusement*. But the story also contains some elements which are frankly improbable, and a sardonic smile betrays incredulity and even *ridicule* (Aw, come *on*!). The advice given by our social worker turns out to be inappropriate, so later we find him explaining to his boss what went wrong. Now his smile is sheepish, a gesture of appeasement and *submission*.

These types of smile are distinct, but they all serve to oil the wheels of everyday social intercourse.

[800 words]

Now, turn back to the passage and read it *completely*. Calculate your reading rate (i.e. 800 ÷ _____ minutes = _____ wpm.) Have you improved your reading rate?

Now let's look at the facts.
1. (a) Where are laughter lines to be found?
   (b) What is characteristic about them?
2. (a) What's another name for body language?
   (b) Why is it so effective?
   (c) What two aspects of body language are important?
3. In terms of muscle movement, how is laughter related to smiling?
4. What two feelings is the professional smile designed to convey?
5. What is the general social purpose of smiling?

Scanning

This technique is speed reading across the page with the aim of extracting the basic framework from a piece of writing.

Activity 16.D   Scanning

1. Below are 8 possible titles for the passage. Scan-read the passage then select the title that most appropriately sums it up.
   (a) The Ark Makes History
   (b) Noah Gets Angry with God
   (c) The Missing Unicorns
   (d) Difficulties with the Animals of the Ark
   (e) Some Problems Are As Old As The Ark
   (f) The Technical Troubles Of Building The Ark
   (g) God Makes Noah Pay For Building The Ark
   (h) The Blame Rests With Noah

And the Lord said to Noah: Where is the ark which I have commanded thee to build?

And Noah said unto the Lord: Verily, I have had three carpenters off ill. The gopher-wood supplier hath let me down. Yea, even though the gopher-wood hath been on order for nigh 12 months. What can I do, O Lord?

And God said unto Noah: I want that ark finished even after seven days and seven nights.

And Noah said: It will be so. And it was not so.

And the Lord said unto Noah: What seemeth to be the trouble this time?

And Noah said unto the Lord: Mine sub-contractor hath gone bankrupt. The pitch which thou commandest me to put on the outside and on the inside of the ark hath not arrived. The plumber hath gone on strike. Shem, my son who helpeth me on the ark side of the business, hath formed a pop group with his brothers Ham and Japhet. Lord, I am undone.

And the Lord grew angry and said: And what about the animals? The male and the female of every sort that I ordered to come up unto thee to keep their seed alive upon the face of the earth?

And Noah said: They have been delivered to the wrong address but should arrive on Friday.

And the Lord said: How about the unicorns, and the fowls of the air by sevens?

And Noah wrung his hands and wept, saying: Lord, the unicorns are a discontinued line, thou canst not get them for love nor money. And the fowls of the air are sold only in half-dozens. Lord, Lord, thou knowest how it is.

And the Lord in his wisdom said: Noah, my son, I knowest. Why else dost thou think I am causing a flood to descend upon the earth?

[350 words]

2. Now read the passage completely and check your reading rate (300 ÷ _____ minutes = _____ wpm). Has your reading rate improved?
3. Select the correct answers from the following:
   (a) God has (i) ordered (ii) begged (iii) requested Noah to construct an ark.
   (b) When Noah asks the Lord for advice, his answer is (i) helpful (ii) critical (iii) irrelevant.

(c) Noah tells the Lord that the plumber has gone (i) bankrupt (ii) on strike (iii) to another job.

(d) Shem, Ham and Japhet have (i) formed a business of their own (ii) formed a pop group (iii) gone to build a rival ark.

(e) God refers to the descendants of the ark animals as (i) seed (ii) young (iii) offspring.

(f) Noah has found out that unicorns are (i) an endangered species (ii) a discontinued line (iii) a rare genus.

(g) God is causing a flood to descend upon the earth because (i) humans are a problem-bound race (ii) Noah has not done his job properly (iii) that is the only way to get the ark going.

(h) The tone of the article is (i) critical (ii) explanatory (iii) entertaining.

COMPREHENSION SCORE ____/8 (answers on page 234).

Key Reading

This technique involves skipping the unimportant words in a piece of writing ('the', 'a', 'an', 'and', etc.) and picking out the important or key words.

Many people key-read without even being conscious of their highly selective approach to a piece of writing. In key-reading, your aim is to get as fast as possible to the words that contain the ideas. The unimportant words have been skipped in this news item:

unusual car accident, argument, learner driver, boyfriend supervising her driving. Approaching T-junction, argue turn—left, right? Both attempted steer, car went straight ahead mounted pavement through double doors, public bar, hotel, scattering blaspheming drinkers, rest front wheels, turning slowly hanging over bar counter. Barmaid rose occasion, floor, dusting herself asking sarcastically 'stubbies, cans?'

It sounds like a telegram but you'll find the basic meaning here, as you'll see when you compare it with the original:

An unusual car accident occurred as a result of an argument between the learner-driver of a car and her boyfriend who was supervising her driving. As they were approaching a T-junction they began to argue over which way to turn—left or right? The girl wanted to turn left, her boyfriend right. They both attempted to steer their separate ways, but the car went straight ahead, mounted the pavement and passed through the double doors of the public bar of a hotel. Scattering blaspheming drinkers, it came to rest with its front wheels, turning slowly, hanging over the bar counter. The barmaid rose to the occasion by picking herself up off the floor, dusting herself down and asking sarcastically: 'stubbies or cans?'

[Note: by skipping unimportant words, your key reading tally is 54 words compared with 124 words in the original!]

Activity 16.E   Key-Reading
To help you, the key words and phrases are printed in italics.

The Ugly Death of a Drunk Motorist
by Tess Lawrence

One of us *will die tonight.* It will be an *ugly death.* It will be a *useless death. You* probably *won't give a damn.*

How can I make the *death* of an *accident victim mean* anything more than a *statistic* or *newspaper headline* to you?

How can I make *you understand* what it's *like to pull* a *lifeless* but *warm corpse reeking* of *grog* from a *car* that has *bulldozed* into a *telegraph pole?*

How can I show you the *bibs of vomit* that drip off *dead passengers, ejected from* their *bellies* in suffocating *fear* as their *last act* of *consciousness?*

How dare I speak of the urine that *stains* the *clothes* of the *Dead?* Because that is the *way* we *humans die.*

Urinating in fear. *Blood, urine, vomit* and *grog*—they are the *last rites* of the *average accident victim.*

Then there are the *screams,* the *song* of the *wounded dying* and the *dead.*

My own *mind* is *scarred* with such *horror.* Do not suppose it melodrama. It is a *perversity committed on life* that can *never* be *captured ruthlessly* and *honestly* on *paper.*

I *remember* working one *New Year's night,* the *police radio* cracked into life. A *car* had *rammed* into a *tree. Two passengers.* One male, one female. The male was dead, the female thought to be dying. *What confronted me* is to this day a *recurring nightmare.* I cannot even share it easily with myself.

The *car* had been *concertinaed* to half its normal size. The *occupants* were still *trapped inside.*

The *girl slumped* on her *dead companion's chest.* He had his *arm around her.* His *arm* was *raised* and *pinned* up by the deformed *metal.*

The arm was thus in drinking position and the *hand held* a *beer bottle.* The *bottle* was *rammed* down his *throat.*

Slivers of *glass* had *sliced* through his *throat.* The *neck* of the *bottle protruded* from the base of his *own neck.*

His *eyes* were *open.* They were *white* with *fear.* And they were *white* with *death.* They were white with the eyes of an animal shot in the head at point-blank range.

I *vomited. I* could *smell* their *blood* and I could *smell* the *alcohol.* The *night destroyed me.*

I had *thought we* were all *invincible.* I had thought *death* crept only into upstairs bedrooms to *close* the *eyes* of the *aged. I never stopped to think* it *hurtled* into *trees* at *100 km/h.*

I never stopped to think of *mothers drowning* in *hysteria,* being brought to *identify* their *dead children,* beating their chests and pulling their hair.

The *mother* of this *boy did.* The *car crashed* only a *couple of hundred metres* from his *home.*

She came *running* down the *street* like a woman *possessed. She bit* and *fought* with the *ambulancemen.* She *wanted* to *tear* the *bottle* from his *throat.*

She was *screaming.* And screaming. She *couldn't understand* why her son wouldn't answer her; *take* the *bottle out himself.*

She *seemed not to notice* his *throat* was *cut.* And that *he* was *dead.* Her mother's heart had punctured her mother's eyes. He was *buried* with most of the *bottle still* in his *throat.*

The *night destroyed her.* But her *night* will last a *lifetime.* But this is a *pantomime* of *death* we *repeat nightly.* The *longest* running *show* on *earth* with a *willing cast* of thousands.

Like drunken lemmings, we *drink* and *drive;* drink and drive.

Sometimes the *guilty kill themselves.* More *often* they *kill* the *innocent.* We are *impervious* to *death.* Because we are *protected* from its *obscenities.*

We *don't see* the *casualty sections* of our hospitals that sometimes look like the *inside* of *abattoirs.* We don't see the *contents* of the *cranium spilling* out on to pillows.

We don't see the *accident victims twitching* in the *throes of death. Life force diminishing.*

We are happy to be our own butchers, our *own murderers.* We are happy to *premeditate* the *killing* of *innocent* people.

We are happy to *drink* to *excess* and jump behind the wheel of a car, as *potent* a *weapon* as a *machine-gun.*

And if we *survive* the *evening* we are happy to sit down to *dinner* the next evening and *tut-tut* over the *carnage* of *Northern Ireland.*

So long as we *don't see* the *torn flesh* and the *severed limbs* bleeding in their twisted, steel tombs, we're right. So long as we *don't* see *bodies* being pulled like *broken puppets* from the *car wrecks* or *shovelled* off the *asphalt* we're right.

Leave it to the *ambulancemen* to handle those thankless *lifeless corpses.* They are the *men* who *weep anger* as well as *tears* for this *senseless killing.*

It's *not tasteful* for *television* newsreels to *record* the *moans* and *screaming* of the *injured.* It's *not tasteful* for *newspaper photographs* to *feature corpses* at *accidents.* It's not tasteful to *write about it.* Who wants to read about it? We all know it goes on.

What we *need* is some *bloody tastelessness.* You *need* to *hear* the *screams.* You *need* to see the *dead* sprawled open-legged open-mouthed and without dignity on our roads.

You *need* to see *blood* spurting, *broken children* who will never be mended; who will never grow up; *cut down* by *drunkards.*

You *need* to visit the *abattoirs* that we call *casualty sections.* You need to understand that it *COULD* and *WILL happen* to you if you *don't take care.*

You need to understand that you have *no right* to *jeopardise* yourself or *anyone else* and that *if you do* you are as *culpable* as *anyone* who *lies in wait* to *kill.*

If you *must go out* and *drink,* leave your car keys at home. *Take a cab.*

[1000 words]

Re-read the passage completely and check your reading rate (1000 ÷ ____ minutes = ____ wpm). Have you improved your reading rate?

1. Your attitude to yet another road death will probably be one of (a) heartfelt concern (b) indifference (c) revulsion.
2. We humans die (a) cleanly (b) bravely (c) messily.
3. The last rites of the average accident victim are (a) body contents (b) prayers (c) feelings expressed in words.
4. The (a) screams (b) sighs (c) pleas constitute the 'song' of the wounded, dying, dead.
5. The horror that is committed on life is termed (a) outrage (b) atrocity (c) perversity.
6. What confronted the journalist was a nightmare that came (a) suddenly (b) again and again (c) prematurely.
7. The occupants of the car were (a) thrown clear (b) rescued (c) trapped inside.
8. The driver was killed by the crash and (a) a beer bottle (b) slivers of glass from a broken window (c) petrol fumes.
9. His eyes were white with (a) fear and death (b) horror and fear (c) panic and death.
10. As the journalist smelled the blood and alcohol, the night (a) enveloped (b) destroyed (c) tortured him.
11. He had thought life was (a) invincible (b) vulnerable (c) whimsical.
12. He never stopped to think of mothers (a) drowning in pity (b) drowning in despair (c) drowning in hysteria.
13. The mother couldn't understand why her son wouldn't answer her or (a) respond to her (b) remove the bottle (c) tear himself loose.
14. Her night will last (a) a lifetime (b) forever (c) eternally.
15. What we repeat nightly is a (a) charade (b) revue (c) pantomine of death.
16. 'Like drunken lemmings we drink and drive.' Lemmings are animals that (a) commit mass suicide (b) stray onto roads in thousands (c) make driving hazardous.
17. Since the (a) horrors (b) ugliness (c) obscenities of death are not obvious to us we are protected.
18. From its context 'impervious' means (a) not alarmed by (b) not to be penetrated or affected by (c) not responsible for in any way.
19. We are happy to (a) prevent (b) assist in (c) premeditate the killing of innocent people.
20. The (a) ambulancemen (b) police (c) relatives weep anger as well as tears.
21. The killing is (a) senseless (b) avoidable (c) vindictive.
22. TV, newspapers, written material avoid the realism of accidents because it is (a) not profitable (b) not tasteful (c) not necessary.
23. The message of this article is that we need to (a) understand what is happening and care enough to stop it (b) give assistance when and where we can to accident victims (c) take care ourselves on the roads so that we do not become accident statistics ourselves.
24. The accidents are caused by (a) the unskilled (b) the careless (c) the drunkards on our roads.
25. The advice of the article is that if you do get drunk (a) drive slowly and carefully (b) take a cab instead of driving yourself (c) wash and wait for a while before driving.
Comprehension score: ____/25 (answers on page 234).

Phrase Reading

This is a technique for increasing your span of recognition—the words you can effectively recognize in one fixation—and hence your reading rate.

Since it is only possible to see a few letters round the actual point of fixation, there is a need for you to draw on your own familiarity and experience with words that are often grouped in phrases. This helps with ideas that are more often expressed in groups of words than in isolated ones.

Activity 16.F Phrase Reading

1. Using, if possible, only *one* fixation per phrase, read across the phrases from left to right. Fixate at the middle of each phrase. Concentrate on seeing the whole phrase each time. Try not to linger on any one fixation, but move swiftly to the next.

this ad	will sell
time for	a commercial break
the TV set	in the corner
on the air	as of now
the new serial	on the radio
the final episode	of Private Lives
in the interest of	the individual consumer
all products shown	are freely available
this is called	a buyer's market
needless to say	sales are limited
a sensational taste	a thrilling experience
a cast of hundreds	and spectacular locations
wandering and mingling	looking for something original
when she reads a magazine	it definitely stays read
profits were grossed	at around quarter of a million
sign there on the dotted line	and you'll never be the same again
in-flight eye-level movies	are a built-in non extra
new ideas are flying around	in our new V jet
smoking is a health hazard	so don't fume if you can't light up

Activity 16.G Comprehensive Phrase-Reading

Now phrase-read the Phillip Adams article. Phrase-read *down* the columns. Then test yourself on your comprehension of it.

A simple guide to advertising

Since 1956
Almost every time you blink
There's another telly spot
Saying what to buy or think.
Pouring from the picture tube
Like lava from Mt Helen
A cacophonous kaleidoscope
Wreaking havoc in one's melon.

Sprinkle Milo in the washing
Stir Omo in your drink
Pour Dettol on your Kornies
And Pepsi down your sink.
Let Castrol fix your pimples
And Clearasil the budgie
That's what the ads are telling us
From Mirboo North to Mudgee.

Ads with plastic children
And pretty plastic wives
In their trendy plastic houses
Leading pretty plastic lives.
Obsessed with their detergents
(Omo sapiens and Fab lemonists)
Each claiming whitest washing
And angering the feminists.

Where your pagans and your heathens
Once sang songs for Mammon
We now raise our voices
To toilet rolls and salmon.
Like congregations singing hymns
(Those jingles to Lord Jesus)
Telly's choirs remind us
What friends we have in cheeses.

Every meat pie has its anthem
That puts Elizabeth's to shame
In a 20-grand spectacular
For that's the price of fame.
Hear the soundtrack's raves and rantings
While the Mortein choir sings
'Come on, come on Mozzie'
To surging brass and strings.

It's a world of conjuring
With a bunny in each topper
It's a whirl of white lies
The little fib, the whopper.
So when your program takes a breath
You know what you must do—
Whizz out and make a cuppa
Or detour down the loo.

Just as the little dicky bird
Designates photography
Advertisers have pursued
What could be called faunography.
Like Noah who filled his Ark
With creatures two by two
Advertisers stuff their ads
With floggers from the zoo.

Like Harry Butler finding
Something strange beneath each log
Grosby, Goodyear, HMV
Have come up with a dog.
While Hilton, Esso, Uniroyal
Have pussies on the prowl
Walpamur? They've got a chimp
And Telecom an owl.

Olympus have a simian
The Dolphin torch, a porpoise.
Our biggest bank? A pachyderm
To symbolise its corpus.
All signed up by Equity
And made to pay their dues
The only creatures left uncast
Are yaks and sloths and gnus.

Now ads have gone all sexy
As Lolitas smooth as silk
Are used by dairy farmers
To flog their flavoured milk.
(Close ups of pert buttocks
And come-hither thighs:
While amazing selling points
Are thrust before your eyes.)

But sadly the blandishments
Of each pneumatic wench
Produce in ageing males
A thirst that milk can't quench.
So far from feeling grateful
When the Big M girls are frisky
To lull the pain and calm our nerves
We lurch off for a whisky.

Hear Ita flog the Weekly
With her million-dollar lithp
While verbose breakfast Bubbles
Tell you that they're crisp.
And if you think that's clever
Just wait until next week
When Cyngell makes Rice Bubbles
Go snap and pop in Greek.

Well, now my pome is over
And I've showed you how to flog
Fixatives or laxatives
Toffy cars to toffee log.
And now you know the tricks
Of media's Machiavellies
You should be that much smarter
When you next turn on your tellies.

[500 words]

1. Phillip Adams compares advertising to (a) a water spout (b) a volcanic eruption (c) an atomic disaster.
2. The phrase, 'a cacophonous kaleidoscope' includes both (a) sound and colour (b) sound and colliding shapes (c) high pressure selling and colour.
3. There is humour in the second stanza because (a) Phillip Adams has chosen corny products (b) The places mentioned are unlikely to use such products (c) The products and their functions do not coincide.
4. In the third stanza the word 'plastic' is repeated because (a) the word has a good sound (b) it suggests the shallow and the artificial (c) many things are made of plastic.

5. Feminists are likely to be angered because detergent ads are (a) aimed at women and children (b) preposterous (c) cannot justify the claims they make.
6. Stanza 4 deals with (a) the way products advertised on TV cause us to sing (b) the superficial nature of TV as a modern religion (c) a comparison between singing on TV and using the product shown.
7. Stanza 5 brings out the discrepancy between (a) meat pies and insect sprays (b) knowing that a song or product is bad and doing something about it (c) the subject of a song and the extravagance of the music that accompanies it.
8. Phillip Adams sees the world of advertising as composed of (a) tricks and lies (b) programmes and advertising breaks (c) lies and white lies.
9. Animals are used in advertising to (a) help the public recognize certain species that are in danger of becoming extinct (b) make any chosen animal famous (c) link the quality possessed by an animal to a product.
10. Sex is used to sell (a) a flavoured milk (b) the physique produced by drinking milk (c) the 'smooth as silk' look.
11. The stanza beginning 'But sadly the blandishments . . .' says the use of sex in advertising (a) succeeds every time (b) may backfire (c) is without subtlety.
12. Phillip Adams calls breakfast Bubbles 'verbose' which means (a) delicious (b) talkative (c) lacking nutrition.
13. The purpose of the poem is to (a) teach us more about (b) expose (c) mock TV advertising techniques.

You may like to check your reading rate on this section (500 ÷ ____ minutes = ____wpm). Compare this with your previous efforts.

Activity 16.H   Reading for Comprehension

Pre-read the following passage by Clive James. Glance at the comprehension questions that follow the passage, and according to your judgement,

- key-read
- phrase read, or
- skim or scan

the passage for the answers.

Deadly Spiders

This description is by Clive James who grew up in a suburb of Sydney but then, as a young man, went to live overseas. He looks back at familiar things . . .

Two of the worst Australian spiders are the funnel-web and the trap-door. One is even more lethal than the other but I can't remember which. It doesn't matter, because either can put a child in peril of its life. The funnel-web spider is a ping-pong ball in a fox-fur coat. It inhabits a miniature missile silo in the ground, from which it emerges in a savage arc, ready to sink its mandibles into anything that breathes. The trap-door spider is really a funnel-web plus cunning, since it conceals the mouth of its silo with a tiny coal-hole door. Both kinds of spiders can leap an incredible distance. A wood-pile might contain hundreds of each kind. If you even suspected the presence of either species in your garden you were supposed to report immediately to the responsible authorities. After the war an English immigrant lady became famous when she was discovered gaily swatting funnel-webs with a broom as they came flying at her in squadrons. Any one of them, if it had got close enough even to spit at her, would have put her in bed for a year.

I somehow managed to avoid meeting trap-door spiders or funnel-webs. Quite often I came face to face with a harmless relative, which Aunt Dot called a tarantula and I called a tiantelope. Actually it was just a common garden spider called the huntsman, whose idea of a big thrill was to suck a wasp. The huntsman wove big vertical webs which I used regularly to walk into when heading tentatively down the back path to the lavatory after dark. Getting mixed up in the web, to which I knew the triantelope must be at some point attached, was a frightening sensation which I attempted to forestall by inching forward very slowly, with one hand held out. It didn't help.

But the real horror among spiders was more likely to be encountered in the lavatory itself. This was the red-back. The red-back is mainly black, with a scarlet stripe down where its spine would be if it were a vertebrate. Looking like a neatly rigged and painted single-seater that might once have been flown by von Richthofen, the red-back has enough poison on it to immobilise a horse. It had the awkward habit, in unsewered areas like ours, of lurking under the lavatory seat. If a red-back bit you on the behind you were left with the problem of where to put the tourniquet and not long to think about it. Nor could you ask anyone to suck out the poison, unless you knew them very well indeed. I saw plenty of red-backs and actually got bitten by one, luckily not on the behind. I think it was a red-back. Certainly I told my mother it was. The site of the wound was my right foot. My mother knelt, sucked and spat. We were both frightened but she was not too frightened to act.

1. How is the shape and covering of the funnel-web spider graphically conveyed to us in the passage?
2. What is up-to-date and everpresent in the description of the funnel-web's habitation?
3. Why is the trap-door more cunning than the funnel-web?
4. What activity is common to the funnel-web and the trap-door?
5. Why did the English immigrant lady become famous?
6. According to Clive James, what degree of danger was she in?
7. Is there any one word that particularly pinpoints the idea of aerial warfare between the lady and the spiders?
8. What confusion existed between Aunt Dot and Clive about the naming of the harmless relative of the funnel-web and the trap-door?
9. What was the huntsman's idea of a big thrill?
10. Getting mixed up in the web was a frightening sensation. Why?
11. The real horror among spiders was the red-back. Where was it likely to be found?
12. What does Clive James compare the red-back to?
13. What points in the comparison appeal to you as being particularly apt?
14. What would *you* compare the red-back with?

15. According to Clive James, how powerful is a red-back's poison?
16. Because of its lurking habits, what are two problems that would immediately arise as a result of a red-back's bite?
17. Clive James was bitten by a red-back. Where was he bitten?
18. How was his bite treated?
19. What indications does Clive James give that his descriptions of deadly Australian spiders are based on long-term recollections?

You may like to check your reading rate one last time (520 ÷ ____ minutes = ____ wpm). Check this figure with your result on the first passage, 'Confronting the Future'.

17   Working With People

While organizations may be encased within the four walls of a building, and the strength of an organization may be seen in terms of material assets, capital and manpower, the real strength of an organization lies in the ability of its staff and employees to carry out their duties efficiently. This not only involves individuals being productive in carrying out their day-to-day functions, it involves them liaising, talking, conferring, interviewing, instructing, directing, empathizing, sharing and, most importantly, working together. The successful organization is one in which individuals work harmoniously in groups to achieve set objectives.

Activity 17.A   The Great Card Tower Company

The object of this exercise is to construct a tower using playing cards and paper clips. For each group participating in this game you will need one pack of playing cards and 50 paper clips (the twisted wire, slide-on type). Each group has to construct a tower from its pack of playing cards using only the paper clips to connect the cards.

Divide the class into groups of between three and five persons. You have thirty minutes to discuss the construction of your tower, and to practise constructing it. During this period of time no one group should be visible to any other group, so find an area where you can work undisturbed.

At the end of thirty minutes each group should return to the classroom. You now have five minutes in which to reconstruct your tower. You are competing against the other groups to construct the tallest tower using the least number of cards.

Rules governing the building of the card towers:
(1) The card tower must be constructed within the five-minute period.
(2) All groups construct their towers at the same time.
(3) Any number of group members can help in the actual construction.
(4) If two towers are the same height on completion, the tower using the least number of cards wins.
(5) No artificial props can be used. The tower must be freestanding.
(6) Paper clips must only be used as fasteners; they cannot be bent or distorted in any way.
(7) Cards cannot be mutilated or folded in any way.
(8) If the tower falls during the five-minute construction time, continue to rebuild as you will be judged on your performance after the five minutes has elapsed.

Group Participation

Within organizations, groups meet to solve problems and make decisions, to be informed of tasks and to work manually to produce goods and services.

In the 'Card Tower' game you were engaged in each of the above types of activities. Each member of the group was allotted a task, problems had to be solved regarding how the cards could be joined, and you had to decide whether you would aim for height in building your tower regardless of the number of cards used. Which group won? Why was its strategy better than that of the other groups?

Your ideas about the playing of the 'Card Tower' game will act as bases for understanding and perhaps learning more about how people work in groups.

Activity 17.B   After the Game is Over

1. Before class discussion, answer all of the following questions. This is most important.
   (a) How did you select one another? How did your group form?
   (b) How did you feel about the group that resulted?
   (c) How many persons were in your group?
   (d) How did the size or composition of the group affect the performance of your group?
   (e) Which diagram best illustrates the communication network of your group? Which of these networks would result in the most effective communication flow? Why?

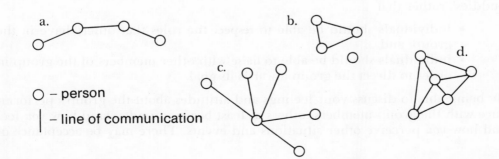

○ – person

| – line of communication

    (f) Were you committed to the task? Why were you committed or how did you become committed?

    (g) How were tasks assigned to members of your group; through delegation, volunteering, mutual consent?

    (h) Were the other members committed to the task? What motivated them?

    (i) Did a leader emerge? If so, was he elected formally or informally, or did he emerge as you became involved in the activity?

    (j) How did the element of competition (that is knowing that you had to build a taller tower than the other groups) affect the performance of your group in the thirty minute preparation stage? In the 5 minute construction stage?

    (k) Apart from ideas mentioned above, did anything else influence your group?

    (l) How did people behave in your group? Write down three words that best describe the behaviour of each of the group members (e.g. helpful, aggressive, dominant, shy, thoughtful) include yourself in the appraisal.

2. When you have answered all the questions, meet again in your 'card tower' group to discuss your answers.

    (a) What did you learn about individual perception by having to answer each question before meeting in the group?

    (b) How did your individual perceptions of the roles of group members differ?

    (c) How did your individual interpretation of the group's performance differ from the perception of others in your group?

    (d) How did the competition affect individuals within the group?

    (e) How did the competition affect the relationship among the members of the group?

Maintenance of Groups

Groups, like machines, need maintenance. Short of major surgery, people cannot have worn parts replaced, oil changed and moving parts synchronized and tuned. However, they can be overhauled and serviced in other ways. In the above discussion you have been performing this operation.

The maintenance took place because each group member had the opportunity to think about the functioning of the whole group and the role of individuals within that group and then discuss their thoughts with the other members. We all need to know how we are being perceived by the persons with whom we have to work, live and socialize. Possibly the greatest cause of communication breakdown within any organization occurs when groups of individuals fail to work harmoniously. This does not imply that all group members need to be 'great buddies', rather that

- individuals should be able to **respect** the roles that others have in the group; and
- individuals should be able to **liaise** with other members of the group in order to direct the group towards its goal.

By being able to discuss your feelings and attitudes about the group's perform-ance with the group members, others at least begin to understand how *you* feel and how *you* perceive other situations and events. There may be acceptance of your views by other members of the group. You may even change your own views, or you may be influential in changing the attitudes of others. What is most important is that individuals have had the opportunity to appraise the workings of the group.

You might ask yourself, 'What did I learn about the others through the playing of the game?' and 'How was this information altered through the discussion that followed?'

Group discussions or group meetings designed for the maintenance of the group sometimes allow members to blow off steam, to clarify ambiguous or ill-defined roles or simply to chat with the other members in order to find out more about the individual's place within the group. Sometimes group maintenance takes place quite informally in coffee or lunch breaks. At other times there may be a deliberate attempt to discuss problems or group functions in a formal setting.

Formal and Informal Groups

Within any organization there are both formal and informal groups. Formal groups are set up by management, supervisors or officers to enable a team of employees to work together on a specific operation or task. A production or assembly team is an example of a formal group. Informal groups emerge when a number of employees identify some mutual tie or common interest. Employees who have lunch together, or who play sport together after work constitute an informal group. Some informal groups are highly cohesive while others are loosely formed. As all of the needs of individuals within an organization cannot be met by the formal group, the informal group has a valuable function within any organization. The informal group provides interaction for its members that may not be possible in the day-to-day operation of the organization. It is quite often through the informal group that the grapevine operates and that individuals have the opportunity to understand how other persons perceive individuals and group roles and needs.

Conflict may exist when an individual is drawn between his responsibility to the formal group and the standards set by the informal group. A foreman may have outlined the specification for a job to a new employee and the employee may work to those standards only to have pressure exerted on him from an informal group to comply with *their* standard or level of work.

When this kind of conflict arises, the employee is faced with the possibility of doing as he has been instructed or following the accepted norm of the informal group. It is when this type of conflict arises that the individual working within the organization has to consider just how important mateship is, when lined up against his responsibility as an employee. In order to understand more about this dilemma it is important to understand the concept of 'role'.

In *The Psychology of Human Communication**, John Parry writes: 'The concept of role has received considerable attention from sociologists and social psychologists, largely in connection with the place of individuals in formal organizations and the need for clear definition of function. Such need originates frequently in the practical necessity of dividing work and responsibility'.

---

* London. University of London Press Ltd, 1967, p. 169.

Roles

In any social system (factory, business, home, team, society, interest group or class) any individual can be seen to play certain parts. This is the idea behind the concept of 'role'. The roles played by any individual will depend on the situation in which a person finds himself and any significant others who see the person in that situation performing the specific roles.

Each individual plays many different roles and will almost certainly behave in different ways when playing each role. At work Bob is a mate, co-worker, employee and storeman. What differences would you *expect* in Bob's behaviour between each of these roles? What demands may Bob have to confront when performing each of these roles? *Within* each role, Bob will behave in ways which conform broadly with the conceptions that others have about how anyone performing that specific role will behave.

The concept of 'role', however, is not as straightforward as that, because there is a difference between how someone *should* behave, how they *probably will* behave, and how they *actually* behave.

An individual actually performing the role, known as a 'role incumbent' is bound by norms, expectations and actual behaviours. **Role norms** indicate how a person or group *believes* the role incumbent should behave. These norms tend to be generalizations: storemen should always be meticulous; supervisors should always be patient with employees. They provide only an outline from which the incumbent can adapt his behaviour. **Role expectations** indicate how a person or group thinks the role incumbent probably will behave. So it might be expected that a storeman would at least keep complete records, and that the supervisor would be patient most of the time. **Role behaviour** indicates how the role incumbent will actually perform the role. In other words, Bob in his role as storeman may keep reasonable records and occasionally lose files and misplace stock lists. In the second example, the supervisor may actually be a complete tyrant and by impatient most of the time.

For each role that we play there is a group known as a **role set**. This consists of those persons who have an influence over the role incumbent.

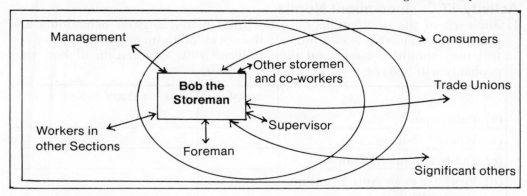

In the illustration you can see that there are several persons and groups who influence Bob when he is performing the role of storeman. One 'set' indicated by the inncer circle has most influence, followed by other individuals, groups and significant others (those persons unstated who may have influence over the role incumbent). The role incumbent's behaviour usually conforms to the norms and expectations of at least some of the persons who comprise the role set.

How do you think each person or group would influence Bob in his role as storeman? How could their expectations create conflict for Bob in his role as storeman? **Role conflict** occurs when a person holds two positions simultaneously and when the expectations of one role are incompatible with the expectations of the second role.

At any one time an individual may occupy several roles, and each role may demand different attitudes and values. This can create conflict between the roles, resulting in one role being dominant and the behaviour associated with that role dominating the incumbent's personality. From time to time we have probably all wondered whether the boss is as authoritarian at home as he is at work or whether a teacher is as patient out of the classroom as he is in the classroom!

Role conflict can occur when the norms and expectations of different members of the role set, as perceived by the incumbent, do not appear to him to be compatible. An unskilled worker may feel that the behaviour which is acceptable to the foreman will be unacceptable to his co-workers. Therefore his behaviour will change in order to accommodate his co-workers.

Conflict can also arise when an individual's personality needs conflict with the demands of the role. A person working in a complaints department may need to be 'cool, calm and collected' all the time, but the actual role incumbent may in fact have a sharp tongue and a fiery temper.

Activity 17.C   Incumbent Norms

1. For each of the occupations or roles listed below, suggest behaviours and personality traits that would indicate the norm for an incumbent, i.e. how you feel they should behave; and then indicate your expectation of how they probably will behave.

	NORM	EXPECTATION
(a) Policeman		
(b) Wharf Labourer		
(c) Fan at a Football Match		
(d) Protester at an Anti-Uranium Demonstration		
(e) Road Worker		
(f) Doctor		
(g) Teacher		
(h) Housewife		
(i) Husband		
(j) Student		

2. After comparing your responses in class, discuss whether or not you could agree on role norms and role expectations for the respective roles. What does this tell you about the nature of roles?

3. Why haven't you been asked to include any details about the incumbent's *actual* behaviour?

4. **Roles and You**
   (a) How many roles do you perform?
   (b) Of these, which are:
      (i)   the most important to you?
      (ii) the most time consuming?
   (c) Do any of these roles make quite distinct demands on your personality or behaviour? Which roles are they, and how do the demands differ?
   (d) How did you decide on the appropriate behaviour for each role? Were you taught formally or instructed, or did you observe another incumbent or simply perform the role and hope for the best?
   (e) What kinds of jobs do you think you are unsuited for? Why do you think you are unsuited to them?

The Self in Communication

In examining the importance of roles in the previous section, it is possible to develop an awareness of an individual or self as a parent, employee, housekeeper, spouse and so on. We each decide at various intervals in our life just how we will divide our energies between these roles, but the concept of role should not detract from the importance of the self. There is but one 'persona' behind the various masks we use when playing out these roles.

An examination of the self brings various questions to mind: How much of our real self do we reveal to others? How much do we guard from others? What is the effect on each of us of 'self disclosure'? What is the difference between our 'self image' and our 'self concept'? In this section we will discuss the importance of the self in communication and in so doing find answers to these questions.

We are continually looking to others for confirmation about who we think we are. Each of us has an image of ourselves in various public situations. This is our **self image**. We may imagine ourselves to be 'good company at parties' and 'confident and articulate at presenting talks and delivering addresses at meetings'. When we get confirmation from those around us, that is we get invited to parties and never appear as a wall flower, and at meetings people comment on what we have said and offer support, we can in fact confirm the image that we have of ourselves. Obviously support of this kind does more than confirm our self image. It provides us with **self esteem** or a feeling of personal worth.

The idea of **self concept** is more difficult to grasp because we can never be totally objective about ourselves and therefore we are never quite sure how we actually look, appear, sound, or present ourselves to others. The self concept we have of ourselves is actually our perceived self. It is what we believe about ourselves, what we believe we are!

Finding out about Ourselves

Human nature being as it is, we all try to 'sum one another up'. The first day in class we sum up the teacher and our classmates. As the basis for this 'summing up' we use our power of observation in addition to any information that the other parties are prepared to reveal about themselves, either intentionally or unintentionally. If the person whom we are observing sends out messages through his behaviour or actions that we find irritating, confusing or pleasant then we will judge him accordingly. The irritator we may switch off completely, the confusing personality we may decide we need more information about, and we may try to establish a relationship with the person who was pleasant.

As we all have some idea of who we want to be, and know how we want others to react to us, it is reasonable to assume that if the feedback we get from others confirms how we feel about ourselves, then our self esteem is boosted. Then we can confirm our self image, and our self concept is strengthened and, at least for the time being, affirmed. It is a relief to know that the image we portray is a close approximation of how we feel about ourselves.

Some persons seem afraid to reveal who they really are, so they mask their behaviour, create a façade so we never really know where we stand with them.

How do people do this? What effects does it have on people around them?

Who am I?

There are things I know about myself . . .
There are things I don't know about myself,
There are things you know about me, and
There are things you don't know about me.

Therefore if I enter into a relationship with you there will be things that I offer freely about myself: you will know my name, address, phone number, preference for entertainment, choice of records and so on. But there will be things that you find out about me that I don't know and probably never will know, that it is useless for you to tell me. I don't know what my voice really sounds like, I don't know if I have any irritating personality traits and I can't tell whether I have bad breath or even whether my taste in clothes appeals to you.

At the same time there will be things that I do not disclose to you. Things that I know that I feel are safer known only to me. I won't tell you that I was arrested in an anti-uranium protest three years ago because I don't know how you might react. I won't tell you about my previous relationships, because you don't need to know about them. And then there are things that neither of us know about me. These things may have not yet penetrated my consciousness, some of these things never will. They may be inner fears, curiosities or deep needs.

As I get to know you I will encourage you to tell me about myself and in doing this I will be soliciting feedback. At the same time as I get to know you I will tell you more about me or disclose details of my self. All in all our relationship is quite complex.

Attitude Formation

'Censorship should be tightened up in this country.'
  'I hate pineapple donuts!'
  'You shouldn't smoke cigarettes!'
  'War is a terrible thing!'
  'Annette has nice eyes!'
  'Girlie magazines should be banned altogether!'
  'Doctors scare me!'
  'I'm not going to church this Sunday!'
  'I'm an atheist!'
  'The boss is a slave-driver!'
  We all express attitudes—but what are attitudes? How do we form them?
  Klausmeier and Goodwin* define an attitude as 'a learned, emotionally toned predisposition to react in a consistent way, favourable or unfavourable toward a person, object or idea'.

* Klausmeier H. J. and Goodwin, W. *Learning & Human Abilities* Harper International, 2nd edn, New York, 1966 (p. 343).

We learn and develop attitudes as we grow. They form the basis for all of the decision-making in which we are engaged. In addition to significant individuals there are groups of people who become influential because they impose values, attitudes and beliefs on us. In fact, these groups help mould the attitudes that we develop. The process of moulding may be quite deliberate; on the other hand it may be unintentional or unconscious.

Within our society there are several significant or influential groups which perform this function. They are the school, the family, the church, the mass media, clubs and societies and, in some societies, the government directly. These groups because of their status within society determine how individuals will behave and act, because they all contribute in influencing the formation of attitudes. However, it is obvious that these groups do not contribute equally in the formation of one's attitude. Every individual will be influenced according not only to his access to one of these groups, but to his level of involvement and the degree of respect that he holds for persons who comprise these groups. However, each group exerts social pressure on us to conform with the tastes, attitudes and values of that group. Consider these questions.

- How does the influence of these groups change throughout our lives?
- With regard to which specific beliefs are each of these social institutions most influential?
- Do any of these groups support one another? Which groups?
- What is the relationship between the groups?

Tastes, Attitudes and Values

Attitudes can be placed in a continuum. In one direction the attitudes are merely tastes or preferences that may change from day to day; in the other direction the attitudes can be firmly entrenched values that rarely, if ever, change. If you refer to the list of statements on page 214, it becomes obvious that

some of the statements simply indicate a taste or preference and that other persons will not be affected by our preference. No one gets particularly upset if you have a preference for iced rather than pineapple donuts, as it doesn't have any dire consequences for other persons.

However, at the other end of the scale where values are involved it could become extremely difficult to maintain harmony within a group where individuals are in disagreement or reveal inconsistent attitudes. This could help explain why we refrain from expressing in general terms our attitudes towards religion, sex and politics. Another reason why we tend to guard our values more closely than our tastes and preferences is that values are more central to our existence. Our tastes may change without any major affect on our personality or behaviour but with significant changes to our value system there could be changes in personality or behaviour. If a person who we have known for a long time develops a strong religious conviction we may find it difficult to accommodate the change in personality and we may stop seeing that person, or even go out of our way in order to avoid him.

Tastes refer to specific objects or events, whereas values are general and encompass whole concepts. Hence there is a significant difference between the two statements: 'The boss is a slave-driver' and 'I couldn't work under a boss'.

Opinions: Stating our Attitudes

At one time or another we all come into contact with an individual or a group of persons with whom we have differing attitudes. When this occurs there are four ways of dealing with the problem.

First, we may decide that the opinion is going to be of no consequence within our relationship, so the difference of opinion can be ignored or overlooked. This amounts to personal preference, such as when one person smokes and another doesn't.

Second, we may seek a compromise, by settling the dispute by mutual concession. As you work with the other person it may be agreed but not even stated that the other person does not smoke when you are together, or you may avoid working in close proximity to that person. Within the organization where the smoker works it may be a policy that while dealing with customers no one smokes—so this compromise is made.

Third, we may find ourselves on a collision course with the other party, particularly if the issue involves an attitude which is quite central to us, such as a socially accepted custom or belief, be it political, racial, religious or sexual in nature. Because of the confrontation either or both parties may try to convert the other party or argue, if not fight out the difference of opinion. You may often hear it said that one person is trying to 'impose his values on another person'. When values are involved it is rare for one party to yield. The confrontation usually polarizes the debate and confirms in both parties' minds that each is and was right all along.

Fourth, we can retreat either physically by leaving the other party, or by avoiding contact with him. By doing this, we can remove the threat. It can be appreciated, though, that often this is difficult to do, particularly if you have to work with others.

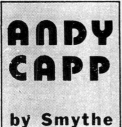

ANDY CAPP appears daily in THE SUN

Opinions and Social Pressure

There is a strong tendency for people to change their attitude about a person or event or perception of a situation in order to conform. No one really likes to be seen to be different. What this suggests is that people will disregard previously held beliefs or attitudes, become apathetic, disinterested or even change their attitude in order to conform with a group, or at least to the point where they are not seen as being different. Writing on the effects of other's opinions on our own, Solomon Asch* states:

> Life in society requires consensus as an indispensable condition. But consensus, to be productive, requires that each individual contribute independently out of his experience and insight. When consensus comes under the dominance of conformity, the social process is polluted and the individual at the same time surrenders the powers on which his functioning as a feeling and thinking being depends. That we have found the tendency to conformity in our society so strong that reasonably intelligent and well meaning people are willing to call white black is a matter of concern.

Propaganda, because it is directed at groups, and is designed to appeal to the individual's need to belong to groups, is one example of how social pressure can be exerted in order to get large numbers of persons to conform to policies and ideas.

Social pressure can also be effective in the workplace. Sometimes attitudes are not even stated as opinions, it is just assumed that individuals will comply with the group norm.

BAA! BAA!

---

* Asch, Solomon. E. (1955) 'Opinions and Social Pressure'. *Scientific American*, Nov. 1955. Vol. 193, No. 5 pp. 31–55.

Activity 17.D   Group Pressure
Consider the following case study.

Ian worked as a plumber for Drainage Enterprises. He had only just received his ticket and he was now eager to earn some extra money at weekends doing odd jobs, as all the other plumbers who worked for Drainage Enterprises did. Until now he had only been able to 'help out' for other plumbers at weekends.

Ian had been asked by a friend to put in some drains. Having measured up the site and organized the job for the following weekend, Ian went off to work to tell his mates about the job and find out where they bought their hardware for their weekend work.

Ian asked Stan, a mate with whom he had worked many weekends doing odd jobs, where *he* normally bought hardware. Stan replied: '*Buy* hardware! You've got to be joking. The only way to make weekend jobs pay is to knock off the stuff from the shed after 4 o'clock on Friday. That way you get free hardware and you can charge the customer for it to boot! If you're worried about taking the stuff, don't be, 'cause everyone does it!'

Ian thanked Stan for his advice, and went on with his work.

1. What does it tell you about
   (a) the attitudes of individuals working in groups?
   (b) the effect of social or group pressure?
2. What can Ian do? What options are open to him?
3. Depending on the option he selects, how should he approach Stan and his workmates, particularly as Stan is bound to ask whether he is going to take the goods?
4. 'Attitudes' and the issues of voicing opinions and being influenced by social pressure raise the question of *honesty* in communication.
   (a) Should you always communicate to others exactly the way you feel and therefore at least be honest with yourself?
   (b) Should you remain silent or appear uninterested or disinterested when discussions come around to controversial topics?
   (c) Should you yield to the pressure of the group, and at least by doing this maintain harmony within groups?
5. (a) What are the effects of pursuing any of the above directions?
   (b) What other options are open to you?

18 Working in the Organization

In Chapter 17 we concerned ourselves with the needs of individuals working in groups. This chapter develops this theme by considering leadership, motivation and problems that can cause communication breakdowns within organizations.

Lead On

Humans will always rank themselves, some persons emerging as leaders, others as followers. There appear to be at least some biological determinants that govern this process of ranking, as occurs with other high-order species in the animal kingdom.

Stature, size, strength, physical prowess and, in humans, dominant personality and superior intellect and ability to be persuasive, all feature as possible attributes for leaders. Depending on the nature of the enterprise in which the group is engaging, the more capable persons will emerge and if there is not observable rank they will struggle for leadership positions. Described in these terms, gaining leadership sounds very much like a game of survival of the fittest. But it's not that simple.

If man engaged only in feats requiring physical strength, then it follows that the strongest person would emerge as the leader as he would be the person who could command the greatest respect from the others in the pecking order. But leaders within organizations require more than brute strength; and leadership is not necessarily granted to those persons who are most capable or who show greatest skill and expertise. In fact, organizations quite often promote individuals into leadership positions without considering the prerequisites for such a posting. Seniority, nepotism and sheer cunning sometimes direct persons into leadership positions.

What this means is that a leader can be a leader in name alone without having the necessary attributes for leadership, resulting in those who are being led becoming completely disillusioned by the lack of direction given, the lack of control and the lack of support that individuals need when working in groups. Non-leadership can result in poor quality of work, the inability of individuals and groups to identify their function within the organization, low morale, and even hostility.

When a leader is ineffective or weak one of four things may happen.

- The group may be able to maintain momentum and function successfully without the leader. Roles may be so specific that job definitions and worker interaction are maintained in spite of the poor leadership.
- The employees may stage a formal revolt by showing disrespect for the leader, questioning orders, ignoring instructions or by making formal appeals to others within the organization for the removal or replacement of the person.
- The group may identify a 'natural' leader from within the group who can provide leadership functions without either the formal title or renumeration. This person may emerge in the day-to-day functioning of the section as individuals identify this person as someone to whom they can take problems and get reasonable help and feedback. The original leader may maintain rank, but little else.
- Productivity, staff morale and job satisfaction will decrease. The organization will continue to function, but no one will be able to pinpoint the dissatisfaction.

Activity 18.A   The Image of the Leader

Below is a list of leaders who have all managed at one time or another to rally support and be influential in guiding people or motivating them to act in a predetermined way.

1. What was it that made each person successful as a leader? List the qualities on the chalkboard.

    (a) Mahatma Ghandi
    (b) Adolf Hitler
    (c) Mao Tse-Tung
    (d) Karl Marx
    (e) Margaret Thatcher

    (f) Sir Winston Churchill
    (g) Ayatollah Khomeini
    (h) Sir Robert Menzies
    (i) Gough Whitlam
    (j) Mickey Mouse

2. Is there any common trait? What is it?
3. If you were asked to compile a list of qualities that *any* leader should have, what would they be?
4. How do the qualities of the above leaders differ from those qualities that you might expect to find in the leader within an organization?

Styles of Leadership

There are probably as many styles of leadership as there are leaders, particularly when you consider that leadership style is a product of biological determinants, personality, the individual's perception of the leadership role, and the leadership function within the organization. How any one person behaves as a leader and carries out the role is the result of such a complex input that stereotyping leadership into three or four styles seems a futile activity.

To enable you to see how the leadership role is perceived we have selected nine terms that are commonly used to describe leadership. Four terms refer to style; five terms describe leader behaviour.

In the grid that follows is indicated the **behaviour** that might be expected of someone who conforms to one of the styles or whose behaviour could be described using one or many of the terms. There is overlap between the styles and terms, and no one group should be seen to be exclusive.

What we would like you to do is describe the possible outcomes that you might expect from a leader who could be described by these terms. In other words you are asking the question: 'If we had a leader who displayed this kind of behaviour, what effect might it have on subordinates and production?'

Be prepared to make both positive and negative comments. If you can use specific examples to illustrate your ideas, please do so. When you complete the grid discuss the results of your findings in class.

Term	Expected Behaviour	Possible Outcomes
1. Team Leader	Tries to instill teamwork and co-operation among the work group. Rather than instructing or lecturing by making statements like, ('You should do this . . .' and 'I have been able to . . .') he uses third personal plural 'we' ('We must get this job out by 4 pm.' and 'We have a deadline to meet.').	
2. Dependent Leader	Tries to gain support for ideas by asking superiors; fears making decisions and implementing ideas because of possible reprisal; i.e. shifts responsibility.	
3. Paternal Leader	Tries to remain the figure-head as the term suggests, as a father-like figure. Is always available for discussion and consultation, but makes few meaningful decisions.	
4. Diplomatic Leader	Tries to get along with both superiors and employees, as he values personal advancement.	
5. Commanding Leader	Tries to maintain close control over activities for which he is responsible, limits communication with subordinates, gives orders and directions.	

Style	Expected Behaviour	Possible Outcome
1. Dictatorial Leader	Tries to hold fear over the heads of employees, threatens punishment as a means of motivation.	
2. Authoritarian–Autocratic Leader	Tries to make sure that workgroup reaches its objective because he feels totally responsible for failure or success of the group. He decides what the group should do, gets the group to accept his ideas.	
3. Democratic Leader	Tries to avoid dominating the group. Helps group identify its problem, or goal. Participates as a member of the group, encourages participation and assistance from others.	
4. Laissez-Faire Leader	Doesn't try. Gives total freedom to the group, minimum leadership, leader in name alone.	

In describing the possible outcomes of these leadership behaviours you have probably been quite ruthless in disregarding some terms and styles, arriving at the conclusion that 'this would be a very poor form of leadership'. If this has been the case, reassess what you have written. Remember, every group of people is different; therefore the needs of each group are different, and what might appear to be weak leadership may in fact be necessary for a particular type of group. As an example, the laissez-faire leadership style may develop because the group members are all highly motivated and are all experts in their field. In this case the 'style' may develop through observation of the group, through developing an awareness that any form of interference may stifle the contribution of group members.

Another point worth considering is that any type of leadership can result in non-leadership if the personality of the leader, the responsibilities of the position, the personalities of group members and the task assigned to the group do not gel.

Successful Leadership

A leader is likely to be successful if:

- He knows exactly what his objectives are and respects the fact that there are limits on what he can achieve and on what he can expect others to achieve.
- He plans in advance individual and group work and responsibilities, but is flexible enough to realize that during implementation plans may need to be changed to accommodate individual and group needs.
- He succeeds in establishing good relationships with his group through being empathic, while being able to maintain the respect of the group.
- He avoids posing as a teacher or prophet, but maintains control of the group's activities.
- He needs to be able to instill a feeling of self-worth in individuals.
- He allows ideas and views to come from the group rather than imposing his own views.
- He does not impose his leadership on the group. The successful leader should not have to assert his position, by *trying to appear* more knowledgeable and skilful than others. The successful leader will gain the respect of the group because he is skilful, knowledgeable and diplomatic in the way in which he carries out his role.

Motivation

Anything which induces a person to act is called a motive. Fear, anger, desire, tiredness, hunger, the need for friends, safety, security and the need for self-fulfilment can all provide people with motivation or drive them to act in some way. Hunger drives us to find food, anger may drive us to become violent, our need for selfrespect makes us seek out those who will compliment us, and tiredness can lead us to do as little as possible or fall asleep.

Motivation may be provided through the influence of either a positive or negative stimulus. In other words, depending on the situation and people involved you might have equal chance of motivating someone by saying 'you have done your work well, keep it up' or 'if you don't maintain your standard of work, you'll be fired'. The thing that is different in these two statements is the need to which the person is appealing. In the first statement the appeal is to an **ego** need, particularly if the statement is made publicly. What is being said is: 'I will praise you in front of your co-workers to boost your ego and motivate you to perform this well all the time'. (In this context the appeal is being made to the co-workers as well.) In the second statement, the appeal is to a **security** need, the motivation being implicit in the threat. In other words, the statement is saying: 'If you don't do your work properly, you won't have any work'.

Often supervisors and employers approach problems of employee behaviour in the wrong way. When an employee's work is unsatisfactory, or the employee fails to meet expectations, punishment is inflicted on the employee. Threats are made which exacerbate rather than solve the problem. Instead of finding the cause of the problem, offering positive motivation and trying to improve morale, the action taken causes further frustration, usually for both parties involved. When faced with the threat of punishment ('you'll lose your job', 'you won't ever get promoted'), the person being chastised can become exasperated, anxious or even fearful of the consequences if the threat is carried out. Self-esteem is flattened.

People who are faced with the problem of motivating others should be aware of the needs of others and know how to appeal to those needs. As we all have different needs, it stands to reason that motivation which is appropriate to the individual and his needs must be used. Having wrestled with someone with a 'work' problem for some time, it may be that disciplinary action needs to be taken. This action may involve reprimanding the person or even making a threat ('You'll lose your job if your work doesn't improve'. I'll check your work again this Friday').

However when this approach is used there are two things that should be remembered:

- If threats are made you should be able to carry them out. There is little point in telling someone he'll be sacked if you have no power to sack him.
- If you provide a person with an option you have to accept that he might select either alternative. To tell someone to 'shape up or ship out' means that you are prepared to meet the consequences if he does elect to leave.

If an employee is not reaching desired goals or his work is sub-standard, it is obvious that some attention should be given to his work behaviour. The only effective way of dealing with the matter is to examine the problem and find the cause. Once the cause is removed, the problem can be rectified.

> Tom, I've been watching you all bloody morning and you've spent the best part of it daydreaming. Keep your mind on your job, man! We've got enough problems with shoddy work slipping through. If you can't keep your mind on it, you may as well stay at home.

(1) The problem will not be rectified if Tom stays at home. It will only create an additional problem, that of finding someone to replace Tom.

(2) The problem will not be rectified by telling Tom that he is part of a larger problem.

(3) The problem will not be rectified by simply letting Tom know that you know he is daydreaming.

In fact, there is no easy solution to the problem, and there is no formula for solving it. Before the problem can be resolved, Tom and his boss need to be able to establish a relationship in which it is possible for Tom to be approached so the boss can find out what it is that is bothering Tom. Then perhaps you can get to the cause. Only then do you have any chance of rectifying the situation by deciding on the alternative courses of action that are open to you.

A Hierarchy of Human Needs

People go to work in order to satisfy their needs. If they had no need to work, they wouldn't. Abraham Maslow* a psychologist, suggests that there are five basic needs by which we are motivated.

(1) **Physiological**: The need for food, water, sleep, in other words our immediate bodily needs

(2) **Safety** (and security): The need for clothing, shelter and protection from harm and the environment

(3) **Social**: The need to belong, to be loved and accepted by others, and a need for friendship

(4) **Ego**: The need to be respected and the need to have self-esteem

(5) **Self-fulfilment**: The need for self-realization, to develop oneself to one's highest potential.

Maslow states that the lower-level needs must be satisfied before the higher-level needs are satisfied. According to the theory, even though a person will try to satisfy needs at all levels at the same time, he will spend more energy trying to find food than trying to be admired. An understanding of this hierarchy is important if we are to understand how people function when working in organizations. In our society, at least, most of our basic needs are satisfied through the provision of adequate wages. Wages make it possible for us to obtain food, clothing and shelter.

---

* Maslow, A. (1954) *Motivation & Personality*, New York, Harper & Bros.

But within the workplace a person still needs to be able to satisfy a range of needs. When you consider the length of time that a person spends 'at work' relative to the time spent at other activities, you can begin to appreciate the importance of this time for the satisfaction of his needs.

Examine Maslow's 'need hierarchy'. At each level of the hierarchy there are needs that should be satisfied at work. What are they? How can they be satisfied at work? Who is responsible for satisfying these needs? Discuss your answers to these questions in class.

Incentives and Staff Morale

You may have listed items such as 'the provision of reasonable work periods' in order to overcome fatigue and tiredness (physiological need), the provision of safety regulations and safety clothing (safety need), the provision of recreation clubs (social need), the attention and support of co-workers and supervisors (ego need) and the opportunity for self-advancement within the organization (fulfilment need) and perhaps a range of other needs in answering the above questions.

If a person works in an organization where his needs can be met, it follows that he will then contribute to that organization. However, an employee must be able to see that the incentives offered are related to his wants, as it is easy to over-satisfy, to offer too much security. Too many privileges, concessions and incentives can result in saturation, the employee no longer placing value in the incentive, and as a consequence he can become unproductive and complacent.

Activity 18.B   Motivation
In the following list, which factors do *you* think would provide you with the greatest motivation?
1. Select the *five* factors that you consider most important. Then write the entire list up on the chalkboard and tally the responses from the class.
   (a) Recognition for work well done
   (b) Delegation of responsibility
   (c) Job security

(d) **Adequate working conditions**
(e) **Wages or salary**
(f) **Opportunity for advancement**
(g) **Feeling of achievement**
(h) **Sound interpersonal relationships with co-workers**
(i) **Sound interpersonal relationships with supervisors**
(j) **Competent supervision of your work**
(k) **The work itself**
(l) **Sound administration**
(m) **Your status relative to others.**

2. Discuss the result of your class tally.
   (a) Which factors were voted the best motivators?
   (b) Why do you think these specific factors were selected?
   (c) Was there strong consensus on these factors?
   (d) Were any factors rejected by the majority of the class? Which factors were they? Why do you think they were disregarded as motivators?

3. (a) If you regarded your class as an organization in which each class member is working, what kinds of incentives would you need to implement in order to:
      (i)   provide motivation for the members?
      (ii) maintain staff morale?
   (b) How are these two points different?

Some of the factors are necessary to maintain the smooth functioning of the organization. These may not in themselves provide motivation, but their absence can lead to dissatisfaction. Other factors do provide motivation, as you have found from the above exercise. People do like to be recognized, seen to be responsible; they like to be achievers; people are motivated by the opportunity for advancement, and the nature of the work being done can provide individual motivation.

In the following cartoon: How is the Chief catering for the Indians' needs by asking their opinions? To which need is he appealing?

The manager, supervisor or foreman who fails to understand the importance of motivation also fails to understand the importance of an individual's needs and the satisfaction of these needs. If individual's needs cannot be met and satisfied within the organization it is inevitable that communication will break down as people see that no one is really interested in them or in what they contribute to the organization.

'Breakdown' on the Job

The responsibility for effective communication within any organization lies with each and every member of that organization. Often the urge to blame others for a breakdown in communication seems too great for some people and in bypassing problems in this way, the real problem is overlooked. More often than not there is more than one reason for the breakdown, more than one person who is responsible.

When a breakdown occurs it is a breakdown in the relationship. As we have said before, the only productive way to tackle the problem is to find the cause.

To find the cause is sometimes difficult. You need to know where to look and what to look for. This section outlines some of the main causes of breakdown within organizations. The issues raised relate specifically to breakdowns in communication that can occur on the job.

Communicating Status

In any organization when we communicate we not only pass on information and ideas, we also communicate our rank and status within that organization. Status differences can be communicated quite inadvertently by not giving full attention to subordinates when they are telling you something, by allowing others to wait while you, as their boss, walk through narrow doorways, or by unintentionally extending greetings only to some people.

Status relationships quite often develop on the assumption that it is the responsibility of superiors to provide information, ideas, motivation and subordinates to accept. Thus communication becomes a one-way flow where there is no provision for dialogue and no opportunity for feedback.

The Vertical Flow of Information

Moving messages through the organization can be particularly difficult when the vertical flow of information is only downward through the hierarchy. Managers pass information to supervisors who in turn pass it on to foremen and so on. By the time the message has reached the person who has to perform the task, distortion of facts, omission of details, carelessness with language and assumptions have all taken their toll on the original message. Organizations that stick so rigidly to this path of communication must be faced with inefficiency and the members of the organization must become frustrated.

While these levels are necessary, they should always be flexible enough to allow persons at all levels face-to-face contact.

The Horizontal Flow of Information

Co-operation between departments is essential for the smooth running of organizations. When this co-operation is required, access should be provided so that individuals at all levels in all sections can meet to sort out problems and make decisions and decide on strategies.

Organizational Climate

If a person at the managerial or supervisory level within an organization feels that his ideas and decisions are not subject to question, he may believe that meetings are a waste of time and consider that staff are underqualified. This can create a poor working and communication climate. The person may be unable to delegate responsibilities and duties; he may be unprepared to meet staff needs.

Number of Authority Levels

The problem of having to move through a number of authority levels is closely linked with the above three points. Authority is necessary within organizations to maintain security and safety. If all authority comes from the top of the organization nothing will ever get done. Authority needs to be delegated; people need to be made responsible for their actions. Levels of authority should be established and the severity or importance of the problem should determine who is in a position to grant authority.

People working within organizations quite often become paranoid and they feel that unless they 'centrally control' all authority then the organization will cease to operate. Alternatively they may feel that some higher authority will crash down on them if they don't have total control. (See also style of leadership pp. 221–23.)

Insincerity and Lack of Confidence

In the previous section on motivation we mention that self-esteem is a need of all persons working within organizations. When insincerity is communicated, we get the feeling that the other party is not genuinely concerned with our interest. This can result in lack of confidence and disenchantment both in our relationships with those persons and with the job itself. All too often people will criticize and provide negative commentary, when in fact they should provide the opposite— that is, offer encouragement and praise.

Fear of Reprisal

Rather than risk reprisal, an employee may hold back a frank and honest statement or criticism. This can result in limited communication. The employee may limit his communication to comments and remarks that he believes will not offend others, particularly if the person to whom he is speaking has control over his future in the organization.

Fear of Message Distortion

Within organizations, especially when you consider the grapevine and its influence, people at all levels become aggravated when they are misquoted and misinterpreted. When misinterpretation is a problem, more care should be taken in selecting a suitable medium and unambiguous message content.

Physical distance can be influential in regulating the amount of communication that can take place within an organization. People will communicate with people closest to them. If decisions need to be made by a group of people then they should be within close proximity. As the distance between individuals becomes greater so the opportunity for face-to-face contact diminishes.

Face-to-face contact is vital within an organization. People not only need to be seen, they need the social contact that is only possible in face-to-face meetings. With electronic media and efficient courier and mailing systems it becomes all too easy to avoid others and use media and channels that cannot hope to give us the efficient feedback that is possible with face-to-face contact.

The Grapevine or Communication Chain

Even though grapevines exist within all organizations we cannot assume that information will flow to everyone through the grapevine. Therefore it is important to understand how the grapevine works.

There are four main ways by which information can spread informally through organizations by way of a grapevine.

(1) The communication chain may be **linear**, whereby one person passes on a message to a second person, and so on.
(2) It may exist in a **gossip** chain, whereby one person seeks and tells everyone else.
(3) The information may pass **randomly** through the organization, whereby there is a probability that the message will reach everyone.
(4) **Clusters** of people may form, one person tells selected others, and so on.

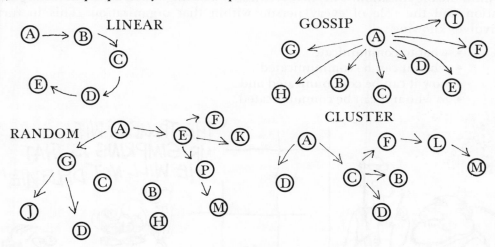

Interdepartmental Jealousy

Interdepartmental rivalry can be used productively as it can provide motivation and help develop a sense of satisfaction on the job and group harmony as well as providing the impetus for getting the job done. When the rivalry turns to jealousy, problems usually follow. Individuals feel insecure or antagonistic toward others and usually the grapevine operates in such a way that friction develops not only between these groups but within the organization as a whole.

Individuals become more concerned with what the other group is doing, roles become poorly defined and departments fail to function effectively. People sometimes become guarded in their behaviour and limit their contact with others within the group or department until they are sure of their loyalty to the group. More often than not the jealousy or rivalry stems from gossip, assumption or inference making.

Poor Supervision

The supervisor's position in an organization is a difficult one as he is responsible for translating information and ideas travelling in both vertical directions within the hierarchy. The supervisor is the filling in the sandwich.

The supervisor needs skill in communicating ideas, requesting information and making commands. Because of his position, a supervisor can become a self-appointed censor blocking the flow of information. He may not invite employees to contribute ideas because of jealousy or insecurity. If the supervisor provides information without a complete understanding of the issue, further misinterpretation and misunderstanding by others is inevitable. Often supervisors will fail to attend to the emotive content in a subordinate's message. This may make further communication difficult. The supervisor may be under the misconception that 'personal' problems are none of his concern.

The major barrier to successful communication is our tendency to judge, evaluate, criticize, blame, approve or disapprove the actions or communication of others. Willingness to communicate alone is insufficient to create effective communication. People need to be made aware of the channels available to them within the organization. This involves understanding the structure of the organization and the role of every person within that organization. This in turn involves knowing

- what to communicate
- when it can be communicated
- how it can be communicated and
- to whom it can be communicated.

"THE TROUBLE WITH MR. SIMPKINS IS THAT HE WILL NOT DELEGATE!"

Answers

Activity 3.B   Perception Test

1. 'A new word'.
2. (a) A cube has regular or square sides, e.g. 3 cm × 3 cm.
   (b) A cube has six faces.
3. If Adam was on the Ark, who was in the Garden of Eden with Eve?
4. You do not bury survivors.
5. One hour.
6. The men were not playing one another.
7. The man is living.
8. (a) This is not a question.
   (b) Machinery is not a British name.
   (c) Syllabification does not help with the pronunciation of these names: Cholmondeley is pronounced 'chum-ley' and Sidebotham is pronounced 'Side-baum'.
9. Eleven.
10. You could not date coins BC.
11. The match.
12. $(60 \div \frac{1}{2}) + 10 = 130$ not $30 + 10 = 40$. The question is asking 'how many $\frac{1}{2}$'s are there in 60, then add 10.'

Activity 10.G   Brain Teasers

1. Say the soldiers are on side X of the river and the boys and boat are on side Y. One boy rows the boat from Y to X, gets out and one soldier rows back to side Y. The soldier gets out at Y, the second boy gets in the boat and rows to X. Both boys now row back to side Y. These four steps have to be repeated for every soldier carried from side X to side Y.
2. Call the slices of toast A, B and C. Toast A and B on one side for 30 seconds. Remove A, turn B and add C to the pan. Toast B on the second side, C on the first side for 30 seconds. Remove B, add A and toast A and C on the second side for 30 seconds. Thus it takes one and a half minutes to toast all three slices of toast on both sides.
3. Using a trial and error approach, you will be able to establish that the Japanese owns the zebra and the Norwegian drinks water.
4. He piled the earth in a mound until he reached the skylight.
5. Put the trousers on backwards.
6. Three of diamonds, four of diamonds, four of hearts.
7. Twelve.
8. Ten centimetres. Since it is the record that turns and not the stylus that travels round the record, the number of grooves is irrelevant to the problem. From the outer margin, the stylus travels 10 centimetres towards the centre of the disc—half the diameter, less the sum of the outer blank and half the inner blank.
9. She had been waiting inside a building.
10. $15. The horse cost $70 and the pig $15, a total of $85.
11. As easily demonstrated, this is a physical impossibility.
12. Pick up the coin at the top of the longer leg and place it on top of the coin where the two legs meet. You now have five coins in each leg.
13. Drop the egg from a height of 2·1 metres. It will not break until *after* its 2-metre fall.
14. Fold the note in half lengthwise, then fold each half again, lengthwise, giving the note an accordion look. Now it is strong enough to support the coin.

234 *Answers*

15. *Voilà!*

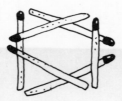

16. As soon as he begins taking off his shoes, you do the same with your own. Get it?

17. Using two hands, carefully roll up one end of the dollar. When the rolled portion reaches the bottle, keep rolling—gently—to nudge the bottle off the note without touching it.

18. Arrange the three matches in a tripod, Indian-tepee style. (Wooden matches work best.) Set their heads afire with the fourth match. Blow the flame out. The three matches will be fused, so you can lift them with the fourth.

20. The two mothers and two daughters consisted of a grandmother, a mother and a daughter.

19.

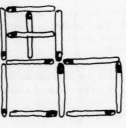

21.

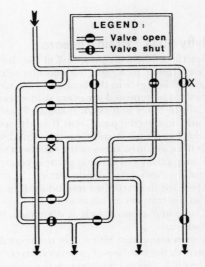

LEGEND :
Valve open
Valve shut

Activity 16.D   Scanning

(a) (i)   (b) (iii)   (c) (ii)   (d) (ii)   (e) (i)   (f) (ii)   (g) (i)   (h) (iii).

Activity 16.E   Key Reading

1. (b)   2. (c)   3. (a)   4. (a)   5. (c)   6. (b)   7. (c)   8. (a)   9. (a)   10. (b)   11. (a)   12. (c)   13. (b)
14. (a)   15. (c)   16. (a)   17. (c)   18. (b)   19. (c)   20. (a)   21. (a)   22. (b)   23. (c)   24. (a)   25. (b).

Activity 16.G   Comprehensive Phrase-Reading

1. (b)   2. (a)   3. (c)   4. (b)   5. (a)   6. (b)   7. (c)   8. (a)   9. (c)   10. (a)   11. (b)   12. (b)   13. (c).